Career Paths and Career Development of Business Librarians

Contributors provide insights about business librarianship in various types of institutions, explore traditional and non-traditional career paths in business librarianship, and discuss numerous strategies for professional growth (from earning an MBA degree to working abroad). Among the topics covered are the following: recruitment of business librarians (including recent data on the supply and demand of business librarians); the special concerns of early career and mid-career business librarians; the importance of mentoring; leadership development; and business librarians on the job in academic, public, and corporate libraries. This book will appeal to a wide audience: practitioners; directors of public, academic, and special libraries serving the business community; library and information science educators; and those considering business librarianship as a career, including students, generalist librarians, and individuals seeking a career change.

This book was published as a special issue of the *Journal of Business & Finance Librarianship*.

Diane Zabel is The Louis and Virginia Benzak Business Librarian (and endowed position) at the Schreyer Business Library at Penn State University's University Park campus. Ms. Zabel is an active member of the American Library Association (ALA). Ms. Zabel is a member of the Editorial Board of the *Journal of Academic Librarianship*. Additionally, she serves as a member of the Editorial Board of the *Journal of Business & Finance Librarianship*. She served on the Editorial Board of the *Publications in Librarianship* series, a monographic series published by the Association of College and Research Libraries, for the period 2001-2008.

Career Paths and Career Development of Business Librarians

Edited by Diane Zabel

Routledge
Taylor & Francis Group

LONDON AND NEW YORK

First published 2009 by Routledge
2 Park Square, Milton Park, Abingdon, Oxon, OX14 4RN

Simultaneously published in the USA and Canada
by Routledge
270 Madison Avenue, New York, NY 10016

Routledge is an imprint of the Taylor & Francis Group, an informa business

© 2009 Edited by Diane Zabel

Typeset in Times by Value Chain, India
Printed and bound in the United Kingdom by MPG Books Group

British Library Cataloguing in Publication Data
A catalogue record for this book is available from the British Library

ISBN10: 0-7890-3794-7 (hbk)
ISBN10: 0-7890-3795-5 (pbk)
ISBN13: 978-0-7890-3794-7 (hbk)
ISBN13: 978-0-7890-3795-4 (pbk)

CONTENTS

Foreword   vii
    Diane Zabel

1   Demand and Supply of Business Information Professionals:
    A Study of the Market from 2001–2005   1
    Lisa O'Connor and Stacey Marien

2   Growing Our Own: Mentoring Undergraduate Students   13
    Doreen Harwood and Charlene McCormack

3   The Orientation and Training of New Librarians
    for Business Information   28
    Ryan Womack

4   Early Career Librarianship in the Business Library   38
    Gene Hayworth

5   Development of Midcareer Librarians   51
    Cory Tucker

6   Growing Your Own Leaders:
    Succession Planning in Libraries   59
    Judith M. Nixon

7   Reframing Leadership: The ACRL/Harvard Leadership
    Institute for Academic Librarians   71
    Sally W. Kalin

8   The UCLA Senior Fellows Program   81
    Juliet Rumble and Bonnie MacEwan

9   Transition from Staff to Faculty in an Academic Library   97
    Cheryl McCallips

v

10 Transitions to Academic Libraries for Business Librarians
   and Librarians' Response to Adjunct Teaching   104
   Christopher LeBeau

11 Taking Business (Librarianship) Public   119
   Mark E. Andersen

12 Transitioning to Corporate Librarianship   128
   Emily Rimland and Glenn Masuchika

13 Successful Mentoring Programs: Examples from Within
   and Without the Academy   142
   Bonnie A. Osif

14 The Mentoring Role of Professional Associations   155
   Diane Zabel

15 Keeping Up With Business Reference   168
   Celia Ross

16 Networking Strategies for Business and Economics
   Librarians   176
   Bobray Bordelon

17 Burnout Strategies for Librarians   183
   Kevin Harwell

18 The Career Choices of Business Librarians:
   A Survey and Discussion   195
   Todd M. Hines and Amia L. Baker

19 The MBA and Academic Business Librarians:
   More than Graduate Education for Subject Specialists   209
   Glenn S. McGuigan

20 The Value of International Experience   222
   David A. Flynn

   Index   234

Foreword

Diane Zabel

When I began my investigation of mentoring in professional associations I was struck by the lack of resources on the professional development of business librarians. What started out as a single article on the role of professional associations expanded into this full exploration of business librarianship as a career path. This book gives prospective and new librarians a glimpse into the work life of business librarians. For more experienced business librarians, it offers advice on career advancement. Beginning and seasoned librarians (generalists as well as business librarians) can benefit from the articles on professional development.

Practicing librarians, library educators, and library administrators share their perspectives on opportunities in business librarianship, professional development, and career advancement. Many of the articles are enriched by the contributors' accounts of their career progression. Contributors provide insights about business librarianship in various types of institutions, explore traditional and nontraditional career paths in business librarianship, and discuss numerous strategies for professional growth (from earning an MBA degree to working abroad).

This book is targeted to academic, public, and corporate librarians and is especially relevant to new, beginning, and midcareer librarians. However, directors of public, academic, and special libraries serving the business community should find it useful. Several of the chapters are particularly pertinent to library and information science educators. Finally, many of the chapters will be of interest to those considering business librarianship as a career, including students, generalist librarians, and individuals seeking a career change.

I am most grateful to the hard-working group of contributors who produced this outstanding compilation of chapters. Of course, I also need to thank Gary W. White who thought that the time was right for a book on the professional development of business librarians and that I was just the person to compile such a volume. I would not have been able to take on this task without the support provided by my institution, The Pennsylvania State University Libraries. In particular, I want to thank Dean Nancy Eaton and Associate Dean Sally Kalin. I am also grateful to the university for the award of a six-month sabbatical. Finally, I want to acknowledge the assistance provided by Lissette Szwydky, the gifted doctoral student who served as an editorial assistant, thanks to financial support provided through the Louis and Virginia Benzak Business Librarian Endowment.

Demand and Supply of Business Information Professionals: A Study of the Market from 2001–2005

Lisa O'Connor
Stacey Marien

LITERATURE REVIEW

The possible shortage of librarians due to the graying of the profession has been written about extensively. Although there is disagreement about whether profound shortages will be realized, the impending retirement of large numbers of librarians is well documented (e.g., Davis, 2005; Kyrillidou, 2006; Lynch, 2005). For example, Ard, Clemmons, et al. (2006) wrote that in 2009 over 25% of librarians will reach or pass age 65 and nearly out of three current librarians will retire by the end of this year (2007). Because these professionals must be replaced in the near future, recruitment and retention of younger librarians has become a focus for the library profession. The Institute for Library & Museum Services has allocated more than $29 million to recruitment efforts by universities, libraries, and library organizations ("ALA Receives $1.6 Million," 2007; Albanese, 2007). The American Library Association (ALA) is also addressing this issue by funding campaigns to recruit diverse individuals to expand and enhance the librarian labor pool ("Recruitment and Retention," 2003).

The potential for labor shortages in the profession is even greater in the area of subject specialties, particularly those that require backgrounds in disciplines with traditionally higher status, such as science, engineering, and technology. Liu and Wei (1993) found that more than 60% of science and technology librarians in the University of California and California State University system libraries did not possess academic degrees in their area of specialty. Hooper-Lane (1999) found that 57% of the 67 science and chemistry librarians surveyed also lacked educational backgrounds in their areas. Stuart and Drake (1992) indicated that a major barrier to recruiting librarians with science backgrounds is the typically low salary of professional librarians. Libraries simply cannot compete with business and industry in recruiting able science and technology graduates into their ranks. As a result, few professional librarians have such backgrounds, and for those who do, the competition for them within libraries is fierce. Ard and Clemmons, et al. (2006) pointed out that libraries are now also competing with the private information sector for qualified subject specialists.

Difficulty recruiting subject specialists with educational qualifications in their areas has also led to a discussion of whether competent subject specialists can be developed without such backgrounds. Fritzler (2006), for example, discussed the debate on the importance of the science degree to science librarianship. He described the difficulty in recruiting scientists into librarianship and asserted that the solution may lie in developing librarians without science backgrounds into science librarians.

The same challenges in recruiting qualified science, engineering, and technology librarians are faced in the business subject specialty. Individuals with business degrees are simply not entering the profession in significant numbers. Kendrick (1990) found that among 162 responding business librarians, 3% had undergraduate degrees in business administration, 3% in economics, 1% in accounting, 1% in management, 1% in marketing, and less than 1% in finance. MBA degrees were held by 17% of respondents. Liu and Allen (2001) further demonstrated this trend. Of 147 respondents, 56% held degrees in humanities, 16% in social sciences, 10% in professional disciplines, and 3% in science and engineering. Only 15% of respondents possessed undergraduate business degrees. Twenty-four percent of respondents held master's degrees in economics or business. The majority (66%) of respondents with second master's degrees earned them in the humanities. As with science and technology, business careers may offer better paying options for graduates than do library careers.

O'Connor and Marien (2002) studied job ads and surveyed employers to assess their satisfaction with the labor supply. They demonstrated that demand for business information professionals outpaces the supply. Employers were disappointed with the quantity and quality of applicants for their positions. Thirty searches for business librarians were analyzed. An average of 17 people applied for positions, though only eight on average met minimum qualifications. An overwhelming 70% of responding employers were dissatisfied with their applicant pool. Forty-three percent indicated dissatisfaction with the overall quality of applicants, 60% with the quantity of applicants, 13% with the educational backgrounds, and

40% with the previous work experience. Sixty-three percent of the responding employers attributed the poor supply to an overall shortage in
qualified candidates, 43% attributed it to competition within the library
profession and with other types of organizations for qualified candidates
and 27% to low salaries in the profession. Forty percent of these searches
were reopened due to lack of qualified candidates, though nearly all of the
positions were ultimately filled. O'Connor and Marien demonstrated that
recruiting qualified candidates was difficult for most libraries.

This study expands and updates the 2002 data. Its purpose is to describe
the current job market for business librarians, determine what types of
qualifications employers are seeking for business library positions, and
assess whether shortages in qualified business librarians and information
professionals have persisted over time. Job advertisements were examined from January 2001 through December 2005 from the following four
journals: *American Libraries*, the *Chronicle of Higher Education*, *College
& Research Libraries News,* and *Library Journal.* Surveys were either
mailed or e-mailed to employers, depending on the contact information
provided in the ad. Position advertisements included in the study met one
of three criteria: (1) their title included the words *business* or *corporate*
and *librarian* or *information*, (2) ads specified skills that are typically considered to be those of a business librarian or information professional,
or (3) the employer was clearly looking for someone to staff a business-
oriented library or information center (example: director in a business library). Employers were asked to complete the nine question survey within
two weeks. Reminders were sent out twice during the study period via
e-mail only.

LIMITATIONS

Researchers wanted to include job postings to the Special Library Association (SLA) Website and BUSLIB-L. Unfortunately, SLA does not
archive their postings, and BUSLIB-L archives were unavailable during
the study period because the list was being moved to a new institution. For
that reason, the data are highly skewed toward public, academic, and very
traditional special library positions. Positions in small special libraries, in
nonlibrary environments, and in organizations seeking business information skills without necessarily designating their positions as "librarian"
positions are highly underrepresented by these findings.

FINDINGS AND DISCUSSION

The Job Market

Researchers collected 112 total job ads. Thirty nine of the ads were listed in multiple journals. The number of ads that were exclusive to a single journal included: 33 from the *Chronicle of Higher Education*, 23 from *American Libraries*, 16 from *College & Research Libraries News*, and one from the *Library Journal*. Ninety-four (84%) ads were for positions in academic libraries, 15 (13%) were for positions in special libraries, and three (3%) in pubic libraries.

The most surprising finding is the disbursement of ads across years in the study. Figure 1 demonstrates a strong trend in a shrinking market. The final year of the study (2005) produced less than one half of the position listings from the first year of the study (2002). In 2002, the *Occupational Outlook Quarterly* predicted that librarianship would grow faster (by 87%) in business services industry than any other area from 1998 to 2008. Three possible explanations exist for this discrepancy: (1) this prediction is incorrect, (2) employers are increasingly likely to advertise positions in nontraditional formats such as the SLA's job board and listservs such as BUSLIB-l, and (3) that this growth is occurring in the smaller, private sector employers not covered by this study as discussed in the limitations section (or perhaps some combination of one or all of these possibilities). The 2007 *Occupational Outlook Handbook* predicted slower than average growth beginning in 2004, so perhaps our data demonstrate an earlier and more severe slow down than expected. Further research would be necessary to confirm this conclusion.

FIGURE 1. Position Advertisements, 2001–2005.

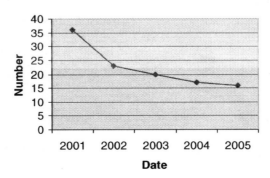

Job titles utilized in ads varied widely. Samples of these titles are listed in Table 1. Qualifications were also varied. Twelve ads (11%) include no minimum requirements. Ninety-four (84%) positions require the MLS or its equivalent, and two positions prefer it. Four positions require an undergraduate degree or higher in library science or related area. One position requires 12 hours of business course work, and two others required an undergraduate degree in business or a related field in addition to the MLS. Most requirements related to the business aspect of the positions are expressed in general ways, such as "academic or work background in business or economics." Although none of the positions requires an MBA or second master's degree for hiring, one ad indicates that a degree would be required for obtaining tenure at that institution. Much of the subject expertise is expressed in terms of preference (as opposed to required).

Seventeen (15%) of the positions prefer an MBA or related graduate degree. Fifteen (13%) prefer an undergraduate degree in business or related area. Four ads indicate a preference for a business degree but do not specify undergraduate or graduate, and three prefer some course work in business or related field. Seven (6%) ads state a preference for "relevant experience" or a "background" in business information services. Other preferred qualifications include certifications of various types and specific technology skills or experience.

Compensation also varied widely across position advertisements. A disappointing 57% ($n = 64$) provided no salary information other than generic statements such as "dependent upon qualifications and/or experience" and "competitive." The average salary listed for all positions is $41,419, ranging from $30,000 to $76,860. Where salary ranges are included, the average minimum salary is $38,476 with a range of $30,000–$70,000, and the average high salary is $47,707 with a range of $33,000–$76,860.

As shown in Table 2, the special libraries in this study that included salary information tend to offer the highest salaries at an average of $41,850.00, but they also are less likely (only 13%) to include this information in their ads. In contrast, 46% of academic libraries included compensation information with an average salary of $41,666. All three of the public library advertisements included salary information with an average salary of $38,108.

Labor Supply

Of the 112 surveys distributed, 41 (37%) were completed and returned. This low response rate, though not desirable, is consistent with response

TABLE 1. ob Titles.

Assistant Head of Business Library	Business Librarian, Instruc tor Assistant Professor	Head Librarian
Assistant Reference Librarian (Business Specialty)	Business Librarian, Social Sciences Team	Instructor in Library Services Business Librarian
Assistant Associate Librarian (Business Sub ect Specialist)	Business Reference Librarian	Librarian (Business Reference)
Bibliographer for business & economics collection management	Business Research Librarian	Librarian for Business (Public Services)
Business Management Librarian	Business Services Librarian I II	Librarian for Public Administration & Government Info.
Business and Agribusiness Librarian	Business Documents Librarian	Management and Economics Librarian
Business and Economics Librarian	Business Electronic Access Librarian	Manager, Information Resource Center
Business and Engineering Sciences Librarian	Business Management Librarian	Records Administration Analyst
Business and Finance Information Librarian	Business Patents Reference Librarian	Reference Librarian Business Specialist
Business and Social Science Librarian	Collection Librarian for Business and Public Affairs	Reference Librarian Business Management
Business and Technology Librarian	Commerce Information Services Librarian	Reference Business Resource Librarian
Business Collection Librarian	Consultant	Research Center Manager
Business Electronic Services and Reference Librarian	Economics Librarian	Research Librarian for Business
Business Instruction and Reference Librarian	Electronic Information Resources Librarian	Research Specialist
Business Liaison Reference Librarian	Electronic Pro ects Business Librarian	Technical Analyst
Business Librarian	Electronic Selection Librarian E ecutive Director Government Documents Coordinator Business Liaison	

TABLE 2. Advertised Salaries.

Library Type	Average	Average Minimum	Average Ma imum	Percent Reporting
Academic libraries	41,666	38,613	48,230	46
Special libraries	41,850	39,600	44,100	13
Public libraries	38,108	35,811	45,000	100
All libraries	41,419	38,476	47,707	43

rate norms for this type of survey. Surveys were completed by 35 (86%) academic, 3 (7%) public, and 3 (7%) special libraries. Compared to the overall makeup of the survey population, special libraries are slightly underrepresented in the response rates. Twelve (29%) of the respondents carried out their searches in 2001, 10 (24%) in 2002, 7 (17.5%) in 2003, 7 (17.5%) in 2004, and 5 (12%) in 2005. The respondent pool is closely representative of the survey population in terms of disbursement across years (see Figure 1).

A range of 3 to 50 and an average of 21.2 individuals applied for each position. A range of 3–29 and an average of 11 applicants met the minimum qualifications for the advertised positions. When asked if they were generally satisfied with the applicant pool, 36 respondents answered this question. Twenty (56%) of them were satisfied, and 16 (44%) were not satisfied with their applicant pool. This represents a significant improvement in employer satisfaction with applicant pools since the 2001 study in which only 30% were satisfied. If rates of employer satisfaction are examined by year (see Figure 2), they demonstrate a trend among these respondents

FIGURE 2. Percentage of Employers Dissatised with Applicant Pool.

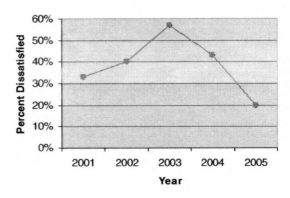

toward substantially greater satisfaction in 2005 than any previous year. It is interesting to note that the average number of minimally qualified applicants remained relatively stable when examined by year.

Respondents who were not satisfied with their applicant pool were asked to select from one to five reasons for their dissatisfaction. Eight (50%) were dissatisfied with the overall quality of applicants, 9 (56%) with the quantity of applicants, 3 (19%) with the qualifications of applicants regarding education, 11 (69%) with the qualifications of applicants regarding experience, and 6 (38%) with the qualifications of candidates regarding skills. Other comments provided in response to this question were:

"We, ultimately, had only one very well-qualified candidate and hired her."
"We found ONE shining star."
"We required an MLS, but put the business reference experience and a degree in business as 'preferred' rather than required knowing that we would have difficulty recruiting someone who had the 'preferred' qualifications. We were correct in our assumptions because we did not get many candidates with the 'preferred' qualifications."

When asked whether they perceived their searches for qualified business librarians as being difficult, 24 (59%) employers answered *yes*. Of those 24 respondents, 11 (46%) attributed the difficulty to a low supply of business information professionals, six (25%) to the high level of qualifications required, five (21%) to the salary advertised for the position, four (17%) cited too much competition with other academic and public libraries, and four (17%) answered there was too much competition with private sector employers. Four (17%) respondents attributed their difficulty to the geographic location of their institution. Other reasons given were:

"This was a fairly specialized position."
"The combination of responsibilities for this position: business AND government documents."
"We do not have enough resources such as travel funds especially since we have promotion and tenure requirements that require professional service and research."
"This [name omitted] library is much larger than other academic business libraries, so applicants from academia tend to be underqualified. Better qualified people come from the corporate world but tended not to apply."
"The nature of the position; that is the perception that a business library is dry and boring."

"The position was offered to two candidates in turn, each of whom declined; third strongest candidate withdrew to accept another position; so we closed the search."

Only three (7%) of the 41 respondents indicated their searches were reopened or readvertised due to a lack of qualified candidates. In none of those searches was the salary increased or the qualifications decreased to attract more applicants. Thirty-nine (95%) of the searches were ultimately successful and resulted in the hiring of a librarian or information professional for the position. One respondent indicated that, in lieu of an experienced applicant, they "trained and mentored a new MLS graduate who really wanted the job and had the drive to succeed."

Respondents were also asked to indicate why they were conducting a search at this time. Five positions were newly created. Two positions had become vacant due to retirements. Eleven positions were vacant because the previous employee had accepted a position in another academic or public library. In three cases, the former business librarian had accepted another position unknown to the respondent. Only one position was known to be vacant due to the previous employee entering the private sector. Three respondents indicated that the former employee was promoted within their institution. Five respondents indicated their former business librarian left the state to follow their spouse as they moved into a new position.

CONCLUSION AND RECOMMENDATIONS

Although it appears from these data that employer satisfaction with the availability of business information professionals is on the rise, this trend seems to correlate more with a declining demand than a rising supply, as the number of minimally qualified applicants did not change significantly over time. If the prediction for increasing retirements over the next decade is realized and is experienced substantively in the business subject specialty, one would expect to see the job market for business information professionals begin an upturn. Whether rising demand would be answered by an increase in supply is not clear. What is evident from the results of this study is that a significant increase in demand could not be supported by the current supply of business information professionals. Thus, this situation should be monitored carefully during this period of predicted retirements to assess shifts in market and supply.

Two important recommendations for future study emerge from this work. First, it is evident to researchers that response rates might have been greatly improved by compiling data annually. Surveys were typically completed, not from official records, but from the records of an individual, generally the chair, of a specific search. As time passes, such individuals and their records are less likely to be available to researchers. Position descriptions should be compiled annually, and surveys should be mailed to employers approximately 6 to 12 months after the end date in the advertisement. This method would yield more reliable results from a greater number of respondents.

The second recommendation from this study is that the market constituted of nontraditional (or nonlibrary) employers of business information professionals requires further investigation. Advertisements on SLA's job board and from the BUSLIB-l listserv are a vital component of the market for such services. Data from both sources should be gathered as it is posted, and employers surveyed in a shorter time frame than are academic libraries, which typically have a slower hiring process. An understanding of the supply and demand for business information professionals will only be complete once it includes data on this area as well.

NOTE

1. This advertisement is fictitious but is based on information obtained in *College Journal: The Wall Street Journal* (2006). Available online at http://www.collegejournal.com/salarydata/mba/mbas.html

REFERENCES

ALA receives $1.6 million in IMLS grants. (2007). *American Libraries, 38*(7), 10.

Albanese, A. (2007). IMLS: $28M for recruitment. *Library Journal, 132*(3), 20.

Ard, A., Clemmons, S., et al. (2006). Why library and information science? The results of a career survey of MLIS students along with implications for reference librarians and recruitment. *Reference & User Services Quarterly, 45*(3), 236–248.

Bureau of Labor Statistics, U.S. Department of Labor. (2002). Librarians. *Occupational Outlook Quarterly,* Winter 2000–2001, 9.

Bureau of Labor Statistics, U.S. Department of Labor. (2007). Librarians. *Occupational Outlook Handbook.* Retrieved November 1, 2007, from http://www.bls.gov/oco/ocos068.htm

Davis, D. M. (2005). Library retirements: What we can expect. *American Libraries, 36*(8), 16.

Fritzler, P. (2006). Made from scratch: The creation and development of a sciences librarian. *Science & Technology Libraries, 27*(1/2), 99–111.

Hooper-Lane, C. (1999). Spotlight on the subject knowledge of chemistry librarians: Results of a survey. *Issues in Science and Technology Librarianship*, 23. Available at http://www.istl.org/99-summer/article1.html.

Kendrick, A. (1990). The educational background and work experience of academic business librarians. *RQ, 29*(3), 394–401.

Kyrillidou, M. (2006). The future of librarians in the US workforce. *ARL, 246*, 5.

Liu, L., & Allen B. (2001). Business librarians: Their education and training. *College & Research Libraries, 62*(6), 555–563.

Liu, M. X., & Wei, W. (1993). Science/technology librarians in California: their background, performance and expectations. *Journal of Educational Media & Library Sciences, 31*(1), 28–40.

Lynch, M. J. (2005). Retirement and recruitment: A Deeper look. *American Libraries, 36*(1), 28.

O'Connor, L., & Marien, S. (2002). Recruiting quality business librarians in a shrinking labor market. *Bottom Line, 15*(2), 70–74.

Recruitment and retention: A professional concern. (2003). *The Bowker Annual Library and Book Trade Almanac*, 291–302.

Stuart, C., & Drake, M. A. (1992). Education and recruitment of science and engineering librarians. *Science & Technology Libraries, 12*(3), 79–89.

Growing Our Own:
Mentoring Undergraduate Students

Doreen Harwood
Charlene McCormack

INTRODUCTION

Our campus at the University of Washington Bothell (UWB) is relatively new, having opened in 1990 in a small business park. By 2000 the
expanding campus moved to a beautiful 128-acre site about 20 miles north-
east of the Seattle campus where it currently resides to help meet demand
for higher education in the Puget Sound region. As a small campus, UWB
has always enjoyed a strong student-centered focus and faculty–librarian

collaboration, as well as having access to a rich resource base through the UW Libraries. The business program was not established until 1993 but has continued to grow steadily, becoming the second largest discipline on campus. As the business librarian, I have continued to monitor the ongoing changes in the Business program and work closely with faculty to see how the Library Media Center and all of Academic Services can support these rapid developments. For example, the program has added new classes, options, faculty, and graduate degrees, as well as experienced an increase in student enrollment and the establishment of new ventures on campus such as the Center for Student Entrepreneurship and the Business Development Center. Due to this continued expansion and the complexity of business projects assigned, our library has experienced high demand for research assistance from business students—by e-mail, chat, phone, drop-ins at the reference desk, and for individualized small-group consultations. Librarians staffing our reference desk call me for help with difficult business questions, and with only myself as the business program liaison, I realized I needed to find a more sustainable way to manage this demand.

Shortly after arriving at the Bothell campus in 1998 as the new business librarian, I began creating an online *Business Research Guide* (http://library.uwb.edu/guides/BusWeb/BusWebContents.htm) to support student research and as an aid for our librarians helping business students at the reference desk. It also became a learning and teaching tool for myself as well, for I am one of the majority of business librarians who do not possess a business degree (Liu & Allen, 2001; O'Connor & Marien, 2002). My master's degree in administrative leadership proved advantageous for designing and presenting the 30 or more in-class research instruction sessions I do each year on campus. Moreover, management classes I took as a graduate student helped me to understand some of the operations and management principles taught in the Business program; coursework I did in accounting, economics, institutions, and investing provided additional subject expertise. However, I never actually developed a marketing or business plan, and it became apparent that I needed to develop this skill, especially as I found myself spending more and more time meeting with students due to the specialized nature and challenge of their business assignments. Some of these students were from other disciplines taking elective business classes and had virtually no business background or knowledge of business resources. The class-specific research guides I created were not a solution, nor were the in-class instruction sessions or the online *Business Research Guide*. Although I have acted as a "consultant" in some classes such as for Entrepreneurial Management where students develop business plans, this has required my presence at a series of class sessions, as well as individual meetings with students outside of class. A more manageable solution was needed.

THE SEARCH FOR A BETTER SOLUTION

Students said the business research guides I posted on the Web were helpful, but I know these guides do not provide the step-by-step guidance needed for intricate core assignments such as creating marketing and business plans or doing business in other countries. Complicating the issue is not only the seemingly overwhelming number of sources available to students but also the overall faculty preference for students to use more relevant library resources for class projects. As a result, I periodically talked with faculty about the need to develop more comprehensive learning tools for core business assignments and to build more awareness of the wide selection of resources available to students through the libraries, beyond the free Web. A Marketing faculty member and I discussed the possibility of developing "An Interactive Annotated Guide to Writing a Marketing Plan," but we never found time to collaborate on the project. However, it was an idea that I kept returning to as a means of addressing more of the overarching problem, for a source with centralized information had the potential to reach a wider audience on a distance platform and also help to increase awareness and use of library resources. Also, I saw it as a way of channeling information to students sooner and relieving some of the sheer demand at the reference desk. However, I knew the project would be a large undertaking, requiring extensive collaboration with faculty and students alike, and I did not know how I would find the time or the help essential for creating and maintaining these tutorials.

I considered tapping into Information School (iSchool) students who might be interested in this project, but until now the iSchool interns our library engaged usually did not possess business backgrounds or much interest in business and, as a result, they were hesitant about and some-times disinterested in working on business projects beyond their scope of expertise. One particularly motivated iSchool intern worked under my supervision to update an international business research guide but strug-gled with sources and guidelines business students needed for their global assignments. I appreciated the effort this intern made and finally accepted the fact that I really needed someone with a business background or a definite interest in business and preferably someone who could work for a longer time. At this point, my attention turned to the possibility of work-ing with a business student interested in improving research skills or in becoming a librarian—someone who could devote enough hours to make it worthwhile to train; someone who would have the motivation, talent, and interest needed to develop Web tutorials and to help update business research guides. I reasoned that such a student, if properly mentored, might even be able to meet with other students seeking research help for busi-ness assignments. In addition, this person could add an invaluable student perspective to our library services and resources, and I welcomed the op-portunity to consult with him or her and gain his or her viewpoints. To accomplish this, I felt it would help if they understood the assignments by having done them or by doing them or a similar class project. Furthermore, the candidate must be well grounded in business resources. It seemed an upper division business student would satisfy these requirements. As for finding a business student interested in becoming a librarian, several stu-dents employed in our library had attended the Information School at the University of Washington while working for us, but none so far had come from the business program. I decided that if the field of business librarian-ship wants to increase the number of business librarians who have degrees in business (O'Connor & Marien, 2002), maybe we need to start mentoring our own. In the summer of 2006, Charlene McCormack, my first Library business intern, appeared. The following section details what we did and how the internship developed an interesting life of its own.

THE FIRST LIBRARY BUSINESS INTERN

Charlene was one of those students who stand out—always open to new ideas, thriving on different research approaches, quick witted, congenial, and optimistic with an air of maturity. She had become a familiar face to us in the library from spending many hours working on assignments over the last 2½ years in what she called her "second home," our library. Now toward the end of her junior year, Charlene was working on a marketing plan assignment that necessitated searching Simmons, and as I assisted her in the library we began discussing how Web-based tutorials would help students for this assignment. When I mentioned needing assistance to develop the tutorial, she remarked how much she would appreciate an opportunity to work on this trial project under my direction and how well this would fit her plans of becoming, of all things, a librarian! It was on this basis we were able to obtain approval from the business program for her to work a three-credit library internship that summer of 2006. Charlene did so well that in the fall of 2006 our library created a paid internship position for her so she could continue working on the marketing plan tutorial and other anticipated projects. This was the beginning of the Library Student Internship Program in our library with Charlene being a role model for succeeding interns. Success of this piloted internship program revealed the added potential for librarian and student collaboration with faculty and for professional development projects, which is discussed later in this article.

WHAT HAVE OTHERS DONE?

An Internet and literature search did not turn up tutorial projects similar to ours. Most sources referred to information literacy tutorials at a more basic level such as searching databases and evaluating sources; or they discussed the effectiveness of online tutorials and, in particular, for distance learning; or they provided tips for creating tutorials. Because some of the sources may prove useful, included in the list of references is a Web link to "A Selection of Resources for Tutorials" we compiled (Harwood & McCormack, 2007c).

We were also curious if there was anything in the literature about mentoring college students in the library field. There are mentorship programs in graduate schools, businesses and professional organizations, but again, we did not find programs comparable to what we are doing here. As Cramer and Scanlon (2005) mentioned, "Most existing mentoring programs in academic libraries focus on getting recently-hired librarians through the tenure process," and the Business Librarianship in North Carolina (BLINC) mentoring program they refer to matched peers from different libraries. This is beyond what we tried to accomplish since Charlene was an undergraduate and, initially, we intended to obtain assistance for handling high demand from Business students for research assistance. The extent to which our internship program also became a mentoring relationship was not foreseen.

There are numerous articles on how to be an effective mentor and, though none reflected our particular situation, the information was useful. Some provided roles and characteristics (Field, 2001), others defined what a mentor is and who should be one (American Library Association Science & Technology Section, 2007), and some referred to specific types of mentoring programs, including from business and librarianship. Krause (2007) wrote an interesting article, "The ABCs of Being a Mentor," which helped me to think more deeply about the importance of mentoring and the benefits provided all-around for mentors, mentees, and the profession.

Partly, our internship experience relates to articles on recruiting for the profession, but although I certainly welcome the opportunity to contribute to business librarianship, that development was only a by-product and not our original intent. O'Connor and Marien (2002) wrote an article "Recruiting Quality Business Librarians in a Shrinking Labor Market." Their findings might also imply the need for further recruiting from the ranks of business programs, as well as the advantage of soliciting student perspective.

COLLABORATING ON THE MARKETING PLAN TUTORIAL

The product we envisioned and produced included incremental procedures and helpful guidelines for developing a marketing plan and embedded annotated sources for books, free Web sites, and restricted databases. Some of the most time-consuming tasks included (1) designing an initial template that could also be used for other tutorials we foresaw doing, (2) getting Charlene up-to-speed on available resources to help design the tutorial and for strategic sources to include in the tutorial, and (3) collaborating with faculty and students.

Throughout the tutorial development, we kept in close contact with marketing faculty and students for continual feedback—by phone, e-mail, in person, and survey response. One of the larger issues we dealt with concerned different fundamental perspectives expressed by faculty while we tried to keep the marketing plan tutorial more universally usable. Charlene's student perspective in helping to design the tutorial and an accompanying student survey, as well as her persistence in working with faculty and her connections with students, contributed greatly to the project's success.

We launched the Marketing Plan Tutorial (http://library.uwb.edu/ guides/Tutorials/MarketingTutorial/FramedMarketingPlanIndex.html) on November 1, 2006, in an Introduction to Marketing Management class and received great interest from students in this class and in succeeding marketing classes. We encouraged and continued to receive input and support from Business faculty and students, which enabled us to further refine the tutorial. According to feedback we received from students, the tutorial evolved into an effective learning tool. One student remarked "This is exactly what I need!" and another student pronounced it "Cool!" Faculty noted that marketing reports submitted by students who used the tutorial were enriched with resources provided within the tutorial. Our librarians found the tutorial a useful teaching tool with guidelines and resources they needed to render better reference service for marketing assignments. With the marketing plan tutorial well endorsed and utilized, we experienced a noticeable decline in requests for reference assistance and individual consultations for marketing reports. In addition, with more students using the tutorials, I found that I no longer needed to spend as much time covering resources and research procedures for marketing plans in the Introduction to Marketing Management classes, leaving me more time to experiment with research instruction in these classes. For example, in one instruction session I reviewed a sampling of marketing reports from prior quarters and discussed what was done well in terms of using and citing sources and what could have made the reports better. I also examined first drafts of each team marketing report and provided detailed source feedback. The result was improved final reports, which made me wonder if developing more tutorials would help to replicate this experience for other core classes.

THE PATH TO MORE INTERNS AND OTHER PROJECTS

With the Marketing Plan Tutorial completed (other than occasional tweaking) our attention focused on developing a Business Plan Tutorial in time for winter quarter's Entrepreneur's Workshop, an advanced class for business plan development with a competition judged by the business community. Charlene was currently taking the Entrepreneurial Management class where she was developing a business plan and grappling with how to approach this new tutorial. She planned to take the Entrepreneur's Workshop in winter quarter as well, contributing to her enthusiasm and knowledge-base. Several measures enabled us to save time: (1) entrepreneurial faculty did not express significantly divergent core philosophies; (2) we had a template to use but decided to dispense with frames since our campus does not currently support them, although we lamented losing some navigational ease; (3) we linked users to a few "Marketing Plan Tutorial" sections, enabling us to concentrate more fully on other aspects of business plans; and (4) we could adjust this tutorial when more feedback rolled in from faculty, students, and alumni, for the class would consist of all three, plus guest consultants, business owners, and venture capitalists. Thus, we were able to roll out the beta version of the "Business Plan Tutorial" (http://library.uwb.edu/guides/Tutorials/BusinessPlanTutorial/BusinessPlanIndex.html) on the first day of class and we received enthusiastic response from students, faculty, and alumni present.

The next project we tackled was the development of a research guide for the Business Policy & Strategic Management capstone classes. Fresh from taking this redesigned class with new faculty, Charlene was ready and excited about helping to work on this project. She based the design and content of the research guide on her "Strategic Challenges" assignment for the class and on guides I had developed for prior capstone class assignments. By now, Charlene had acquired a firmer grasp of strategic business resources and coupled with her student experience (which turned out to be exactly what was needed), the final product (http://library.uwb.edu/guides/Bus470Hoehn-Weiss.html) again met faculty approval and received a positive reception by students.

Another avenue pursued in the spring of 2007 was peer tutoring, which interested me for two reasons, besides the need for help with research demand. I noticed students do not always know how to begin class projects, and I thought perhaps having a peer familiar with the assignment to provide direction would help. Students tutored in a Research Mentor Program (Fensom, McCarthy, Rundquist, Sherman, & White, 2006) commented on the difficulties in beginning new assignments: "I had no idea where to start. She grounded me" (p. 67). "In research you feel swamped with information. The tutor helped me with direction and to learn to pinpoint stuff" (p. 67). I also noticed students consult each other, seeming to be more at ease seeking research assistance from peers. Auerbach (1998) wrote about tutored students receiving "free, individualized help in a relaxed atmosphere from a non-threatening peer" (p. 50). Reports in the literature concur with this (Auer, Seamans & Pelletier, 2003). White (Fensom et al., 2006) explained during peer tutor training how college students are hesitant to seek research assistance from reference librarians and, as fellow students with friendly faces, they "can be approached without embarrassment" (p. 54). Therefore, to accommodate business students on our campus, I arranged some limited hours for Charlene to peer tutor students needing research assistance with their marketing and business plan assignments.

After I guided Charlene in research and consultation methodologies, I observed as business students consulted with her and she provided intuitive peer tutoring, relating well to her peers and enjoying the respect and trust her new position offered. Charlene even persuaded students to use some excellent print sources and directed them to proprietary databases, convincing them of their value instead of using just the free Web. The outcome seemed a win-win situation because Charlene had the security of being able to consult with me further on any challenging questions, the students had the comfort of consulting with a peer, and we were able to accommodate more requests effectively. I only wish we had more interns to partake in this venture so we could offer additional peer tutoring hours to accommodate all of the demand we received, especially for guidance in using complex databases included in the tutorials such as Simmons and SimplyMap.

The success of these projects provided reassurance to contemplate more projects for future library business interns. In fact, it was Charlene who recommended her successor, Eliece Gazaway, who began working a five-credit internship with us during the summer of 2007, bringing her Web design skills, finance option expertise, diplomatic finesse, and sharp analytical skills. She is helping with Web design changes for the tutorials and the *Business Research Guides*, and she is interested in collaborating on the development of a Web-based tutorial for analyzing financial statements. Eliece agreed to accept a paid internship at the library during her senior year 2007–2008 so she can work on these projects. Charlene will help train Eliece on business resources and some of the projects she worked on, including the SimplyMap tutorial she began in Captivate this summer. Eliece has already started to review the *Business Research Guides* and make content and design suggestions for a few of them, but future interns can pick up where Eliece leaves off, including the development of a Web tutorial for "Doing Business in Other Countries."

A MENTORSHIP IS LAUNCHED

It seems pretty amazing what these two interns have already accomplished and how this internship has progressed. Their enthusiasm and interest in learning and growing were crucial to making the internship program and mentorship so successful. I may have learned as much from this experience as they have, but Charlene will share more about this in the next section on "What It Means: The Mentee's Perspective."

According to *Merriam-Webster Online* (2007), a mentor is "a trusted counselor or guide," and though I certainly endeavored to be this to Charlene, our relationship really began as part of a timely internship program that gradually grew into a mentorship as well. As a result, program guidelines or goals were not initially crafted for this internship/mentorship, other than the projects we focused on and others we contemplated doing, as we sped along to meet deadlines and accomplish as much as possible. Our agenda was fashioned by our completed projects and professional development opportunities that materialized. However, in an article for *Academic BRASS* regarding mentorships involving the pairing of more experienced librarians with younger librarians (Cramer & Scanlon, 2005)—about as close as we could come to our situation—provides mentor and mentee responsibilities to consider, most of which we think we met such as:

- create a welcoming environment for mentee
- listen well and respect the mentee's opinions and contributions
- respect confidential and sensitive information
- be willing to use examples and illustrate anecdotes (good and bad) from one's professional career (Cramer & Scanlon, 2005, appendix).

As they further suggested, we tried to "establish limits, where appropriate (For example, the mentor may not be interested in co-authoring a research article. . . .)" (Cramer & Scanlon, 2005, appendix). Fortuitously, Charlene expressed interest in professional development, seeing it as stretching her potential and advancing her toward her goal of being a business librarian, so we drafted proposals for conference presentations and consequently were able to copresent on the outcome of our collaborative tutorial project (Harwood & McCormack, 2007a and 2007b) at the Pacific Northwest Conference for Higher Education Teaching and Learning Conference in spring 2007 (http://library.uwb.edu/guides/BusWeb/PacNW. html), and at the 2007 American Library Association (ALA) Annual Conference Poster Session (http://library.uwb.edu/guides/BusWeb/ALA2007. html). This was the first time Charlene presented to a professional audience, and I know it elated and concerned her; I also know she captivated our audiences and did far better than she expected. To attend the events, Charlene learned the intricacies of applying for available student travel funds from our campus Teaching and Learning Center, the Chancellor's Office, and the Business Program. While traveling, Charlene and I had more time to talk and get to know one another better. I suggested to her some of the highlights of the conferences such as the BRASS Annual Program. She visited some of our vendors' exhibit booths to chat with them and stopped by one of my committee meetings and met some of the members, including the outgoing BRASS chair, which, to Charlene, were exhilarating experiences. Her curiosity about librarianship has been appreciably expansive, and I have enjoyed this opportunity to provide guidance and support during her career-searching journey and internship with us, finding this to be one effective way to help recruit another gifted business student to the field of librarianship. In the *Academic BRASS* article on recruiting future business librarians, Korzenko (2004) referred to the efficacy of "channeling students directly from undergraduate programs." Even if they do not join the field of librarianship immediately, they may join later as my new intern, Eliece, mentioned to me she had not thought about being a librarian but it was a possibility!

As a mentor, I tried to share with Charlene many of the facets of running a library and being a librarian—in my case, an academic business librarian. For instance, Charlene was given a collection development project, invited to attend our Library Learning 2.0 sessions this summer, and offered the chance to present to our librarians the SimplyMap tutorial she developed and further demonstrate more complex features of this demographic mapping database from Geographic Research, Inc. We discussed different research instruction approaches we might experiment with during the next academic year such as (1) using a Wiki as a learning tool for students to develop a marketing plan tutorial, (2) using clickers in classrooms, and (3) setting up a blog for marketing students to ask questions and obtain responses from their classmates, the business student intern and the business librarian. Thus, I have had the advantage of my student interns' illuminating perspective on connecting with their peers. Eliece and I are anticipating trying some of these techniques—and Charlene may return as an iSchool intern to assist with them.

According to Krause (2007), "Both professional and personal development must occur to make mentoring relationships beneficial," and I believe Charlene and I reached this plateau. Certainly, mentoring Charlene helped me grow as well and enabled me to follow my philosophy of giving back to the profession. Charlene has grown tremendously in this position—in confidence, research capability, collaborative skills, and determining and supporting learners' needs. I feel confident in passing a future mentor's torch to Charlene.

WHAT IT MEANS: THE MENTEE'S PERSPECTIVE

I am a nontraditional student who decided to return to school so I could have a career matching my interests in business and librarianship, and for the first time I can fully pursue those interests. I was gifted with an incredible opportunity, a job in the library on campus where I attended school to complete my undergraduate degree in business administration. I plan to get my master's degree in library & information science so I can be a business librarian. When Doreen offered me the library internship, I was excited to be able to work with the business librarian so I could improve my research skills with her guidance. I was given an office of my own to work in and more support than I imagined possible from Doreen and the other librarians.

From working with Doreen in the library, I have a skill set few of my peers possess: (1) I honed my research skills in finding and evaluating resources to refer others to, (2) I practiced assimilating information from many sources into a cohesive report, and (3) I learned to transfer this new knowledge to others through peer tutoring and the Web-based projects I created. All of this will benefit me when I attend iSchool.

The "Marketing Plan Tutorial" was my first project, and it seemed like it would be easy to put together because I had just completed a marketing plan for an Introduction to Marketing Management class and I felt I understood the components required for an in-depth plan. However, I quickly realized as I worked on the "Marketing Plan Tutorial" with Doreen that writing one specific plan is very different from writing a tutorial to support students having different learning styles and focusing on varied products and services. Creating the tutorial allowed me to apply what I learned in class but on a different, more encompassing level. For instance, the project compelled me to structure large sets of information in an easy-to-follow format for the students. I also had to evaluate the sources more critically than I had for my own paper to limit the information and to verify it would support different products and services. This was by far the largest project I had ever undertaken; it took five months from the initial research to the posting of the Web site that will continue to be revised.

The project built momentum incrementally, with each section feeding into succeeding ones. This corresponded with classes Doreen suggested I take so I would possess the knowledge and skill set necessary to work on upcoming sections and projects. Because Doreen was aware of assignments I would receive in my classes, she planned my library projects accordingly. This strategy helped me with my class research and my understanding of what I could do to support students with my library projects. Likewise, by being given the opportunity to peer tutor others using the "Marketing Plan Tutorial" and some of the resources within it, I came to understand how the students were using the tutorial for their own projects and where changes could be made to support them more fully. Any confusion I experienced usually served as an indicator for the amount of assistance other students might also require and I could then develop the tutorials or class guides to better support these students' needs.

Doreen provided structure by breaking large projects into sections so they were manageable while allowing me to switch to different areas if I needed a change of pace. Also, having Doreen available to answer questions and provide suggestions about the arrangement, content, and resources needed for the tutorial enabled me to continue developing my writing style and resource knowledge.

Once the "Marketing Plan Tutorial" was posted online Doreen suggested presenting what we created to our professional community as a way to share information, so we applied to a number of conferences. The process of each application carefully written, revised, rewritten, and finally revised again was a unique learning opportunity for me. We used separate approaches, making a point of promoting aspects of our tutorial project that matched each conference's overarching theme—be it Technology Innovation, Student/Faculty Collaboration, or Innovative Educational Collaboration through Community Involvement with Sustainable Environmental Business Practices. I had only presented with my peers in classroom situations so copresenting in a formal setting was a new experience for me. The first presentation was in a small room with an audience of college faculty and librarians, which I found to be very intimidating. Doreen encouraged me to make it an intimate conversation with the audience, and I was thereby able to overcome my trepidations and actually enjoy myself.

In accepting the position with the library, I expected to increase my understanding of library processes and confirm how I want to spend my career; fortuitously, I received that and so much more, but the most significant growth I have had has been to my confidence. Realizing how fortunate I am to have this opportunity, I plan to continue to share my knowledge with others so I can give back to the library and the business community, as Doreen so graciously showed me by example to do.

I am thankful to Doreen for everything she taught me, shared with me, and hoped for me. In turn, I promise to try to give others what she gave to me so they can benefit from being mentored by someone who cares and wants to see them succeed.

CONCLUSION

Through the piloted Internship Program, our Library derived invaluable student perspectives and an effective alternative means of meeting research demand with limited resources. The internship developed into a win-win situation for the intern and library, as well as for the Business program. Moreover, the collaborative process originating from the many projects we undertook strengthened relations among the library, students, and faculty. Overall, the experience for the intern proved enriching for her personal and professional life. She acquired research skills, professional development, and mentoring toward her goal of being a librarian and gained confidence from her many accomplishments during the internship. Although intern training, guidance, and possible mentorship in some situations need to be provided, the outcomes achieved from the internship far outweigh the time invested. Based on our library's experience, the internship was well worth doing and has the potential of being expanded to other programs as well. Internships focusing on projects such as peer tutoring, development of Web-based tutorials, and class research pages can be a sustainable alternative for supporting research needs where resources are scarce. We look forward to the next year with our new library business intern, Eliece. With so many projects under consideration now, Charlene and Eliece jested they cannot leave until they find a suitable successor, and they thought this a good thing—keeping the internship going, for we have all found it so beneficial.

REFERENCES

American Library Association Science & Technology Section. (2007, May). *STS Sci/Tech library mentors learn about mentoring*. Retrieved July 25, 2007, from http://www.ala.org/ala/acrl/aboutacrl/acrlsections/sciencetech/stsmentors/mentorinfo.cfm.

Auer, N. J., Seamans, N. H., & Pelletier, L. (2003). Peer advising in the research process: A year of student success. In J. K. Nims & E. Owens (Eds.), *Managing library instruction programs in academic libraries* (pp. 25–30). Ann Arbor, MI: Pieran Press.

Auerbach, B. (1998). Jenny & her trig problem. *School Library Journal, 44*(1), 50.

Business Plan Tutorial (University of Washington Bothell). (2007). Available online at http://library. uwb.edu/guides/Tutorials/BusinessPlanTutorial/BusinessPlanIndex.html

Cramer, S., & Scanlon, M. (2005). Mentoring fellow business librarians: One model from BLINC. *BRASS Business Reference in Academic Libraries Committee, 2*. Retrieved July 25, 2007, from http://www.ala.org/ala/rusa/rusaourassoc/rusasections/brass/brasspubs/academicbrass/acadarchives/vol2no2/acadbrassv2n2a2.htm.

Fensom, G., McCarthy, R., Rundquist, K., Sherman, D., & White, C. B. (2006). Navigating research waters: The research mentor program at the University of New Hampshire at Manchester. *College & Undergraduate Libraries, 13*(2), 49–74.

Field, J. (2001). Mentoring: A natural act for information professionals? *New Library World, 102*(7/8), 269–273.

Harwood, D., & McCormack, C. (2007a, May). *Meeting research demand in a limited resource environment: Streamlining with technologies.* Presented at the Pacific Northwest Higher Education Teaching & Learning Conference, Vancouver, WA. Retrieved July 9, 2007, from: http://library.uwb.edu/guides/BusWeb/PacNW.html.

Harwood, D., & McCormack, C. (2007b, June). . *Meeting research demand in a limited resource environment: Streamlining with technologies.* Poster session presented at the annual meeting of The American Library Association, Washington, DC. Retrieved July 9, 2007, from http://library.uwb.edu/guides/BusWeb/ALA2007.html.

Harwood, D., & McCormack, C. (2007c, May). *A selection of resources for tutorials.* Retrieved July 9, 2007, from http://library.uwb.edu/guides/BusWeb/ALA2007Bib.html.

Korzen, K. J. (2004). Association for Library and Information Science Education. *Educating library and information science professionals for a new century: The KALIPER report.* Retrieved July 9, 2007, from http://www.alise.org.

Korzenko, J. (2004). Recruiting future business librarians. *BRASS Business Reference in Academic Libraries Committee, 2.* Retrieved July 25, 2007, from http://www.ala.org/ala/rusa/rusaourassoc/rusasections/brass/brasspubs/academicbrass/acadarchives/vol2no1/acadbrassv2n1a2.htm.

Krause, M. K. (2007, May). The ABCs of being a mentor: A primer for being both a mentor and a protégé. *Healthcare Executive, 22*(3), 62, 64, 66.

Liu, L., & Allen, B. (2001, November). Business librarians: Their education and training. *College & Research Libraries, 62*(6), 555–563. Available online at http://web2.ala.org/ala/acrl/acrlpubs/crljournal/backissues2001b/november01/liu.pdf.

Merriam-Webster Online. (2007). *Mentor.* Retrieved August 7, 2007, from http://www.m-w.com/dictionary/mentor.

O'Connor, L., & Marien, S. (2002). Recruiting quality business librarians in a shrinking labor market. *The Bottom Line, 15*(2), 70-74. Retrieved July 9, 2007, from ABI/INFORM Global database.

The Orientation and Training
of New Librarians for Business Information

Ryan Womack

INTRODUCTION

Business librarians do not enter into the world fully formed and often do not begin their library careers with a clear focus on business. Many different factors in individuals' educational, work, and personal backgrounds combine to lead librarians on the path to business librarianship. When librarians enter the field without a common starting point of shared experience, an initial orientation to the unique aspects of business information provides an essential foundation for success. This article discusses issues involved in the training of entry-level librarians in the basics of business librarianship.

ENTERING THE PROFESSION

Studies of the educational background of academic business librarians have consistently shown that only a minority in the field have formal training in business or related disciplines at either the undergraduate or graduate level. Liu and Allen (2001) found that 23.8% of practicing business librarians at accredited business programs had a second master's, such as an MBA or degree in a related field, and an additional 15% had business training at the undergraduate level. This was only a slight increase from Kendrick's (1990) finding of 17% of business librarians with master's degrees and 10% with undergraduate business degrees. The cultural and compensation differences between the library and the business workplace make it difficult to attract large numbers of previously trained business experts to libraries. As Liu and Allen (2001) stated, "The overall picture, then, is of professionals working in a specialized area who are scrambling to obtain the expertise they need to function effectively in that context" (p. 562). The authors went on to suggest potential joint programs between library and business schools to remedy the problem, but this seems impractical in today's educational environment where funding and time are in short supply.

If this is the state of affairs in larger academic programs, small college libraries and public libraries must have even more difficulty finding formally trained business librarians. In the U.K. context, Considine (2005) discussed the shortage of business expertise in public libraries and the consequent need to train librarians in-house to provide business services. O'Connor and Marien (2002) provided further evidence on the recruiting dilemma for business librarians.

In addition, the number of library schools offering specialized courses in business reference (as well as the number of students taking those courses) appears to be on the decline. Given these realities, it is unrealistic to expect new librarians in a business library setting to enter with much of the knowledge needed to function effectively. On-the-job training and retraining is the rule for most business librarians.

Corporate librarians are a special case. Librarians entering this sphere tend to have more direct business experience, whether from prior work or education. However, the world of corporate librarianship is also changing.

As physical collections and staffs are reduced, librarians are redefining themselves and integrating themselves into the workplace as embedded information professionals (Chindlund, Chochrek, Scanlan, Shumaker, & Stich, 2005). Due to corporate librarians' unique experiences and the fact that they often work solo, much of their training and orientation will have to be self-initiated.

UNIQUE BUSINESS NEEDS

Regardless of setting, business reference and collection development present special challenges. Lavin (1995) provided an excellent discussion of the unique nature of business reference, describing the typical business patron's urgent need for current information. Atkinson and Figueroa (1997) provided early empirical evidence of the business patron's time-sensitive approach to finding information: patrons would often simply end their search abruptly when their time budgeted for the task was reached. According to Wilkins (1999), "patrons are more likely to be demanding, time sensitive, and carry high expectations about the results of the library visit regardless of their individual fluency with libraries" (p. 40). Librarians must develop reference strategies and techniques for simultaneously speeding up their delivery of information and slowing down patrons to the point that an effective reference interview can take place. The training of new librarians must develop comfort with not only the content, but also the style of business reference interactions.

Another challenge to the new librarian is gaining expertise with the vast array of competing and overlapping business publications available in print and online. Unlike many academic disciplines—which may be structured around a major index, a list of top journals, and a few key reference sources that constitute the core of knowledge in the field—the contours of business information are constantly changing, and patrons' needs can be met in a variety of ways. Each particular type of reference question may have several resources that can provide an adequate answer. Each library will have its own mix of databases and print sources on hand, and this selection may change frequently in response to vendors' new offerings and pricing. The librarian training for business reference must learn to be flexible and to blend his or her knowledge of resources with patron needs to provide a unique concoction for each query. In-depth knowledge of specific sources may come with time, but it should not be an immediate goal when orienting the new librarian.

Wilkins (1999) gave an excellent description of the stages necessary for successful training. Helping the trainee understand the psychology of the patron, the patron's typical questions, and the usual resources that will provide answers gives the trainee the broad context needed to develop comfort and confidence in his or her abilities to respond to questions. This will be necessary to properly negotiate the reference interaction and to recognize the underlying information needs in their various guises beneath business jargon.

Many business information resources also differ qualitatively from the standard range of books, journals, and indexes that library school students are usually exposed to. At a minimum, the new librarian must develop comfort with numerical data sources and be able to deal with requests for the Dow Jones Index with the same ease as requests for the Periodicals Index. Training must also provide practice on databases containing unique bodies of business material such as financial statements, annual reports, or accounting regulations. Although these sources are often not as complex as they first appear, the orientation process must include explanations and demonstrations of these sources, which are otherwise dauntingly unfamiliar.

Another unique need of business patrons is the heavy demand for current demographic and marketing data and forecasts. In addition to knowledge of basic sources, the new librarian must be trained in matching highly specific queries to data that may be available at a more general level, and in making referrals when necessary. If the patron really does need to know a piece of information that is not available from public sources, they can often directly contact industry associations, government experts, or library colleagues through services like the BUSLIB-L list to get an inside track on the information. The nature and scope of referrals to outside contacts is another unusual feature of business librarianship.

Going beyond reference, the new librarian with collection development responsibilities in business will need to appreciate the characteristics of business vendors. With prices driven by the corporate market, most libraries will always find it expensive to acquire key business information resources. The same pressure for currency and specificity of information influences the selection process for business resources. The business selector must begin to learn the art of balancing need and cost to develop satisfactory, if not ideal, collections. Learning about specific vendors can be facilitated by attending conferences with many exhibitors and presentations on resources, such as the American Library Association (ALA) or the Special Library Association.

THE TRAINING PROCESS

Any training program should be founded on sound basic principles of librarianship. General training for all public services staff is useful (Mozenter, Sanders, & Bellamy, 2003) and to be most effective must be supported with release time and appropriate incentives (Buchanan, 2005). For reference, learning basic techniques for keeping patron interactions focused on quality service is very important (Macke, 2005). Business training can make use of any general training components for librarians that already exist at the library.

All librarians and staff who work with business information will benefit from additional training to respond to the specific business needs described above. Often the most comprehensive and complete method to raise awareness is a formal program. As Lavin (1995) stated, "Establishing a formal in-house training program requires effort and may be mistakenly perceived as a luxury, but the payoff can be remarkable" (p. 94). Tucker (2004) provided the most recent and thorough description of a systematic business reference training process in the literature. At the University of Nevada, Las Vegas (UNLV), Tucker developed a program for 29 staff members at two reference desks. Given the large number of staff to be trained, Tucker created a structured process with workshops, lists of resources, and homework assignments in three major categories of business information: company information, industry information, and market research. Tucker reinforced the initial training on specific sources with contextualized sample questions and follow-up quizzes to test mastery of concepts. Specific goals were set for raising information competencies, which were assessed through performance on the homework assignments and a survey.

For large and frequently changing groups of staff such as student workers, an automated tutorial can be an effective introduction (Kathman & Kathman, 2000; Poole, Grieco, & Derck, 2001), but this approach may not be appropriate for the training of small groups of librarians specializing in business.

At Rutgers University, Womack (2007) maintained a training manual for new librarians and information assistants at the Kilmer Library, the primary business library on the New Brunswick campus. The training manual provides context for the individualized on-the-job orientation provided by Womack, covering the most significant local business information sources, along with examples of typical questions and reference issues. This style of one-to-one training is more suited to small numbers of new librarians. Typically no more than three new reference desk staff per semester are hired at Kilmer Library. Hires range from first-year library school students to experienced post-MLS librarians on temporary assignments. The training at Rutgers also covered the three basic areas of company, industry, and market research, along with material customized to the new hire's background. Sometimes new librarians are interested in in-depth learning in an area of potential strength, and sometimes additional training is necessary to bolster areas of unfamiliarity.

Wilkins (1999) provided further detail on the need for training to properly orient new hires to the culture of the organization and the local business patrons. Local operating practices can include special instructions and passwords for accessing business databases, as well as information on tiers of service available to different user groups. If the librarian has collection development responsibilities, there will undoubtedly be a number of local practices and procedures to learn in connection to budgets and acquisitions.

Training also should provide a crash course in the business terminology that creates difficulties in understanding for those not familiar with the field (Muchin, 2000). Librarians must learn the lingo of 10-K's, tickers, and ratios to decipher reference queries and select resources. One specific example is the "risk-free rate of return" that is described in many textbooks and student assignments as though it could be located under that title. To field these questions, the new librarian must be taught the appropriate T-bill and bond rates that serve as measures of the risk-free rate of return in the real world.

Beyond language, the style of many business information needs is quite different from the norm for libraries. Rarely will a patron say, "I need to know more information about X." Instead, the librarian is likely to hear the desire for a specific outcome to a demand and, to be frank, business patrons can be somewhat pushy compared to other types of patrons. Training must include discussion of strategies for defusing such situations and ways to gently guide the business patron towards a suitable reframing of the question and a suitable expectation of an answer. Although actual experience in these situations will always be necessary for the librarian to increase their confidence and ability to handle difficult business reference questions, proper training can speed the learning process. At the same time, new librarians must be cognizant of their limitations and be taught the appropriate point to refer questions to those with more expertise.

Local training programs and materials should also be supplemented with other resources. The Business Reference and Services Section (BRASS) of the Reference and User Services Association (RUSA) in ALA maintains many useful resources for new librarians, including the *Core Competencies for Business Reference* (2007) that reviews key information resources on a number of business topics.

More difficult to formalize, but equally essential to the training process is the inculcation of a curious, problem-solving spirit in the new librarian. Maintaining awareness of business resources and responding to changing patron needs requires active investigation on the part of the librarian after the initial training phase ends. A sense of wonder and excitement at discovering the information that lies behind the newspaper headlines can compensate for many gaps in formal education. Mastering the challenges of a new subject area should be a source of satisfaction and not frustration for the new librarian. More experienced librarians should model these attitudes for their junior colleagues. Informal in-house traditions such as the swapping of difficult questions at reference meetings are often the best way to accomplish this goal (Wilkins, 1999).

On-the-job learning and development continue throughout the business librarian's career, and after an initial structured orientation, the librarian will need an ongoing approach to learning. Formal and informal mentoring opportunities should be made use of at the local library level and at the national professional level (Fiegen, 2002). New librarians should be encouraged early on to take responsibility for staying professionally up-to-date. The role of the professional association in furthering the development and adjustment of the new librarian is described by Juricek (2007).

THE FUTURE OF TRAINING

It may be appropriate at this point to speculate about how the changing library environment affects the need for training in the future. As mentioned above, business information needs evolve rapidly in response to the volatile real world of business, and competition among information providers has resulted in a succession of changes in format and functionality of major resources. A formal training program must be constantly updated to reflect these changes. It should also be designed so that the trainees do not become locked into a particular pattern of finding information, a pattern that will inevitably break down as old sources are discontinued and new information needs arise.

Already librarians have seen the impact of the "Googlization" of reference, with the answers to commonly asked, standardized questions often easily surfacing in a quick Internet search—a result that disintermediates the role of the librarian in the search process. For example, no one asks

City Colleges
of Chicago
Truman

where they can look up stock prices anymore. In contrast to Wilkins' (1999) description of the common buzzwords of sources that patrons would ask for by name—S&P, D&B, SRDS—the patron of today is less focused on specific sources. Instead, patrons often come to the desk out of frustration with a Google search gone awry. Their information needs are much more individualized and require lengthier efforts to solve. Training has to respond to this reality. Neuhaus (2001) describes the need for a continuous, individualized, flexible, hands-on approach to training, arguing that this is more effective than traditional formal training programs. Kutzik (2005) discussed the virtues of just-in-time training for new technology skills, but this approach can be applied to training in business librarianship as well. Training units can be modularized and offered as individual brief lessons in response to emerging needs. Often the same instructional materials can serve patrons and new librarians alike when properly designed.

Taking this atomization of information needs to its furthest extent leads to the development of searchable repositories of specific knowledge. A highly successful implementation of this approach is the business FAQ originating from the Lippincott Library of the Wharton School (Halperin, Eichler, & Khanna, 2006). As technology advances, the capabilities of databases to store and make available knowledge encapsulated in interactive guides, video tutorials, and the like will only increase. The work of training will then become providing new librarians with the basic skills to absorb this knowledge, and on designing of the architecture of the knowledge repository itself. Certainly with a well-defined architecture and interface, the trainees and learners can capture their new experiences as they learn and create their own educational modules to pass along. The success of Wikis in today's environment is only the most visible example of this approach.

The development of dynamic content that can not only be viewed and searched 24/7, but also created and edited continuously from any location, is a powerful tool that has yet to be fully exploited for training. The future development of these expressions of the collective mind of expert librarians should allow the dream of continuous just-in-time training and learning to be realized at some point. However, the subtle inferences at play in the very human interaction of the reference interview, and the development of critical judgment in the use and selection of business sources will continue to demand person-to-person transmission of information to new librarians. Just as electronic resources are taking away some of the routine work involved in explaining to patrons exactly how to use a particular source, the routine aspects of training can be automated to allow the higher level functions of mentoring to come to the fore.

REFERENCES

Atkinson, J. D., & Figueroa, M. (1997). Information seeking behavior of business students: A research study. *The Reference Librarian, 27*(58), 59–73.

Buchanan, R. A. (2005). Library assistant training: Perceptions, incentives, and barriers. *Journal of Academic Librarianship, 31*(5), 421–431.

Chindlund, J., Chochrek, D., Scanlan, J., Shumaker, D., & Stich, J. (2005, December 15). *The future of librarians in the workforce: business librarians, an IMLS white paper.* Retrieved September 23, 2007, from http://libraryworkforce.org/ tiki-download_file.php?fileId=45.

Considine, G. (2005). Response from a dying breed: Public libraries and the business information resources survey 2005. *Business Information Review, 22*(2), 85–89.

Core Competencies for Business Reference. (2007). Retrieved September 25, 2007, from http://www.ala.org/ala/rusa/rusaourassoc/rusasections/brass/brassprotools/corecompetencies/corecompetenciesbusiness.htm.

Fiegen, A. M. (2002). Mentoring and academic librarians: Personally designed for results. *College and Undergraduate Libraries, 9*(1), 23–32.

Halperin, M., Eichler, L., & Khanna, D. (2006). Just the FAQs, ma'am: Sharing a Business Knowledge Database. *Journal of Business & Finance Librarianship, 12*(1), 33–40.

Juricek, J. (2007). Challenges faced by a new academic business librarian. *Academic BRASS, 3*(1). Retrieved September 25, 2007, from http://www.ala.org/ala/rusa/rusaourassoc/rusasections/brass/brasspubs/academicbrass/acadarchives/vol3no1/acadbrassv2n20703.htm.

Kathman, J. M., & Kathman, M. D. (2000). Training student employees for quality service. *Journal of Academic Librarianship, 26*(3), 176–182.

Kendrick, A. W. (1990). The educational background and work experience of academic business librarians. *RQ, 29*(3), 394–399.

Kutzik, J. S. (2005). Just-in-time technology training for emergent needs. *Library Mosaics, 16*(2), 8–10.

Lavin, M. R. (1995). Improving the quality of business reference service. *Reference Librarian, 22*(48), 71–98.

Liu, L., & Allen, B. L. (2001). Business librarians: Their education and training. *College & Research Libraries, 62*(6), 555–563.

Macke, B. (2005). Roaches, guerillas, and "librarians on the loose." *Journal of Academic Librarianship, 31*(6), 586–589.

Mozenter, F., Sanders, B. T., & Bellamy, C. (2003). Cross-training public service staff in the electronic age: I have to learn to do what?! *Journal of Academic Librarianship, 29*(6), 399–404.

Muchin, J. A. (2000). The librarian's self-education of financial terminology. *Bottom Line, 13*(2), 90–92.

Neuhaus, C. (2001). Flexibility and feedback: A new approach to ongoing training for reference student assistants. *Reference Services Review, 29*(1), 53–64.

O'Connor, L., & Marien, S. A. (2002) . Recruiting quality business librarians in a shrinking labor market. *The Bottom Line, 15*(2), 70–74.

Poole, E., Grieco, F., & Derck, H. (2001). Training library student assistants: Bloomsburg university's interactive instructional program. *College & Research Libraries News, 62*(5), 537–538.

Tucker, J. C. (2004). Getting down to business: Library staff training. *Reference Services Review, 32*(3), 293–301.

Wilkins, C. (1999). Training staff for business reference. *Journal of Library Administration, 29*(1), 37–45.

Womack, R. (2007). *Business reference training manual*. Retrieved September 25, 2007, from http://www.rci.rutgers.edu/~rwomack/training.html.

Early Career Librarianship in the Business Library

Gene Hayworth

INTRODUCTION

Like many colleagues, my career in librarianship has followed an indirect path. I began my MLS at Syracuse University while working as a computer support technician at the University of Rochester medical library media center. After completing my degree, I worked for a brief time at CARL Corporation in a position that combined my technical background with my newly acquired MLS. That was followed by one year with another software firm, then three years at a community college library. Although I had conducted a few bibliographic instruction sessions for business classes at the community college and worked with the small business reference collection, these experiences did little to prepare me for my current position as a business librarian at the University of Colorado at Boulder. I came into the position feeling that I was not suitably qualified, but I soon learned that such a situation is common. The literature shows that business librarians come from a wide cross-section of the population, and that only about one in four business librarians have an advanced degree in business.

Individuals beginning a career in business librarianship (whether directly out of library school, transferring from a non-subject-specific library position, or from a different subject specialty) may at first be overwhelmed by the breadth of knowledge required to function adequately as a business librarian. Maintaining a working knowledge of finance, accounting, marketing, real estate, and tax law, combined with information from a variety of state, federal, and international agencies, challenges even the most seasoned business librarian. Those who come into the job with a working knowledge in any of these areas will have an advantage, but, like any librarian, relying on the skills developed in school or career will get you far in fulfilling the duties of the new position.

Mentors are valuable assets. My supervisor, Carol Krismann, head of the William M. White Business Library for over 25 years, has been an excellent mentor. She taught me that business librarianship, like any other library discipline, relies on an aptitude for collection development, instruction, and public service skills. Knowledge of business disciplines develops naturally from daily tasks required by the position. Collection development begins with a thorough assessment of the current business collection. This is followed by examining new titles, reading reviews of new materials, and considering library collections and collection policies at other institutions. Schools usually provide a faculty directory that contains an overview of faculty research interests; in addition, most faculty now have Web pages that address publications, interests, and courses. These can be invaluable for an early career librarian to begin to examine the collection and see how it fits into research and the curriculum.

Conducting library instruction sessions requires understanding the course materials and requirements and is greatly enhanced by learning faculty research interests. Public service includes gaining an understanding of the institution. It is essential to know the mission of the school and the vision of the dean. Finally, advancing as a business librarian requires active participation in a professional organization and consistent review of the literature concerning business librarianship.

LITERATURE REVIEW

For those beginning their careers, there has been little scholarship published that provides a focus on the daily routines of business librarianship. Yet there is a wealth of supporting material that can help shape the career of a new business librarian. Articles discussing demographics, business education, and core competencies for business librarianship can be found in journals as diverse as *Library Mosaics* and *One-Person Library*. These sources explore qualifications for business librarians, resources, education, real-world examples, and advice on general librarianship.

Demographics

There have been no recent surveys that examine the demographics of business librarianship. However, a 1999 study analyzed age, gender, ethnic diversity, education, professional development and additional demographic characteristics of U.S. and international business librarians. In "A Professional Photo of Academic Business Librarians Worldwide: the Present Picture and a Future View," Ruth Pagell and Edward Lusk reported on a survey of members of the Academic Business Library Directors (ABLD) and scrutinized other surveys for relevant data. The statistics present characteristics of the ABLD group and business librarians as a whole. The survey revealed a mean age of 50.8 years for library managers in the United States and a mean age of 41.8 years for international library managers. Nonmanagement librarians had a mean age of 41.9 years (in the United States) and 36.7 (internationally). The results also indicated that 9.7% of the professional staff consisted of minority librarians. In addition, results from the study indicated that 46.5% of all academic business library directors were male. The authors also analyzed educational background and noted that "only 23.5% of the group had MBAs, with about a third of the managers and less than one fifth of the non-managers holding this degree" (Pagell & Lusk, 2000, p. 9).

Education and Qualifications for Business Librarians

Three exceptional articles focus on changing trends in education for librarians. Amanda Martin's "Leap into Your Future" (2005) provides advice for those considering library school. Although the article does not address a specific type of librarian, it provides practical advice applicable to a business library career. Martin suggested that those considering employment in librarianship first examine their priorities and interests. The article recommends working in a library prior to beginning an MLS degree program. She also advised working in different types of libraries (such as medical, corporate, and law), before making a commitment, and observing how the library staff interacts with patrons in a variety of areas. Where jobs are not available, there may be volunteer opportunities. It can be particularly helpful to talk to librarians and library staff to discuss what the work means, and it is also a way to find a potential mentor.

A more focused discussion occurs in "Business Information Courses in LIS Programs: A Content Analysis," by Gary White (2004). The author examined the course content of business information courses available from accredited library and information studies (LIS) programs in the United States. White analyzed the number and type of courses, examined the syllabi for courses from 48 programs offered in 2002–2003, and identified the business subjects covered. He considered textbooks and other materials, assignments, projects, and examinations, as well as the use of guest lecturers and tours. White's study shows that although the content of business information courses in LIS programs varies widely, common content includes coverage of online databases, introduction to business librarianship, and company, industry, and investment information.

An earlier article by White, "Academic Subject Specialist Positions in the United States: A Content Analysis of Announcements," (1999) analyzes position announcements to determine what requirements, characteristics, and qualifications academic libraries seek when filling open positions. The article addressed the skills, educational background, and experience sought in candidates applying for 103 positions in business, 104 positions in social science, and 108 positions in science libraries. Skills required for these positions included a familiarity with electronic resources, "oral, written, or interpersonal communication skills," and experience conducting bibliographic instruction sessions (White, 1999, p. 380). Findings also included a list of the desired education most frequently appearing in the position announcements. There was an interesting correlation between these findings and the results presented by Pagell and Lusk. White's study showed that only 24 of the 103 positions in business librarianship required an MBA.

Resources for Business Librarians

In "Core Competencies for Business Reference," members of the Education Committee of the Business Reference and Services Section (BRASS), a subset of the American Library Association's Reference and

User Services Association (ALA/RUSA), described the core competencies guides that the Committee developed and continue to maintain on the BRASS Best of the Best Business Website. The core competencies guides in the series cover the fields of accounting, advertising and marketing, banking, company and industry research, insurance, international business, investment and finance, jobs and human resources, small business, and taxation. These online guides provide a list of resources necessary for business reference. The article discusses the benefits of using the guides, which often include a glossary of terms. Each guide defines the basic terms and "lists the core resources, both print and online, needed to develop a working knowledge of the research area" (Education Committee, 2006).

Lewis Guodo Liu's study, reported in "The Emergence of Business Information Resources and Services on the Internet and Its Impact on Business Librarianship" (2000), considered the rapid expansion of business services and resources on the Internet and how such resources influence the profession. Liu identifies resources in areas such as economics, finance, marketing, international business, and real estate. The article asserts that it is becoming increasingly crucial for business librarians to effectively identify, evaluate, select, and organize subject knowledge in business online, and that business information on the Internet poses a significant challenge. Without subject knowledge, Liu suggested that business librarians will not be able to maintain a high quality of business information services. He concluded that it is time for library and information science schools and libraries to set high standards for recruiting instructors in business information and for employing business librarians.

Advice from Practitioners

Several articles provide advice from individuals serving in the profession. In "A Glimpse of the Future? Virtual Corporate Librarians," Steven Kaye (2006) focused on the virtualization of business libraries. Kaye asserted that the majority of information needed by customers of business libraries will likely be digital in the next 10 years. He argued that business librarians may work in a smaller space or even at home because the virtualization will allow libraries to go to customers rather than customers going to the libraries.

In "The Journey from Corporate to Academic Librarian," Susan Klopper (2006) discussed the change in her career from a corporate setting to the Goizueta Business Library at Emory University. From her perspective, hiring librarians with a corporate background makes the library a better place because such individuals often bring a fresh perspective and an understanding of how organizations run. She contrasted the responsibilities of a corporate librarian (who conducts research) to an academic librarian (who teaches customers how to locate and evaluate resources themselves). She also discusses the need to help students understand that the skill sets learned in the library will be invaluable to them in the corporate world.

The interviews in "Conversations with Charles Popovich & Hal Kirkwood" by Cynthia Lenox (2006) illustrate two impressive careers. Lenox interviewed Popovich, head business librarian at Ohio State University in Columbus, and Hal Kirkwood, instruction coordinator at Purdue University Management and Economics Library. Popovich refered to several memorable mentors who had been there during different stages of his career. When asked about the qualities of a successful academic business librarian, Kirkwood referred to one's willingness to be constantly challenged and the ability to multitask.

In "Paper Number 2: Business School Libraries-Determining New Services," Jan Wallace (2005) examined the ability of academic business libraries to provide value while competing for funds with other groups within the university. Wallace applied Michael Porter's work on the theory of the value chain (a theory that advocates partitioning the organization into specific activities that are key to competitive advantage and identify the linkages among them) to business library services. The study assessed those competitors—the World Wide Web, online libraries, and other university departments—and considers options for competing with them. Results from the study suggest that selecting and positioning services is of crucial importance to the relevance, cost-effectiveness, and value to parent organizations of libraries. Wallace stated that

> When libraries are not involved in the early stages of curriculum planning, they are less able to insert a library research component into course content. Similarly libraries that do not actively promote in-class teaching, especially when library resources are tied to a particular assignment, are less able to ensure their resources are well-used. (p. 32)

DISCUSSION

It is clear from the literature that early career librarians face a wide variety of challenges. It is also clear that my background in the corporate

world and my work in a library prior to receiving my MLS is not significantly different from the background of many of my peers in business
librarianship. Like them, I have learned that there are many opportunities
for education and guidance. Most important is finding ways to interact with
the faculty of the business school.

Two valuable initiatives that were in place prior to my arrival at the
University of Colorado have been discontinued but deserve to be mentioned
in this discussion. As early as 1966 the business school had a library
committee comprising business faculty who collaborated with the librarian
to ensure that library collections would meet the needs of faculty research
and teaching. The committee participated in the interview process for
selecting a library director and provided advice and guidance on matters
related to library operations. It was active for approximately 20 years, but
when the campus mission changed, placing a greater emphasis on faculty
research, interest in serving on this library committee ebbed, and it was
disbanded.

In addition to interacting with business faculty on the library committee, one former colleague worked with business faculty on the business
school's curriculum committee. The objective was to increase the role of
bibliographic instruction in the business curriculum and to provide a voice
for the library in course development. Although librarians here at the University of Colorado no longer have a presence on that committee, when
possible it is a highly recommended avenue for keeping abreast of changes
in the curriculum, providing a voice for the library, and forecasting changes
in library materials to support the new curriculum.

Library instruction provides another avenue for establishing a librar-
ian/faculty connection. Through teaching, I have been able to form close
ties with business faculty and students. The majority of our bibliographic
instruction sessions are conducted for "Introduction to Business," a course
required for all freshmen. We also teach sessions for business writing, marketing, entrepreneurship, and business ethics classes. These sessions have
taught me much more about faculty interests and the variety of disciplines
within the business school.

In addition, my work with students who share an interest in corporate
ethics and sustainability issues encouraged me to develop the Business
Ethics Links Library (BELL), an online resource available at http://libnet.
colorado.edu/Bell/. BELL is a comprehensive starting point for research in
corporate ethics and social responsibility that provides access to codes of
ethics for U.S. companies and trade and professional associations, ethics
sites at college and university business programs, industry information

resources, and company promotion of social responsibility covering such topics as arts assistance, environmental clean up, charitable giving, and community programming.

My technology background has also provided me with skills useful for marketing the library. I am responsible for the library Web pages and use them as another method for communicating with the faculty. I notify the faculty about our monthly New Books list, new trial databases, and special library events. Our new learning commons feature a wide variety of software, and I am often able to assist our students with software questions and to troubleshoot hardware problems.

Professional Associations

Another important strategy for developing a career as a business librarian is to gather support and knowledge outside of the institution. Professional organizations distribute excellent resources for development and can serve as a channel to develop associates with similar interests. Among the many professional associations that exist to promote business education, two prominent groups provide support for business librarians. Through conferences, educational programs, online and print publications, and member networking, the BRASS of the ALA/RUSA division, and the Business and Finance Division of the Special Libraries Association (BFD/SLA) offer opportunities for new members. At my library, we have had individuals who are active in each group, and that representation has served the library well by providing us with perspectives and resources from both organizations.

The Business Reference and Services Section (BRASS)

Because I was a member of ALA when I accepted the job as business librarian, joining BRASS was an easy transition. Established in 1988, ALA/RUSA's BRASS represents the interests of reference librarians, business information specialists, and others engaged in providing business reference and information services. The purpose of the section is to study, promote, and support the role of business reference in academic libraries, serving as a medium for the sharing of information and concerns among interested librarians, publishers, and other suppliers of business reference sources. Members are actively encouraged to participate in a larger arena. BRASS sends representatives to many of the RUSA committees to represent BRASS interests and speak on behalf of the section. Through its programs and projects, the section works to improve the sources and techniques of business reference and information. Members promote the role of business reference in academic and public libraries and address issues facing business reference. BRASS also promotes the professional development of its members through educational programs and through committee service (Business Reference and Services Section, 2007).

The Business Reference Services Discussion Group, for example, provides an excellent forum for learning and sharing information about reference resources with colleagues. The Education Committee sponsors a series of programs designed to disseminate information about the profession and to provide training for new as well as seasoned business librarians. Topics of discussion among members of other committees in the past have included business bibliographic instruction, online and CD-ROM sources, creative funding for academic business libraries, and investment information in academic libraries.

A highlight of each Annual ALA meeting is the preconference sponsored by BRASS. In the past, these have included the following programs: "Follow the Money—From School Buses to Surpluses: Understanding Public Finance," "Beyond Stocks and Bonds: Learning about Futures, Options, Derivatives, and More," "Success by the Numbers: Statistics for Business Development," and "Quick Lubes, Java Joints & Pet Parlors: the Keys to Writing an Effective Business Plan." Handouts and other materials from these programs are later published on the BRASS Education Website.

In June 2005, I attended the Business Librarianship 101 preconference. This day-long session featured Irwin Faye, a retired business librarian, who discussed business reference sources; Bobray Bordelon, Economics and Finance Librarian at Princeton University, who presented strategies for collection development; Becky Albitz, Electronic Resources and Copyright Librarian at Penn State, who spoke about electronic resource licensing; and David Flynn, Head of the Business, Humanities and Social Sciences reference department at the University of Hawaii, who provided information about marketing and outreach services for business libraries.

Special Library Association

One colleague, Martha Jo Sani, has represented our library as a member of the Special Library Association. Established in 1958, the Business and Finance Division of the Special Libraries Association promotes all aspects of business and financial libraries, including planning, collection building, design of services and operations, personnel education, and the development of new business information sources. The division was the result of a

1958 merger between two earlier groups: the Business Group (established in 1934) and the Financial Group (established in 1925).

Sani prefers attending SLA to ALA for several reasons. First, she has found that there is a greater mix of corporate, academic, public, and information services librarians involved in this organization. Because the group is smaller than ALA, she believes that members have better access to vendors and get to see new products first. She also participates in a local chapter of the Business and Finance Division and finds that the local programming brings the group together more frequently. After each conference she shares her knowledge and experience with the business library staff and faculty.

Through five specialized sections and the Real Estate Round Table, the Division offers its members increased depth of service and value. The College & University Business Libraries Section provides a forum for members to focus on issues related to all areas of academic business librarianship including research, collection development, reference, instruction, and service activities. The Corporate Information Centers Section allows members to focus on issues related to the operation of libraries, information centers and services, competitive intelligence groups, and content management units in business settings. Members of the Financial Institutions Section focus on issues related to the compilation, retrieval, and dissemination of key information devoted to banking, finance, and related industry areas, and in the management of libraries and information centers pertaining to these subjects. The Investment Services Section examines how the use of information and the work of the public and academic sectors help capital market; and the Private Equity Section facilitates the networking of members involved in private equity or venture capital internationally. Each of these sections maintains a Website.

The group you choose will depend in large part on your budget, your interests, and your institution. Once you have decided, consider serving on a committee. Your contribution to the profession will not go unnoticed, and you will find this service rewarding and enriching.

Publishing in Professional Journals

The list of journal titles in the field of library and information science is wide and variable. Articles on business librarianship are suitable for most of these titles and are worthy of review for those who are interested in the literature. Journals provide sources for education and awareness, as well as a channel for sharing your own work. At the University of

Colorado at Boulder, librarians are faculty members with a citizenship requirement of 40% librarianship, 40% research, and 20% service. Such a division of labor is not suitable for every individual, but I have found that the research and service components are an excellent counterpoint to my daily work within the business library. Selecting and developing a research agenda provides a focus for learning more about business disciplines. It also requires familiarity with the literature that might otherwise escape notice. I have focused on business ethics research tools and methodologies; I have also completed a series of articles and Web reviews for the *Journal of Business & Finance Librarianship* (*JFBL*).

JFBL is a refereed, quarterly journal that promotes the creation, organization, dissemination, retrieval, and use of business information. Articles cover the business information needs of special libraries, academic libraries, and public libraries, as well as information services and centers outside of the traditional library setting. The journal offers an international perspective, reflecting the multinational and international scope of today's business community. The focus of the journal is practice oriented, but it also provides an outlet for new empirical studies on business librarianship and business information. Aside from articles, this journal offers valuable statistical and meeting reports, literature and media reviews, Website reviews, and interviews.

The SLA Business and Finance Division publishes the *B&F Bulletin*. Recent topics have included a discussion of knowledge databases, techniques for marketing the library, and blogging for scholars. The *Bulletin* provides a peer-review option to article authors but also provides publishing opportunities to those who do not choose that option. The peer-review process is double blind and draws upon a pool of reviewers offering a broad range of expertise. Complete copies of the most recent issues are available online at http://www.slabf.org/bulletin.html.

CONCLUSION

There are many paths that can lead an individual into a career as a business librarian. For those who are new to the profession, there are many resources that can provide guidance and several organizations that can provide peer support. I have been fortunate in the initial stages of my career to have an experienced, knowledgeable mentor. My association with BRASS has allowed me to develop a service record at the national level. Within two months of accepting my position, I was appointed to serve on the BRASS Publications Committee and developed a support network that I have often turned to for guidance and advice. Through the creation and maintenance of my BELL database, I have continued to refine my research interests in business ethics, and after publishing several pieces in *JFBL*, I was asked to serve on the editorial board. All of these activities are considered during my yearly evaluation, and, although not guaranteed, with a little more work attaining tenure seems possible.

Where tenure is not an issue, business librarians may find that there is more time to focus on educational opportunities. In my situation, pursuing an MBA has not been practical. To meet the stringent tenure requirements at the University of Colorado I have focused my time on research and publication. To attain an MBA here would require 60 credit hours, a goal that would take 10 years to complete. Those who can pursue this education will gain knowledge that will be extremely useful, but for those who cannot, there are many other avenues to explore. Many of the skills and much of the knowledge required of a business librarian will come naturally from work with the collection, developing bibliographic instruction, joining a professional association, and review of business library literature.

REFERENCES

Business Reference and Services Section (2007). *American Library Association, Reference and User Services Association, Business Reference and Services Section*. Retrieved August 10, 2007, from http://www.ala.org/ala/rusa/rusaourassoc/rusasections/brass/brass.htm.

Education Committee of the Business Reference and Services Section. (2006). Core competencies for business reference. *Reference & User Services Quarterly, 46*(1), 40–43.

Kaye, S. (2006, October). A glimpse of the future? Virtual corporate librarians. *One-Person Library, 23*(6), 10–11.

Klopper, S. M. (2006, September/October). The journey from corporate to academic librarian. *Online, 30*(5), 14–20.

Lenox, C. (2006). Conversations with Charles Popovich & Hal Kirkwood. *B&F Bulletin, 132*, 9–13.

Liu, L. G. (2000). The emergence of business information resources and services on the Internet and its impact on business librarianship. *Online Information Review, 24*(3), 234–254.

Martin, A. (2005) March/April). Leap into your future. *Library Mosaics, 16*(2), 17.

Pagell, R. A., & Lusk, E. J. (2000). A professional photo of academic business librarians worldwide: The present picture and a future view. *Journal of Business & Finance Librarianship, 6*(1), 3–21.

Special Library Association. (2006). *Business & Finance Division of the Special Library Association.* Retrieved August 18, 2007, from http://www.slabf.org/.

Wallace, J. (2005). Paper number 2: Business school libraries-determining new services. *Journal of Business & Finance Librarianship, 10*(3), 31–36.

White, G. W. (1999, September). Academic subject specialist positions in the United States: A content analysis of announcements. *Journal of Academic Librarianship, 25*(5), 372–382.

White, G. W. (2004). Business information courses in LIS programs: A content analysis. *Journal of Business & Finance Librarianship, 10*(2), 3–15.

Willner, R. A. (1993). Education for library and information management careers in business and financial services. *Library Trends, 42*, 232–248.

Development of Midcareer Librarians

Cory Tucker

INTRODUCTION

While thinking about being a midcareer librarian and analyzing one's career path, I came across a passage in Lewis Carroll's *Alice in Wonderland* where the Cheshire cat tells young Alice, "If you don't know where you are going, any road will take you there." Confusing? Maybe, but the quote illustrates an important point when it comes to choosing a career path. Planning is a crucial aspect of career development for librarians.

The midcareer librarian, in my mind, can be a person working in libraries between eight and 15 years and has worked for their current employer for over five years. At this stage in their work life, the person may be faced with the possibility of career impatience, stagnation with their current job, need of professional growth, or need for achievement

(Sterns & Subich, 2002). Midcareer is a perfect time for self-assessment and renewal. Whatever the case may be, the midcareer librarian is faced with many difficult decisions from changing jobs or careers, engaging in development activities, moving to administration, and pursuing promotions. These can be further complicated by other issues including current work environment, job market conditions, and balancing work and family, particularly when children may be involved (Sterns & Subich, 2002).

This article takes a look at the midcareer librarian and discusses what challenges the person may face in his or her career path. In addition, it will analyze how the person can deal with these challenges through career development.

LITERATURE REVIEW

There are a few articles that touch on the topic of midcareer librarians. Reid (2005) acknowledged the difficulties faced by midcareer librarians and offered suggestions to help people reenergize themselves and survive in a constantly changing work environment. Among the suggestions given by Reid are self-assessment, matching your personality to your job and organization, and changing careers. Another article coauthored by Broady-Preston and Bell (2001) discusses the establishment of a distance learning program to help midcareer librarians acquire the skills and academic credentials to complete in a changing marketplace. Their article is a case study on the effectiveness of the program and also measured the attitudes of professionals in library and information science. A third article that is useful for midcareer librarians was written by Harhai (2002) and reviews 13 popular career self-help books.

Although not specifically related to midcareer librarians, there is another article dealing with career development in librarianship. The article discusses results from the Library and Information Commission report on cross-sectoral mobility in the library and information services (LIS) profession (Dalton, Mynott, & Schoolbred, 2000). This study (conducted by researchers at the University of Central England in Birmingham) was created to look at the barrier to career development within the LIS profession, specifically targeting professionals moving to different sectors of the profession. The issues discussed by the authors include the following: professional segregation, employment strategies, self-confidence, training, and professional support. In an article published in 2004, Jacobsen provided a case study of graduates from the UCLA Graduate School of Library and Information Science. The article discusses the results of a survey of the class of 1988 and how their careers have progressed. Jacobsen offered insights on career development, moving jobs, dealing with office politics and changing technology, salaries, mentoring, and service in associations.

Outside of librarianship, there are articles about midcareer professionals and development that may be useful for librarians at this stage in their career. Power and Rothausen (2003) proposed a model of midcareer development for individuals who are proactively managing their own careers. The model directs workers to define their work, identify its future requirements, and select a developmental direction. Three levels of midcareer development are also proposed: job oriented, work maintenance, and work growth. This new structure allows midcareer individuals to maintain or grow their employment security, income, and career satisfaction in an environment of increasing mobility and salary compression. The model is a useful tool for midcareer professionals as it touches on the economic and labor market concerns that influence one's career path and decisions.

Another article that is not related to midcareer librarianship specifically but might be nonetheless of interest is Montgomery's (2002) discussion about plateauing and long-term career satisfaction. Montgomery discussed the idea of career plateaus and provided a definition for the following three types of plateauing: structural plateauing, which occurs when an employee has reached the highest level one can obtain within an organization; content plateauing, when an employee has mastered the work and there is nothing left to learn; and life plateauing, which is characterized by little fulfillment in any area of life. This article provides possible ways to deal with plateaus.

SELF ASSESSMENT

The midcareer is a point where a person may reexamine and reevaluate personal values and attitude, career goals, and progress (Carney, Wells, & Streufert, 1981). To help make an informed decision at this critical time in one's career, it is important to conduct a self-assessment on a personal and professional level. Self-assessment allows individuals to chart their progress, learning, and development to see how they are progressing on a personal and professional level. Conducting such evaluations will help individuals identify appropriate development opportunities, including staying in their current positions, making a lateral move, or accepting positions with more responsibility. Self-assessment allows an individual to analyze the stages in his or her career and see how these stages have affected his or her development and goals (London & Stumpf, 1982). A couple of interesting exercises can be found on the allbusiness.com Website (http://www.allbusiness.com/human-resources/careers-career-path/12068.html). One exercise involves writing down what you have enjoyed about your career in one column and, in another column, writing down what you could have done without. The exercise can help midcareer professionals identify what has been satisfying and what has not been satisfying thus far. Another recommended exercise consists of writing down your short-term and long-term goals to identify career priorities. This exercise can help you compare earlier to current goals, enabling you to see how these priorities may have changed. A final exercise is to create your ideal job description. This exercise can help with finding what job duties you prefer and what skill sets you will need to enhance.

Personal Growth

Obviously it is important to analyze your personal growth and development. As you go through your life cycle and career path, you may develop new interests or desire new personal and professional challenges. As you change as an individual, you should evaluate how your job fits with your personal interests. It may be helpful for you to identify specific interests or skills that you cannot pursue in your current position. Once these interests have been identified, you can begin searching for internal and external opportunities to achieve these goals. Such an evaluation may result in an internal move within your current organization, a move to another organization, or a career change.

Professional Growth

Professional growth can be analyzed by looking at your past, present, and future career path. According to Carney et al. (1981), there are several stages in career decisions, and the midcareer librarian tends to be in the reevaluation stage. The person in this stage may begin to examine more closely whether the job is fulfilling his or her expectations. The person may want to reevaluate goals and alternatives. During this reevaluation stage, it is a good idea to analyze your entire career path, from past to present to future.

Past Career

When analyzing one's career, a good place to start is with your past career as a librarian. Upon entering librarianship, you had an idea of what job you wanted and established specific goals for the first five years of your career. A simple question to ask is: did you meet all of the goals you established? If not, are these goals still applicable for your career? What events did you experience that may have altered your career path? How did these events and decisions affect your career path?

Current Career

Once you have delved into your past career as a librarian, it is important to look at yourself in your current position. What are you doing now? Are you happy with your job and workplace environment? What skills have you obtained in your current position? How will these skills help you in another job? How have your goals and aspirations changed? Are you still motivated to perform your job? Do the organization's goals and beliefs match your own?

Future Career

How have your values changed? Do you want more responsibility? Do you want to be a leader?

ORGANIZATIONAL ISSUES

When analyzing your career path, it is important to chart the course of your career within your current organization (Carney et al., 1981). Schein's (1971) model charts growth within an organization inwardly, vertically, and horizontally. According to Schein's model, inward growth does not involve a visible change in position, nor development of new skills; instead, this growth is measured in terms of interpersonal relationships. The next form of growth in this model is vertical, representing movement up the career ladder. Finally, the last measurement of growth is horizontal, which encompasses a rotation across a series of functions within an organization. This usually involves exposing employees to different facets of an organization. This model is helpful for an individual because it provides a picture of how one has experienced growth and professional development within an organization and may provide valuable insight into whether a person is ready for change or satisfied in his or her current environment.

One of the items related to the organization, and a major individual career path issue, is your development as a professional librarian. When looking at your current position, identify skills or interests that you have not achieved or fulfilled. Organizations should provide development opportunities. Thus, it is appropriate to ask yourself: are my needs being met? In this self- and career assessment, it is vital to have a clear picture of where you are personally and professionally, what you want to do with your personal and professional career, and how you can achieve these personal and professional aspirations.

CAREER DEVELOPMENT

Once you have conducted your personal and professional evaluations, you can identify specific goals and explore ways to achieve these goals. Whatever the career path you have chosen, there may be additional skills or opportunities you need to consider to meet your goals. These may include professional development opportunities, leadership and management training, and mentoring.

Professional Development

Depending on the career path you choose, you may need to take continuing education classes through universities or professional organizations. Continuing education may also be an option through self-training. If you happen to choose the path to administration and management, you may be required to obtain another master's degree, MBA, or a PhD. In instances where a person is moving laterally in his or her existing organization, there are several library organizations (or divisions or sections within organizations) that can help build the necessary skills. For example, if a subject librarian would like to move into collection development or management, he or she can join the Association for Library Collections & Technical Services (ALCTS), a division of the American Library Association. ALCTS offers online classes, Webinars, and conference presentations and discussions. A possible option for professional development at the midcareer stage is sabbatical or other types of leave (Hubbard, 2002).

Leadership

No matter what path you take, as a midcareer librarian, you will most likely be looked upon for direction and leadership within your organization or at your new organization. Some people are natural born leaders, and others are not. However, there are opportunities to learn how to be a leader. One option is to learn from existing leaders in your organization. Sit down with these people and discuss various aspects of leadership and obtain their advice. Another option is to research articles and books available on this topic. There are also numerous leadership institutes, such as the ACRL/Harvard Leadership Institute. A good listing of leadership training programs and institutes is available in a 2004 article by Mason and Wetherbee. Most regional and state associations have annual leadership institutes that can be extremely beneficial. Another way to develop leadership skills is taking on specific roles and projects in the workplace. One study indicates that a major influence on leadership development is an individual's ability to cope with job variety, responsibility, new tasks, and unfamiliar situations (Mason & Wetherbee, 2004).

Administration/Management

For a midcareer librarian, taking on management or administrative responsibilities is quite common. A person at this stage in his or her career may become a department head, division head, or other type of manager. This step in the career path can be a big change, especially for those people who have not previously supervised others. Supervision and management responsibilities bring new challenges and require the incorporation of a new skill set. Just as some people are not natural leaders, some people are not natural managers. Like leadership, management skills can be learned in various ways, such as through workshops, continuing education, or through professional organizations. Another option is to speak with people in management positions and attempt to learn as much from them as possible. There are many books published on the topic of becoming a manager that may be helpful as well.

Mentoring

As a midcareer librarian, you probably have had a mentor guiding you professionally along your career path. At this point in your career, you might be ready to become a mentor. Being a mentor can be rewarding in that you can pass along your knowledge, support, and experiences to another librarian who is just beginning his or her career. Mentoring may take place within an institution or within a professional association or organization.

CONCLUSION

Reaching the midcareer point in the profession of librarianship can be a tumultuous time due to personal and professional changes. Although this can be a difficult phase in one's career path, there are several options available to deal with the various issues of a midcareer professional. It is important to carefully weigh your options and assess your career and personal life to choose the appropriate path to take for your future.

REFERENCES

Broady-Preston, J., & Bell, S. (2001). Motivating mid-career LIS professionals: The Aberystwyth experience. *New Library World, 102*(10), 372–381.

Carney, C., Wells, C., & Streufert, D. (1981). *Career planning: Skills to build your future.* New York: D. Van Nostrand.

Dalton, P., Mynott, G., & Schoolbred, M. (2000). Barriers to career development within the LIS profession. *Library Review, 49*(6), 271–277.

Harhai, M. (2002). Maybe it's not too late to join the circus: Books for midlife career management. *Library Trends, 50*(4), 640–650.

Hubbard, M. (2002). Exploring the sabbatical or other leave as a means of energizing a career. *Library Trends, 50*(4), 603–613.

Jacobsen, T. (2004). The class of 1988: Fifteen years after library school, what do their careers say about yours? *Library Journal, 129*(12), 38–41.

London, M., & Stumpf, S. (1982). *Managing careers.* Reading, MA: Addison-Wesley.

Mason, F., & Wetherbee, L. (2004). Learning to lead: An analysis of current training programs for library leadership. *Library Trends, 53*(1), 187–217.

Montgomery, D. (2002). Happily ever after: Plateauing as a means for long-term career satisfaction. *Library Trends, 50*(4), 702–716.

Power, S., & Rothausen, T. (2003). The work-oriented midcareer development model: An extension of Super's maintenance stage. *Counseling Psychologist, 31*(2), 157–197.

Reid, B. (2005). What do I do now: Suggestions for the frustrated mid-career professional. *IEEE Antennas and Propagation Magazine, 47*(5), 159–163.

Schein, E. (1971). The individual, the organization, and the career. *Journal of Applied Behavioral Science, 7*, 401–426.

Sterns, H., & Subich, L. (2002). Career development in midcareer. In D. Feldman (Ed.), *Work careers* (pp. 186–214). San Francisco: Jossey-Bass.

Growing Your Own Leaders:
Succession Planning in Libraries

Judith M. Nixon

Imagine this: You come to work one day to find out that your library director has accepted another job, decided to retire, or (heaven forbid) become ill or had an accident. In any event, you have a top position open. What will happen? The procedure in academic libraries is very familiar. A search committee will be appointed, and a position description will be written and advertised. Occasionally it will be decided to limit the search to current staff members, an in-house search. This will speed up the process. However, if a national search is conducted, the hiring process will take months. Contrast this scenario with one at a major corporation such as McDonald's Corp. Jim Cantalupo, chair and CEO suddenly died. Within days the corporation was announcing a new chair. Before the stockholders reading the financial page had time to respond, McDonald's was back to business as usual.

How can they respond so fast? What planning and preparation make this possible? The answer is called succession planning. Organizations such as Dow Chemical, Eli Lilly, Sonoco, and Dell Computer are anticipating changes in leadership, assessing the skills and knowledge of their employees, identifying those that possess the potential to be effective leaders, and providing training, mentoring, and experience so that when the moment happens the plan is in place. Companies are not just doing this for the top executive, they are pushing this planning down the ladder. Succession planning is becoming workplace planning. William J. Rothwell (2005), author of the major book on succession planning, defined it as anticipating changes in management, creating a strategic plan to identify potential staff members, determining the gaps in their knowledge, and providing training and coaching, special assignments, and experiences so that they are ready to step up when the time comes.

REVIEW OF THE LIBRARY LITERATURE

Are some libraries following the lead of these corporations and adopting succession planning? A review of the literature turned up only one article about succession planning in academic or public libraries in the United States, "Your Library's Future," a 2004 article published in *Library Journal* (Singer, Goodrich, & Goldberg). This article discusses how one library, the Multnomah County Library in Portland, Oregon, developed a program to prepare and train younger staff members for the anticipated upper-level positions. This plan included making staff aware of the future needs, encouraging them to make their interest known, and then providing peer reviews, mentors, and a training program. A side bar called "Succession Planning Tool Kit" gives an excellent but brief outline of the steps to take to set up a program. Besides this article, there is one book on succession planning in libraries, *Staff Planning in a Time of Demographic Change,* which is based on a series of conferences held in Ontario, Canada, in 2002 and 2003 (Whitmell, 2005). Libraries in the United Kingdom, Canada, and Australia have more seriously discussed succession planning, and this book provides a thorough discussion of the issues, many which apply to U.S. library situations. With the exception of the *Library Journal* article and a small set of articles centering on special libraries, there is almost nothing in journal literature about libraries in the United States using succession planning. The lack of articles about U.S. libraries is a red flag. Should libraries use succession planning? Why are U.S. libraries not using such plans? Are libraries just behind the times and missing a technique that could be useful? The primary reason that the business world uses succession planning is the shortage of capable people in the management ranks to fill the senior executive positions. In other words, major corporations cannot hire the leaders they need, so they are growing their own. Are libraries facing the same problem? Is there a shortage of leaders in the library field?

IS SUCCESSION PLANNING SOMETHING LIBRARIANS SHOULD CONSIDER?

A Look at the Leadership Supply in the Library Profession as a Whole

Within the next few years, many librarians, especially those holding the top-level positions, such as directors, deans, associate directors, and heads of libraries, will be retiring. The Bureau of Labor Statistics said that more than three in five librarians are age 45 years or older and will become eligible for retirement in the next 10 years. Mary Jo Lynch, director of American Library Association's Office for Research and Statistics, confirmed that in the near future a surge of retirements will take place peaking between 2015 and 2019. "In total, the decade beginning in 2010 will see 45% of today's librarians reach age 65, representing the early wave of baby-boom librarians reaching the traditional retirement age" (Lynch, Tordella, & Godfrey, 2005, p. 28). Earlier statistics similarly outlined the coming librarian shortage and predicted that 83,366 librarians will be age 65 years by the year 2010 (Hernon, Powell, & Young, 2001). The general conclusion of many articles on the future of the profession is that the cause of the projected shortage is the expected retirements. (For a more detailed look at the retirement data, visit www.ala.org/ala/ors/reports/reports.htm). Not satisfied with this general conclusion Larry Hardesty (2002) took a more analytical look at the recruitment and hiring statistics in his article in *portal: Libraries and the Academy.* He identified and investigated the possible causes: closing library schools, more attractive positions for MLS graduates in information science fields, or low salaries. He concluded, "The most plausible explanation for the current situation is the increased number of retirements" (p. 94).

The problem is even more pronounced in Canada, which may explain why the Canadian libraries have been paying more attention to this phenomenon than U.S. libraries. The Canadian Library Association conducted a questionnaire survey sent to 386 members that focused on retirement trends from 2002–2010 and looked for strategies and the level of preparedness to deal with the future shortage of librarians. The survey found that between 30%–50% of the Canadian librarians will retire by 2010 and most libraries (74%) feel that they are not prepared or only somewhat prepared (Summerfield, 2002). Further data indicates that there is a decrease in the number of librarians in the 25–34 age range; the figure is 12% in Canadian Association of Research Libraries (ARL) libraries. These numbers are far from the ideal figures of 20% at the senior level and 20% at the newcomer level. The full report on the Canadian situation has just been released in a publication by the 8Rs Research Team (2007). Despite statistics that indicate a shortage of librarians and lack of middle-level librarians trained in the competencies of leadership, only 9% of the libraries surveyed have a succession plan in place. Although this is a dismal figure, ARL libraries in the United States are probably even less prepared.

In the past the profession has solved similar shortages by promoting mid-career librarians and filling their positions with new graduates. However, there is now a shortage of midcareer librarians and new MLS graduates. The situation is complicated by the fact that the 1990s were lean times in libraries, and the number of new hires during this time was limited. Many of the jobs went to boomers who changed careers and became librarians later in life. The result is that many librarians in middle management positions are the same age as the directors and associate directors, and they will be retiring along a similar time table.

To further complicate the labor situation, over the past 15 to 20 years, there has also been a shortage of new MLS graduates to fill the ranks vacated by promotions of middle-level librarians (Berry, 1988). This shortage is predicted to extend into the peak baby boomer retirement years, 2015–2019. "Estimated retirements outpace graduations in the United States, even accounting for reduced growth in professional-level library staffing in public and academic libraries" (Davis, 2005, p. 16). The library professional associations have made valiant efforts to address this problem by recruiting more people into the profession, but the prediction is that there is still a shortage of new MLS graduates.

The retirement of the boomers coupled with the shortage of new librarians will complicate the already tight recruiting market, but there is yet another phenomenon occurring that is blackening the outlook even more. That is poor retention of new librarians, or "the five year itch." Many new librarians are leaving the profession dissatisfied and restless within their first five years as librarians. In survey research reported by Markgren and her research colleagues (Markgren, Dickinson, Leonard, & Vassiliadis, 2007), one half of the 464 new librarians who answered their survey said they are thinking of leaving the profession and list some of the top reasons as "limited or no opportunities,"and "position or role is not challenging enough." They feel there are no growth opportunities, that they cannot move up the ladder, and that to advance they need to change jobs. Many are leaving librarianship as a career. So while library managers are despairing because they cannot find qualified staff especially for middle and upper-level positions, the new recruits feel there is no job advancement possible. There seems to be a serious communication gap between the generations (i.e., between the boomers and gen Xers). My own personal experience with gen Xers parallels what is written about them. They are described as self-focused and impatient but also very motivated and success oriented; they want to learn and take on responsibility including management and supervision. The time is ripe for formal succession planning programs that open up the discussion of opportunities for leadership and set up educational and training programs to prepare new librarians to step up.

IS THE SHORTAGE OF LIBRARIANS TRUE FOR BUSINESS LIBRARIANS AND BUSINESS LIBRARY MANAGERS?

Statistics on Business Librarians and the Job Market for Business Librarians

The focus of this journal is business librarianship, and there is data on this niche of the library world. Two articles published since 2000 shed some light. Ruth Pagell and Edward Lusk (2000) did a thorough statistical study of business librarians and found that in the United States the average business library manager was a 51-year-old white and as likely to be female as male. As a group business librarians were well educated with 68% of the 25 managers in the survey holding multiple postundergraduate degrees and about one third of them having a MBA. They averaged 22 years of experience as a librarian and nearly 17 years as business librarians. A major finding of this research was that 50% of the managers indicated that they did not anticipate being an academic business librarian longer than five years. So Pagell and Lusk's research indicates that we should be in the midst of a major shift in the managers/directors/heads in business libraries right now. However, a quick review of the Academic Business Library Directors (ABLD), the same group Pagell and Lusk surveyed, indicates little change in the demographics of this group in the last seven years. The average age now is 55 years; their education level is approximately the same with 67% holding multiple higher education degrees; 37% hold a second master's degree other than an MBA, and 30% hold an MBA; and 55% are female So in seven years the group has aged respectively, but the education level has not altered. New directors were more likely female as the ratio of male to female has altered. However, many business library directors are not retiring yet, as Pagell and Lusk's survey expected. To ascertain when the retirement exodus will begin, I asked when each ABLD member plans to retire. Sixteen of the 27 in the group (or 60%) plan to retire by 2014; but only three of these 16 plan to retire within the next two years. So just as the Census Bureau predicts, the retirement blitz will occur between 2010 and 2015.

Are the upcoming business librarians (the midcareer, nonmanagement business librarians) being prepared for these positions? Some of Pagell and Lusk's (2000) survey results shed some light. They asked how the current managers found out about and were hired for these positions. The major way (36%) was by personal contact, followed by internal postings (28%). It is the internal posting statistic that is of interest to this article. If in the 2000 survey over one fourth of the business library directors came to their jobs by internal promotions, then some rudimentary "succession planning" techniques were happening in their library, even if it was not called that. I found this so surprising that I asked a few related follow-up questions of the ABLD group in August 2007. Sixty percent stated that they were internal candidates. Twenty-two percent were internal promotions without any search, in-house or external. Another 11% were promotions after an in-house search, and 26% were internal candidates in an external search. These statistics clearly show that libraries are "growing their own" business library directors. Business librarians in the ranks are being prepared to manage the library and being promoted from within the same library.

Do midcareer, nonmanaging business librarians feel they are ready and willing to be promoted to leadership positions when the business managers retire? Again some of Pagell and Lusk's (2000) survey results give us some clues as they asked skill related questions. Interestingly, nonmanaging business librarians' self ratings for information skills did not deviate from managers' skills; however, there was a significant gap in management skills in two areas: human resource responsibilities and conflict resolution. There was a wide variation especially in conflict resolution; about 60% of the managers rated themselves high in this area, whereas only 30% of the nonmanagers felt they were able to handle this. So business librarians in the ranks know their subject but feel they lack management skills, and they feel they particularly lack human resources skills such as conflict resolution skills.

The Pagell and Lusk (2000) article did not attempt to determine if there will be enough business librarians to fill the upcoming management positions. However, another article by Lisa O'Connor and Stacey Marien (2002) did address this question. Their research, based on a survey to libraries that had advertised for a business librarian between March 1, 2000 and March 31, 2001, emphasized that at that time there was a lack of available business librarians. The major conclusion was that 70% of the employers were not satisfied with the applicant pool, with the quantity of candidates being the major problem. "Low supply of business information professionals" and "too much competition" for librarians were the major reasons listed by libraries that experienced difficulties in hiring. A huge 40% of the searches were reopened at least once. O'Connor and Marien concluded that "a good business librarian is hard to find" and "recruiting internally and providing extensive professional development and training may also be a cost-effective alternative" to searching for an outside business librarian. Their recommendations have the sound of succession planning. Like major corporations, perhaps libraries need to grow their own.

All the statistics indicate that there will be a major shortage of librarians, starting in 2010 and peaking at 2015, caused by retirements and shortages of young people choosing librarianship as a career. This shortage will affect business libraries. Succession planning seems like a logical approach. So why are U.S. libraries not readily using it? One reason is that in most libraries "the bench is too narrow." In other words, libraries do not have enough staff members to mentor and train new leaders. Major corporations have thousands of employees and hundreds of top-level managers. Identifying a handful of them that have the potential and interest to lead is possible. In a library with a few dozen librarians, this may not work. Another reason is that higher education institutions are actively working on increasing diversity; every opening is an opportunity. And the institutions have stated goals to increase the diversity of the faculty and staff;

internal promotions do not met this goal. The whole diversity problem is a topic for another article, but American Library Association's Office for Research and Statistics is following these statistics closely. They concluded that the "persistent lag in diversity in our LIS schools, the number of librarians and library assistants leaving the profession prematurely, the aging of racial and ethnic minority library workers, and the continued under representation of workers with disabilities, suggest a proportionally less diverse library workforce on the horizon" (*Diversity Counts*, 2006). Furthermore, they suggested strategically planning around human resource development and succession planning (for the full *Diversity Counts* report, see www.ala.org/diversitycounts). A third reason is the "grass is greener" perception. Libraries always want to hire the best candidate, and somehow librarians are not inclined to believe the best is on the staff right now. The last reason is the "new broom theory"; libraries have a strong desire for a change in management. Unlike the business world that is dependent on stockholders' desire for consistency, libraries use upper-level staff openings as an opportunity to bring in new ideas and people that can implement creative strategic changes. Verbalizing and then discussing these reasons can help a library assess whether succession planning or some strategies of succession planning might be useful. Even if a fully developed succession planning program is not the choice, there is much to be learned and borrowed from succession planning.

HOW TO START A SUCCESSION PLANNING PROGRAM

The business literature on the topic is clear on two essentials: succession planning only works if the top-level administrators are 100% behind it; and the program needs to be an open process. It cannot be done by the human resource department alone or by middle managers mentoring and grooming staff members reporting to them. The administration has to be deeply involved; likewise staff members need to be involved, with feedback going to the employees that have been identified as possessing the potential for leadership.

The basic steps of succession planning are:

1. analyze the demographics of your key positions
2. identify potential employees for lead positions
3. assess candidates strengths and weaknesses
4. develop a training program to build competencies.

Analyze Your Demographics

In a large academic or public library this would mean figuring out the age of your current directors, assistant or associate directors, department heads, and any other key positions, such as the main computer technician or business manager. In a smaller library system or a business library within a larger library system this might be a short list including only the managing librarian and possibly the assistant or associate managers. This step is easy to do; the main obstacle, because birth dates may not be readily available, is ascertaining ages. However a fairly close estimate can be obtained by assuming each librarian was age 22 years when the undergraduate degree was earned. This analysis does give some insights. Using the *Purdue Faculty Directory* I did this exercise for Purdue libraries just to see what our demographics are. The average age of librarians in management positions has dropped over the past five years as younger people have been hired. One surprise was the number of internal promotions and in-house hires; over one half of the changes were internal promotions. We are not officially using succession planning, but these internal promotions indicate that we are preparing our midcareer librarians for upper-level positions.

Identify Potential Employees

This step is much more involved. Following the philosophy that top-level administrators need to be involved in the process does not mean that other people in the library system are not included. Even in business setting, identifying potential employees involves many people; in some instances it is done by committee. For each position the qualifications and competencies need to be agreed upon. These might include such additional skills as ability to speak influentially to a large group, or ability to handle multiple projects at the same time, or ability to influence staff. These skills and competencies need to grow from the libraries' strategic plan and emphasize future needs. One way of developing this list of skills is to interview the staff currently in these positions. This is also a good opportunity to ask for their nominations for a successor, recommendations for a training program, and their willingness to mentor candidates for succession. This step is similar to writing job descriptions. Next potential employees are nominated and staff are asked to self identify listing their personal goals. The openness of the process is critical. Doing this step behind closed doors is generally not successful as it leads to staff distrust and accusations of unfair opportunities.

Assess Candidates' Strengths and Weaknesses

Once a list of potential candidates is developed, interview each of these employees to identify his or her interest, experience, and potential skills in librarianship and management. For example, does the candidate have extensive reference skills but lacks supervisory skills? Pay particular attention to management and leadership skills and gaps, and then prioritize the gaps. This needs to be a frank discussion, and help from mentors and supervisors will be critical for the success. At this point it is important to have an agreement with the incumbents about their skill gaps and willingness to address these gaps and build the competencies needed. Is he or she willing to be mentored and willing to outline a self-development program? Is the candidate willing to travel to attend association preconferences and workshops, to take courses at the university that provide needed skills such as financial management or personnel management skills? Likewise the library administration needs to make a commitment to the incumbents. This would include funds for training and travel, release time from current responsibilities, and such things as supporting mentors.

One of the major challenges of succession planning in libraries is "bench strength." In a small library there might not be anyone in the ranks who has the potential or interest in managing or leading the library. If this is the conclusion then the library needs to look closely at new hires in the future and to search for beginning librarians with career objectives of leadership and management.

Develop a Training Program to Build Competencies

There are many choices for meeting skill gaps. Many libraries already have extensive training programs in place, and libraries connected with universities have university employee training programs as well as formal courses available. The major library associations offer many opportunities to learn leadership and management skills. In addition there are leadership institutes available at the University of California–Los Angeles, Harvard and Emory. The Association of Research Libraries also has programs on leadership. Besides these formal training programs, other options are job rotation, job shadowing, or interim positions. Managing a library while the head is on an extended vacation or sabbatical can help fill the management experience gap. Budget planning; staff selection, training, and evaluation; crisis management; and donor relations are all areas that midcareer librarians need training to be ready to step up to director-level positions.

For detailed information on developing a succession plan, I recommend three books. The major one is William J. Rothwell's (2005) *Effective Succession Planning*. A second useful title is *Growing Your Company's Leaders* (Fulmer & Conger, 2004). And as mentioned in the introduction to this article, the third recent book is the Whitmell's (2005) *Staff Planning in a Time of Demographic Change*. It is the only book available specifically on succession planning in libraries. It is a collection papers from a conferences held in Ontario, Canada, and covers mentoring, training, and demographic statistics and information from the business literature. Like many of the articles on succession planning, this book focuses on Canadian, Australian, and U.K. libraries. Whitmell is executive director of the Legislative Library for the Legislative Assembly of Ontario.

CONCLUSION

Although the literature indicates that few U.S. libraries are utilizing succession planning techniques, statistics on the demographics of librarians, and business librarians in particular, indicate that there is and will continue to be shortage of qualified middle-level librarians available for the projected management positions. This shortage will peak between 2010 and 2015. The business world has successfully used succession planning to identify, train, and prepare employees to be ready to step up the executive positions. This idea of "grow your own" leaders could help to accomplish the following goals for libraries: increasing career advancement opportunities for interested staff that will lead to the retention of young librarians looking for a more challenges and career development, encouragement of targeted diversity candidates who have leadership potential, as well as being ensured of leadership at a critical moment when the boomers retire.

REFERENCES

8Rs Research Team. (2007). *The future of human resources in Canadian libraries.* Edmonton, Canada: University of Alberta. Available online at www.ls.ualberta.ca/8rs/reports.htm.

Berry, J. (1988, May 15). The shortage of librarians is back. *Library Journal, 113,* 4.

Bureau of Labor Statistics, U.S. Department of Labor, Occupational (Outlook Handbook, 2008-09 Edition), Librarians, Retrieved from http://www.bls.gov/oco/ocos068.htm.

Davis, D. M. (2005, September). Library retirements: What we can expect. *American Libraries, 36*(8), 16.

Diversity Counts. (2006). Chicago Office of Diversity, Office of Research and Statistics of the American Library Association. Available online at www.ala.org/diversitycounts.

Fulmer, R. M., & Conger, J. A. (2004). *Grow your company's leaders: How great organizations use succession management to sustain competitive advantage.* New York: AMACOM.

Hardesty, L. (2002). Future of academic/research librarians: A period of transition—to what? *portal: Libraries and the Academy, 2*(1), 79–97.

Hernon, P., Powell, R. R., & Young, A. P. (2001). University library directors in the Association of Research Libraries: The new generation, Part one. *College & Research Libraries, 62*(2), 116–145.

Lynch, M. J., Tordella, S., & Godfrey, T. (2005, January). Retirement and recruitment: A deeper look. *American Libraries, 6*(1), 28.

Markgren, S., Dickinson, T., Leonard, A., & Vassiliadis, K. (2007). The five-year itch: Are libraries losing their most valuable resources? *Library Administration & Management, 21*(2), 70–77.

O'Connor, L. & Marien. S. (2002). Requiting quality business librarians in a shrinking labor market. *The Bottom Line: Managing Library Finances, 15*(2), 70–74.

Pagell, R. A., & Lusk, E. J. (2000). A professional photo of academic business librarians worldwide: The present picture and a future view. *Journal of Business & Finance Librarianship, 6*(1), 3–21.

Rothwell, W. J. (2005). *Effective succession planning: Ensuring leadership continuity and building talent from within* (3rd ed.). New York: AMACOM.

Singer, P., Goodrich, J., & Goldberg, L. (2004, October 15). Your library's future. *Library Journal, 129*(17), 38–40.

Summerfield, M. (2002). CLA's human resources and succession planning survey: Analysis and recommendations. *Feliciter, 48*(4), 188–189.

Whitmell, V. (Ed.). (2005). *Staff planning in a time of demographic change.* Lanham, MD: Scarecrow.

Reframing Leadership:
The ACRL/Harvard Leadership Institute
for Academic Librarians

Sally W. Kalin

My office shelves groan with notebooks that testify to the many and wide-ranging leadership programs that I have attended. Their spine labels bear titles such as *Stable Change*, *Building the Future*, and *Excellence in Higher Education* and represent programs that ranged from simple seminars to intensive multiday workshops. All purported to enhance my leadership skills within the contemporary higher education milieu. Some captivated my imagination; some enhanced my capacity as an academic administrator; others failed to engage me. The best of them not only armed me with the skills of administration, but also compelled me to go deep within myself to assess the quality and impact of my own leadership.

Leadership has become a watchword in academic circles. Conventional wisdom says that leadership is an innate skill that can be cultivated and developed, and that leaders can be distinct from administrators or managers. The best leaders provide vision, stimulate innovation, uphold integrity, and foster morale. They bring special abilities and soft skills to the workplace that cannot be easily quantified. In contrast, administrators are charged to develop new rules and guidelines and enforce existing ones, create and direct processes, oversee the creation and expenditure of budgets, and ensure that deadlines are met. Their success is more easily measured because it can be held against norms and standards. In my own organization, some of the most respected librarians are those who hold neither administrative nor supervisory positions; they are simply colleagues whose voice matters and, accordingly, exert special influence on the organization. There have been occasions when I have explained to colleagues that good leaders possess their own power, and that their leadership is not dependent on being an administrator or having a title after their name. The irony is that you can be an excellent leader without being an administrator, but you cannot be an excellent administrator without also being an excellent leader. Therefore, the objective of most leadership programs is to enable their participants to meld the best of their administrative and leadership abilities.

Leadership development opportunities abound. From my personal experiences, I have found that these programs are underpinned by an emphasis on the technical aspects of administration (such as budgeting, planning, and personnel management) upon which a layer of leadership development is then applied. They demonstrate how an administrator can successfully perform by using tools such as assessment, communications, and project management to drive the organization to a higher level but can also apply leadership abilities to spur employee and customer satisfaction, improve workplace climate, and encourage change and innovation. For example, an administrator could create a reduced budget scenario that would be fiscally sound, but a leader would encourage the staff to identify and accept strategic changes in the organization that would mitigate the impact of the budget reductions. An expression often heard in library circles is "there is no constant but change," and developers of leadership programs have responded to this call. Contemporary programs rotate around the theme of transformational change. Many focus on providing leaders with the skills to foster and manage change such as negotiation, political acumen, and partnership building.

I have been fortunate to have taken part in some exceptional leadership programs. I have learned what works best for me, such as traveling off-site to locations where the workday does not interfere, exposure to nonlibrary problems and solutions, being forced out of my personal comfort zone to induce self-examination, the opportunity to build my personal network, and encountering to provocative theories and opinions. I have even participated in outdoor team-building exercises that involved—no kidding—blindfolds, ropes, and someone suspended from a tree. Such experiences might not be everyone's cup of tea, but for me, it was a growth experience. Many of my favorite elements came together for me 10 years ago, when the Provost invited me to be one of five Penn State Fellows in the Committee on Inter-institutional Cooperation (CIC, also known as the Big Ten Universities) Academic Leadership Program. During the academic year, the Penn State team joined Fellows from the other CIC institutions at different universities for several days of seminars and presentations by national leaders in higher education. I was the only librarian out a group of about 50 Fellows.

The experience strengthened my self-confidence because I realized that my experience in library administration was pertinent to the discussions and that I could articulate solutions to the leadership problems that were posed to the Fellows. Leaving the comfort of my home environment to visit other universities allowed me to see and hear how leaders used their administrative acumen to create innovative and productive learning environments. I was able to network with the other Penn State faculty and administrators who made up our leadership team. A sense of camaraderie was fostered by traveling together and enjoying such unique bonding experiences as watching a Penn State versus the University of Michigan football game while seated in a booth at an Ohio State sports bar. The professional relationships that I developed during the program continue to this day. What I appreciated most about being a Fellow was not the content of the lectures nor the quality of the speakers (although both were excellent), but the sustained benefits of the experiential learning.

All of which leads me to my best encounter with leadership development: the Association of College and Research Libraries (ACRL)/Harvard Leadership Institute for Academic Librarians. I was a member of the class of 2004. The first thing I did upon my return was to inform my dean, who had sponsored me, that the experience was one of the most rewarding of my academic career. A collaboration between Harvard and ACRL, the Institute was founded in 1999 at the initiation of Maureen Sullivan, then president of ACRL. It is an intensive five-day program designed to develop leadership skills in the context of each participant's experience and complements similar institutes conducted under the auspices of the Harvard Graduate School for Education for college and university presidents, provosts, and deans (http://www.gse.harvard.edu/ppe/highered/index.html). Like the Association of Research Libraries' Leadership Fellows Program (http://www.arl.org/leadership/rllf/) and the UCLA Senior Fellows Program (http://is.gseis.ucla.edu/seniorfellows/index.htm), most of the Institute's participants already hold administrative positions in academic libraries and many aspire to even higher positions. However, the Institute has more participants—my class had about 100—and represents a greater diversity of institutions, from community colleges to consortia to research universities. It also occurs over a shorter period of time, and its early August schedule allows library administrators to escape from their workplaces during a period of relative downtime, or before the hectic pace of the new academic year commences.

The Institute prepares librarians to be leaders that can enable their organizations to be well positioned for transformation. According to Maureen Sullivan (personal communication, October 22, 2007), its premise "is to reach individual learners, to allow them to come to the topics and discussion from where they are, and to enable them to derive what is most useful to them so that they can benefit from the learning." According to the Institute's Website, the program is designed to answer two key questions: How well positioned is my organization to meet current and future challenges? and How effective is my own leadership? (http://www.gse.harvard.edu/ppe/highered/programs/acrl.html).

Be forewarned: this is an intensive program (after all, it is Harvard). Before arriving at Harvard, we were asked to read Bolman and Dean's (2001) *Reframing Organizations: Artistry, Choice, and Leadership*, which served as the Institute's textbook. Reading the text (nearly 500 pages!) in advance was critical, as it provided the infrastructure upon which much of the Institute's content was based. The pace of the Institute's curriculum and numerous assigned readings did not give us the luxury of reading the text during the Institute. Also in advance, we were required to submit an original case study based on a personal experience with a serious management problem with the understanding that it would be shared with the other Institute participants. I found this assignment to be more challenging than I expected, as the case study had to be concise yet thought provoking, of broad interest, and able to stimulate discussion and problem solving.

We were expected to immerse ourselves in the Institute's program (which also included social activities) almost immediately upon our arrival. In fact, the first afternoon featured discussion of a case study that we were asked to prepare in advance. We had been firmly discouraged from bringing family members with us to Cambridge, Massachusetts, or trying to engage in work-related activities, such as monitoring e-mail, while in attendance. The advance materials that we received from the Institute underscored the importance of this total commitment:

> The Institute has been designed as an integrated whole. The faculty considers attendance by each participant at all classes essential for the program to make a maximum contribution to both the individual and the group. You will be attending the program with the understanding that you will devote your full attention to it.

The first morning of the Institute, Joe Zolnar, the affable but highly professional director of Harvard's Institutes of Higher Education, delivered a miniscolding to us when several participants sauntered in late after a scheduled coffee break, cutting into the time allotted for the next lecture. He informed us that we were at Harvard to learn, affirmed the importance of total focus on the Institute, and reminded us of the investment our home institutions were making in our futures. We needed no more reminders to be on time: no one was late ever again.

The curriculum of the Institute is built around the theory of reframing as outlined in Bolman and Deal's *Reframing Organizations* (2001). This text is also used in the complementary Harvard educational leadership programs; therefore provosts, presidents, deans, and librarians are exposed to the same leadership concepts, providing a common ground for collaboration and problem solving. In their preface, Bolman and Deal explained why managers make poor judgments: "Managers often misread situations. They have not learned how to use multiple lenses to get a better sense of what they're up against and what they might do (p. xviii)." The lenses they refer to are the four frames detailed in the text: (1) structure, or an organization's goals, tasks, and context; (2) human resource, or the people element; (3) political, or the competitive arena; and (4) symbolic, or organizational culture. Through the in-depth examination of real case studies, an instructional technique pioneered at Harvard, Institute participants are encouraged to approach solutions for management problems by applying the four frames. Faculty member Joan Gallos liked to refer to this approach as being "up in the balcony," or placing ourselves in a context where we could view the stage and its actors from different perspectives. Most of the case studies that we studied did not relate to libraries, but to other arenas of higher education and in at least one case to a profit-making corporation. This allowed me to stretch my personal boundaries, and to view the frames in different, yet also surprisingly similar, dimensions.

We were given new assignments each day, consisting of highly readable but complex case studies and supplementary materials. I quickly discovered how critical it was to read the case studies carefully and thoughtfully in advance of each class; otherwise, it would have been impossible for me to contribute to or even follow the discussions the next day. I stayed in a local hotel (the other option was to stay in a Harvard dormitory) and was grateful to have a room to myself because I was reading late into the night, or getting up very early in the morning to finish the readings. Complex and rich in detail, the case studies were based on problems that had actually occurred in a higher education environment. Because the cases were so multidimensional, reframing was a good analytical technique to use when contemplating solutions. With each case, I had to examine the underlying leadership issues and to consider how I might effectively apply administrative skills to solve the problem. Often I went to class believing, somewhat smugly, that I had mastered the elements of a case study, only to discover that my fellow students found nuances of and solutions for the case study that I had never considered. The creativity and intellectual abilities of my classmates definitely enhanced my learning.

All of us were assigned to a small study group of approximately seven members, who discussed the case studies that we had authored and offered solutions based on the four frames and other lessons learned in class. Within these study groups, there was a common understanding about the importance of confidentiality, especially because many case studies dealt with serious personnel issues that sometimes evoked emotional reactions from their authors. Four years later, I still wonder whether some of the seemingly intractable problems that some of my colleagues faced have ever been resolved.

An underlying objective of the Institute is to force participants to examine their own leadership styles through a path of self-discovery covering three themes: how you lead, what you lead, and where you lead from. The first day, we completed a questionnaire keyed to the four frames to determine our personal leadership orientation, and the degree to which we conformed to four types: analyst (structural), humanist (human resource), politician (political), and visionary (structural). A later exercise, developed by faculty members Lisa Lahey and Bob Kegan, professors of adult learning and professional development at the Harvard Graduate School of Education, required us to chart our personal leadership commitments and their value to our organizations, and then to identify the competing interests and assumptions that would have to be overcome if we were to reach our goals (Kegan & Lahey, 2001, pp. 78–79). Among my Harvard course materials, I still have the chart that I had created and derive some satisfaction that I have made strides in reaching some of my leadership growth commitments.

The strength of the Institute is due, in large part, to the quality and stability of the faculty. Most of the faculty has been with the program since its inception. They are very familiar with each other's lecture content, leadership philosophies, and teaching styles, and their comfortable banter indicates that they genuinely like each other. Their collaboration melds the curriculum into a cohesive whole, with each lecture serving as a building block for future content. The Institute faculty include Joan Gallos, professor of education from the University of Missouri-Kansas City; Jim Honan, senior lecturer on education, Harvard Graduate School of Education; Lisa Lahey, associate director of the Change Leadership Group, Harvard Graduate School of Education; Maureen Sullivan, organizational development consultant and former president of ACRL, and Joe Zolnar, director of the Harvard Institutes for Higher Education.

Of all the constructive experiences that I had during the Institute, the opportunity to watch master teachers at their craft rated the top spot on my list. Each of us was assigned a seat in a tiered amphitheater, with the instructor operating from a podium in the middle. The room was small enough to create an intimate setting. The instructors constantly moved about the room, eliciting comments from their students and generating a sense of energy. No one was called upon who did not volunteer or raise a hand; but because the instructors made everyone feel comfortable, we were encouraged to volunteer our ideas and opinions. The course content was immeasurably enriched by the insights and ideas contributed by my classmates who I found to be very smart, articulate, and more than willing to share their personal, and sometimes unpleasant, experiences for the good of the order. Not once did I witness anyone or their ideas denigrated; the instructors and students demonstrated mutual respect. Ed Garten, a graduate of the class of 2003, nicely captured the learning environment:

> Given the likely number of "Type A" personalities in the room, there were few wallflowers in this bunch; indeed, at every opportunity for response to questions posed by faculty, typically dozens of hands

would go up, figuratively crying out: "Pick me, pick me!" Instructors had an almost uncanny way of solidifying a sense of fairness of involvement among participants, drawing forth a rich tapestry of experience and insight, as well as some measure of what could only be called administrative angst. The knowing laughter of recognition of experiences shared, as well as the recognition of the often difficult human issues with which deans and directors are faced, threaded its way through each of the interactive sessions. (Garten, 2004)

The teachers were skilled in integrating the technical elements of the classroom into their teaching. For example, Joan Gallos creatively peppered her presentations with music (swing was especially popular) that served to illustrate the concepts that she was conveying. The instructors' effective use of the built-in sound system and microphones allowed them to leave the center podium and move easily around the room, reducing the perception of distance between them and their students, and serving to keep everyone engaged. The last day of the Institute, after we had completed discussing an especially complex capstone case study, the classroom's speakers began crackling. Suddenly we were chatting with the case study's central character who had been audio-conferenced into the classroom from the Italian coast, where he was no doubt enjoying the sun and vino, to tell us about the outcome of the case and to answer our questions. It was a transformative moment for me. I wrote in the margin of my case study: "make sure we install speakers and microphones in all of our classrooms."

The Institute's faculty is committed to continuous quality improvement. The last day of class, Joe Zolnar asked us to consider three questions that encouraged self-reflection: (1) what are we leaving, (2) what are we returning to, and (3) what have we have gained. Feedback from the Institute's participants is used by the faculty to design future programs and to ensure the inclusion of contemporary administrative issues, such as the critical importance of library partnerships in fostering student learning and faculty teaching. The recent addition of a case study focused on Ohio State's $100 million renovation project reflects the faculty's awareness of the increased emphasis on the "library as place" in academic circles. The Institute is now reaching out to the middle managers in academic libraries. Educating middle managers in the art of leadership means that they will be able to apply their Harvard learning experience earlier in their careers, and to make sustained contributions to their organizations.

In March 2008, in response to requests from the alumni of the Institute, the first Advanced Leadership Institute for Senior Academic Librarians was held under the direction of Jim Honan, one of the Institute's instructors. The Advanced Leadership Institute is designed to focus on leadership challenges associated with taking the academic library to the "'next level' of effectiveness" and covers topics such as the competitive environment in higher education collaborating with members of central administration and developing a vision of the 21st century (http://www.gse.harvard.edu/~ppe/highered/programs/ali.html).

Harvard makes an effort to continue to engage past students. An alumni reception is held at every Midwinter Meeting of the American Library Association; alums are kept informed of forthcoming programs and institutes; and each class has a Website and discussion list that for my class remained active for about a year. Some alums keep Harvard apprised of their career development. ACRL also keeps the Institute in the public eye. Each year, one or two members of the class are selected to summarize their experience in *College & Research Libraries News*. Anyone considering attending the Institute should read these summaries, which are not only informative but reflect the enthusiasm of their authors for the program.

Maureen Sullivan continues to serve on the Institute's faculty, teaching on the subject of leadership strategies for library leaders. Asked how the Institute has changed over its nine year history, Maureen responded that "everyone now accepts the need for transformation; librarians want to be more effective as leaders" (personal communication, October 22, 2007). We discussed the symbiosis that exists between faculty and students in a rich learning environment such as one finds at the Institute. Maureen found that serving on the Institute faculty had enhanced her growth as a teacher because she complemented her knowledge of active and experiential teaching with "how to effectively facilitate learning in the traditional pedagogical model," which she describes as the "role of the expert in front of the room." Each year the Harvard faculty indicates how much they appreciate being with and learning from academic library administrators, regarding them as talented and creative as the other higher education administrators they encounter. Maureen, who believes that the Institute's program gets better every year and cites the growing waiting list for enrollment as evidence, is optimistic about the Institute's future: "It's exceeded my expectations. It's a privilege to be part of it every year."

There is an aura about being at Harvard, a university that has generated so many of the nation's leaders. The last night of the Institute, we were treated to a New England clambake where one of the evening's highlights was the premiere of an original and very clever ditty titled "Reframing," sung by class members Kitty and the Change Agents. After dinner, I walked around an adjoining garden area in the yard of Radcliffe College. A fellow student informed me that the garden had been designed for and dedicated to Helen Keller on the 50th anniversary of her 1904 graduation from Radcliffe, and that the garden fountain was in honor of Annie Sullivan, her teacher and friend. It was impossible not to think about Helen Keller, who overcame her severe disabilities to become a world renowned speaker, author, and civil rights advocate, and of Annie Sullivan, who despite her own visual impairment, guided and directed Keller along her path. The carefully cultivated and lush garden became a metaphor for my experience at the Institute and the promise of leadership growth.

REFERENCES

Bolman, L. G., & Dean, T. E. (2001). *Reframing organizations: Artistry, choice, and leadership* (3rd ed.). San Francisco: Jossey-Bass.

Garten, E. (2004). The ACRL/Harvard Leadership Institute: A five year old spreads its wings. *College & Research Libraries News, 65*, 2. Available at http://www.ala.org/ala/acrl/acrlpubs/crlnews/backissues2004/february04/acrlharvard.cfm

Kegan, R., & Lacey, L. L. (2001). *How the way we talk can change the way we work: Seven languages in transformation.* San Francisco: Jossey-Bass.

The UCLA Senior Fellows Program

Juliet Rumble
Bonnie MacEwan

INTRODUCTION

Established in 1982 at the University of California, Los Angeles (UCLA), the Senior Fellows Program is a professional development program for senior-level academic librarians. The program, which began as an initiative of the then Council on Library Resources, is focused on enhancing leadership in research libraries. The fundamental purpose of Senior Fellows, articulated by its first director, Robert M. Hayes (1989), is to "create through [participants] and their association with each other a cadre of persons who [can] serve as a force for improvement of the strategic positions of libraries within their institutions and the nation as a whole" (p. 20).

The Senior Fellows Program is a three-week residential program held biennially on the campus of UCLA. The program brings together 15 individuals who are library directors or who have been identified as potential library directors. Selection to Senior Fellows is competitive. The program is structured around a variety of learning activities including readings, lectures, group discussions, guest speakers, case studies, and field trips. Since 1982, over 200 individuals have participated in the program. Of these participants, 77 currently direct academic libraries (including 31 Association of Research Libraries [ARL] libraries), 60 are associate directors or directors of major units in academic libraries, four are consortia directors, five work in library and information science education, two are university administrators, and four are employed as consultants.

Over the years, the program's curriculum has been revised to reflect changes in higher education and the academic library environment. Faculty have also taken into consideration the needs and interests of individual Senior Fellows classes when planning program content. For the past several years, general themes have included the following: issues in higher education, public policy issues of importance to academic libraries, organizational changes in academic libraries, and the role of special collections in academic libraries.

The program is structured so that participants can take full advantage of the immersion experience. Sessions are held in the morning, with afternoons typically devoted to study, informal group activities, and recreation. The format of the program is intended to provide time for personal reflection, self-exploration, and networking with other participants. The opportunity for developing long-lasting personal and professional relationships with faculty and with other Fellows is cited frequently as one of the most significant benefits of participation in the program.

Although the Senior Fellows Program is the oldest formal leadership development program for librarians in the United States—and certainly one of the most prestigious—there have been comparatively few reports in the library literature about participants' experiences with the program. In this study, deans and directors from 11 academic libraries were interviewed about the program. Study participants were asked to identify the aspects of the Senior Fellows Program that had been most valuable to them and to reflect on lessons learned, the impact of the program on their personal and professional development, and the support they received from faculty and cohort group members.

REVIEW OF THE LITERATURE

One outcome of the Senior Fellows Program is research and publication. During the 1980s, leadership became an increasingly prominent topic in library literature. Graduates of the Senior Fellows Program were among those contributing to the scholarly discussion. In 1988, a collection of essays authored and edited by a group of Senior Fellows was published under the title *Leadership for Research Libraries*. According to editors Woodsworth and von Wahlde (1988), research libraries, and higher education generally, had been undergoing dramatic changes in the decade of the 1980s. "The nature of the scholarly process, research patterns, organizational culture, economic constraints, and shifting societal and personal values are combining to alter the nature and the face of library and information services in educational settings" (p. viii). Faced with these changes, they noted, "it behooves the profession to take responsibility for defining leadership needs within the context of the field" (p. ix). The volume's contributors approached this subject from a variety of perspectives, including essays by Williams (1988) and Hoffmann (1988) that focused on leadership development and career management for library leaders.

During this same time period, a group of Senior Fellows who had participated in a Council on Library Resources conference, "Options for the Future" (1988), presented their vision of the ideal research library in an article titled "The Model Research Library: Planning for the Future." The article's authors argued that to achieve the future mission of the research library, librarians must become "more active participants" in the scholarly communication process, in the development of information technology, and in the formulation of information policy (Woodsworth et al., 1989, p. 132).

These and related studies pointed to heightened expectations from library constituents and expanding responsibilities for library directors. The convergence of issues in higher education related to scholarly research, technology, and instruction required research libraries not only to work more closely with other units on campus but also to develop strategic plans that addressed the environment outside the university. According to Senior Fellows Program Director Beverly Lynch, these issues shaped the design of the Senior Fellows Program curriculum in 1993. They were also addressed in *The Dynamic Library Organizations in a Changing Environment* (Giesecke, 1994), a collaborative publication project undertaken by members of the 1993 Senior Fellows class. In addition to organizational and environmental issues affecting libraries, this group of Senior Fellows had also been preoccupied with the "question of leadership, how it emerges, is shaped, and is able to change to reflect new situations," Lynch reported (1994, p. 14). The elusive characteristics of leadership were also the subject of a study by Anderson (1984) that compared the career profiles of 25 Senior Fellows to a control group of Association of College and Research Libraries (ACRL) librarians.

Some 20 years after these first collaborative publications by Senior Fellows, research libraries continue to be profoundly affected by the environmental factors identified and anticipated by these studies. As part of their coursework, Senior Fellows analyze this environment and reflect on the challenges and opportunities it presents to library leadership. Horrell (2001), Bracken (2003), and Ferguson (2003) published articles that address current issues in research libraries and that report briefly on their experiences with the Senior Fellows Program. Recently, Lynch and other members of the 2003 Senior Fellows class undertook to replicate Deborah Grimes' investigation (1992–1993) of the concept of academic library "centrality" (Grimes, 1998). The group's findings, published in the *College & Research Libraries* article, "Attitudes of Presidents and Provosts on the University Library," suggest that it is the research library's functional role in service to the university's mission, and not the library's symbolic value, that secures funding and administrative support (Lynch et al., 2007). If there is a common theme that runs through these recent studies, it is the priority given to the library director's role in raising awareness about the contributions made by the research library to the university's core values and mission.

METHOD

This article reports on interviews with 11 academic library directors who have participated in the UCLA Senior Fellows Program. These individuals were asked to identify the aspect(s) of the program that had been most beneficial to them and to discuss other program components related to leadership development. Participants were interviewed by telephone during July and August 2007, with interviews typically lasting around 30 minutes. Interview sessions were recorded and later transcribed.

The questions posed to study participants focused on three key areas: (1) knowledge and insights gained as a result of participation in the program, (2) the impact of the program on personal and professional development, and (3) supportive relationships formed with faculty and cohort group members. The questions were as follows: (1) Which aspect of the program was most important to you? Program content? Professional networking opportunities? Getting away? (2) What did you learn from the program? What was the most important insight that you took away? (3) What changed when you first got back from the program? Later? (4) Has your support group changed as a result of Senior Fellows? (5) What kinds of mentoring did you receive at the program? What role did Beverly Lynch play for you during the program and after? What kinds of mentoring do you do now?

The participants selected for this study included six women and five men, representing eight Senior Fellows classes: 1987, 1989, 1991 (two participants), 1993 (two participants), 1995, 1999 (three participants), and 2001. All 11 respondents are sitting deans or directors at major research libraries across the United States (including nine ARL members). These individuals direct libraries that serve campuses with student populations ranging from 5,700 to 50,000 students. All 11 colleges and universities award bachelor's, master's, and doctoral degrees. Library collection sizes range from approximately 1.3 to 8.9 million volumes.

FINDINGS

Valued Aspects of the Program

Of the 11 library deans and directors interviewed for this study, six reported that professional networking opportunities had been the most important aspect of the Senior Fellows program for them. According to one participant:

> The opportunity of getting to know the 14 or 15 people in the group I participated in who were all about at the same stages of their career was extremely valuable. I might have met some of these folks in other settings, at conferences or other professional settings, but to have that group of individuals all in one place for three weeks was a very unique experience.

Another participant, who was initially attracted to the program's focus on higher education administration and to the prospect of getting away ("It felt a little like a sabbatical"), noted: "[O]nce you get there [to UCLA] you realize pretty quickly . . . that it's the professional networking opportunities. . . . It's the people that you meet. . . . I turn to these people all the time when I have something to discuss or test out informally."

Several respondents indicated that the combination of professional networking opportunities, program content, and time away had been important to them. Regarding program content, one participant observed: "It was certainly a wonderful opportunity for us to have some concentrated time available to explore an issue in depth that one had been thinking about in one's workaday life but hadn't had the opportunity to think about deeply." Seven respondents reported that getting away had been another important part of the program. The three weeks at UCLA (or, in one case, Long Island) had provided a "physical break" from day-to-day job responsibilities and an opportunity to "step back" and focus on "big picture" issues at their institutions and in the profession.

For one dean, program content had been the most important part of the Senior Fellows experience. This respondent identified the parts of the curriculum dealing with personal development and leadership as the most valuable. In particular, coursework that addressed issues about senior leadership had been especially useful: "Very early in my career I participated in ARL's Basic Management Skills Workshop, and that was really good, but, as I had increasingly higher levels of responsibility, it's a very different kind of leadership, and it's not talked about a great deal in our professional world." This Senior Fellow believed that the format of the program was particularly conducive to reflection on these issues, noting that this "kind of conversation is better held in a more intimate setting, more of a one on one, [with] the general idea that it's about you as a leader."

For another Senior Fellow, the process of application and selection to the program had been especially meaningful: "For me, the most important part of any of these [leadership] programs is sort of a validation process. . . . [W]hen you're a young librarian or a young director thinking about what your future can be and should be, just the act of being selected is very affirming."

Important Takeaways

Asked to identify the most important insight that they had taken away from the program, participants responded with a variety of observations about the mission and role of research libraries and with insights related to their personal development as leaders. For a number of Senior Fellows, the timing of the program coincided with a period in their careers when they were considering a move to a library director position. Several mentioned that the program had helped them with this deliberation process. One dean stated that the program provided a "broad vision of the expectations of an ARL dean." Another Senior Fellow reported coming away with a sense of the importance of being strategic in charting one's career: "I think some of us going into the program weren't sure about the next step. . . . I wasn't sure. But I left the program knowing that I needed to develop a strategy." One dean appreciated the opportunity to interact with members of her cohort group who were already sitting deans:

> For me their involvement . . . created a particularly rich content. . . . [M]oving from an assistant dean or an associate dean to a dean's job—that transition and the role is really different from any other movement in a promotion. . . . There are enormous differences in moving from being an assistant dean to a dean, and they have to do with the power situation, how people perceive what you do, things you can and can't do.

This dean felt that ARL directors, perhaps especially those relatively new to the position, would have valuable insights to share with Senior Fellows about the nature of the job and how they had negotiated that transition.

For some participants, cultivating self-awareness as a leader was a key insight gained from the program. One Fellow reported: "I think . . . [a] really important insight that I took away was that, if I was going to be the person who led a library, I could do that my own way. I didn't have to do it the way that I'd seen other people do it or the way that I'd been led throughout my career." For this dean, interactions with other Senior Fellows had contributed to this realization: "[A]t some point—and this happened to me—people would turn to you and expect you to be the leader . . . and, when a group like that respects your leadership ability, you think maybe the way that I do it is okay."

Another Senior Fellow also underscored the importance of understanding one's leadership style and leadership strengths, noting that this was especially important when building an administrative team:

> [Y]ou learn in some way . . . to be who you really are. . . . And I think the thing that I came away with after a program like Senior Fellows is that, as you develop a management team or a leadership

team ... it's important to balance the strengths and expertise [of team members]. . . . [P]utting together an administrative team to have strengths that are different from your own—some certainly that would be complimentary but others that you just don't have but you understand that an organization needs—that's a healthy thing in terms of an organizational team.

Three Senior Fellows highlighted the valuable insights gained from interacting with individuals from multiple sectors within the profession. One dean, referencing the "dominant culture" of a previous workplace, observed: "[O]ne of the things I was reminded of is [my previous workplace] is not the center of the universe. There were lots of people outside [of that organization] . . . that were looking at the world in different ways." These Senior Fellows described cohort groups that had included a rich mix of participants from ARL and non-ARL libraries, public and private universities, and library staff from public and technical services. The program offered a rare opportunity to exchange information and to learn from individuals with whom they had previously had limited interactions. One noted:

> The lesson that I took away from my fellow [Senior] Fellows was that, even though we work in a very diverse profession in terms of the types of libraries and the types of roles within the library profession that we might play, at the end of the day we have a considerable amount in common.

Several Senior Fellows discussed ways in which the program had focused their attention on the broader contexts within which academic libraries operate. According to one:

> [B]eing in that cohort and being on the campus of that great university [UCLA], you learn a lot about what research universities are about. You learn it's not about the library, stupid, it's about the university and the library's place in it. . . . [Y]ou learn that . . . if you're going to become an effective administrator at a major university . . . you [need to] figure out both how libraries relate to the academic mission and how to communicate that contribution to the other deans and the other administrators at the university.

One Fellow had learned a great deal from discussions about the impact of public policy issues on academic libraries:

[A]fter you've surveyed the environment [at Senior Fellows] you come away with a sense of how very different things are very connected in our work in academic libraries—that there are a wide number of facets that all are part of the same big diamond that we get to occupy when we're academic librarians. . . . [E]verything from basic accounting all the way to national policy to library organizational structures . . . . They all end up being connected in one way or another. The curriculum helped to underscore that connectedness for me.

Another Fellow had found the program's accounting module to be especially useful: "[E]verything we do with our time and physical resources is a budget issue," she remarked. This director also commented: "We take a lot of this for granted [today], but, in 1989 at least, I didn't have a sense as true as it is today for the necessity of a collaborative approach among leaders in the profession and among our professional associations to address our common issues in higher education."

Cohort Groups

All the Senior Fellows in the study indicated that they considered their cohort group, or specific individuals from that group, to be part of their support system. Most of the Senior Fellows participated in cohort groups that were (and are) unusually close knit. Eight of the 11 participants are members of groups that still meet twice a year at the American Library Association's (ALA) annual and midwinter meetings. In addition to getting together at professional conferences, participants from two different cohort groups had arranged special class reunions.

One respondent described her Senior Fellows class as "particularly well bonded" and "very engaged with each other"; another stated that her group was a "major extension" of her support system. One Fellow reported that his class "hangs tight": "It was really a blessed group. [R]eally stimulating. It was almost like being an undergraduate again, if you know what I mean. You made friends. . . . [The group] just clicked." Three respondents indicated that, with the passage of time, retirements, and/or cohort members with competing professional commitments, they were no longer meeting regularly with their Senior Fellows class. "That gradually faded away," noted one. Nevertheless, all three commented that they were still in contact with some of the Senior Fellows from their year and that these postprogram connections had been very useful to them. One Senior Fellow described his relationship with his class this way:

[Y]ou have 12, 14, 15 people that you know you can call on, count on, to bounce an idea off of, formally or informally, because you've had that experience together. You know them well enough and vice versa. You're confident and comfortable in doing that. [T]here's a deep level of trust in that way.

In describing what the community of Senior Fellows has meant to them, respondents spoke of "sustaining" professional friendships, trusted colleagues who provided "honest, direct feedback," and a respected peer group that could be called upon to discuss an issue, share information, or help troubleshoot problems. One director reported that when he walked into his first ARL directors' meeting, he knew half of the people there thanks to Senior Fellows. This was a "huge benefit": "[You have] the ability to pick up the phone and call someone you know and have spent time with and actually have some sense of why they respond the way that they do."

A number of Senior Fellows stressed the benefits of developing working partnerships with fellow deans and directors from across the country. A network of library leaders able to collaborate on issues affecting all was viewed as a strategic advantage for academic libraries. The role played by the Senior Fellows Program in building community among senior administrators was praised. One Senior Fellow commented: "I think one of the things Senior Fellows does is to foster an intimate sense of community in a very busy workaday context. It's almost like a retreat, but unlike a retreat where the focus is very individual, it's more like a collective focus."

Senior Fellows also emphasized that community building takes time. Many believed that the closeness enjoyed by their cohort groups had to do with the length of the program and the residential setting at UCLA. Lively conversations over dinner at local restaurants, sharing a bathroom sink with their Senior Fellows roommate, or Sunday morning picnics at the beach were recalled with pleasure, humor—and gratitude. A number of Fellows observed that these informal interactions played an important role in fostering camaraderie between class members. It was the conversations in the van during field trips—"the stuff you can't totally structure"—that brought people together.

Program Impact

Senior Fellows pointed to a variety of ways in which the program had enhanced their professional development. For several, the program was less about acquiring particular skills or changing work habits as it was about validating what they were already doing. As one participant put it: "I had an underscoring that I was very mature in my career and that I was on the right track." A number of Senior Fellows mentioned that participation in the program had enhanced their "credibility" as candidates for library directorships.

Other Senior Fellows reported specific changes in how they approached their work and interacted with colleagues. One Fellow noted: "I learned something about being open to people—to new people, different people. I understood better that different kinds of strength can come together. I need people in my support group who are strong in ways that I'm not." Another Fellow made a related observation:

> [W]hat changed was my . . . propensity to consult others when trying to work through a situation. . . . [Y]ou tend to think—you've got your head down—"I've got to sort this out" and you may not think . . . "I'm going to pick the phone up and see what [my colleague] . . . thinks about this." And I found myself immediately after the program doing much more of that.

One Senior Fellow stated that the program had been a huge confidence builder: "I had a lot more confidence coming out of the program than going into it. . . . I didn't realize how much I knew and that I could make a contribution at that level both with the faculty of the program and with a set of colleagues from all over the country." Recognition of these capabilities had encouraged this participant to seek out a library directorship: "I credit the Senior Fellows experience with giving me the self-image to go out and apply."

Another dean recalled that being away for three weeks had been a reminder that she was not indispensable: "[I]f you have a good organization and you have good people working for you, they'll figure [things] out. . . . It isn't always necessary that the leader weighs in and makes every decision. . . . I'm trying to push down more decision making to lower levels." A corollary insight was "knowing that I had to take care of myself in terms of keeping myself invigorated."

One Senior Fellow reported coming away with a greater understanding of self and a broadened awareness of leadership issues. Another returned to his institution with a revitalized commitment to building collaborative relationships with campus stakeholders in order to build momentum and "keep [the] message alive" that libraries make vital contributions to teaching and learning.

Although all study participants are library deans or directors, most were reluctant to attribute any direct causal relationship between participation in Senior Fellows and the progress of their careers. Instead, as one Fellow noted, "there is a cumulative impact of these kinds of programs that's helped me to be more effective in what I do." Another had this observation about a career change: "It's hard for me to say that the Senior Fellows program was a factor in that change, but it prepared me in some ways to be able to make that change." It was also necessary to integrate what had been learned during the program. "It took time for everything to sink in and sort out for me," said one Fellow. "Three weeks isn't very long—it really just sets you out on a course where you continue to learn and continue to be open to ideas in a different way... .[F]or me it's been a process more than 'I've got this kernel.'" Although the respondents are all senior administrators, more than one noted that it wasn't necessary to seek this type of leadership position in order to get something out of a program such as Senior Fellows:

> You don't necessarily need to change positions to appreciate the value of a program like this. You can go back into your own institution—and the way this profession is—we're reinventing what we do all the time in terms of what the positions are. [T]he skills and the exposure and the relationships that you build in a program like this can easily translate into one's current environment.

Mentoring

Asked to comment upon the mentoring that they received during the Senior Fellows Program, a number of respondents remarked that the mentoring relationship that exists between a protégé and a more senior colleague did not capture the nature of their interactions with cohorts or program faculty. As one noted, "At the point I was at in my career, I wasn't looking for advice about how to conduct myself. It was more [about] looking at stances on issues and how to interpret patterns and changes."

Other Senior Fellows, however, did report being mentored at the program. Their experiences appeared to be of the kind discussed by Williams—namely that which takes place at the "advanced career change level"; as noted by Williams (1988), this type of mentoring is "more likely to be centered around encouragement to take professional risks, including competing for senior administrative positions" (p. 110). Several in this group indicated that Program Director Beverly Lynch had served as a mentor to them during and after the program. "When I think of Beverly Lynch, I think of the adjectives: supportive, nurturing, and a real friend," said one. Another Senior Fellow described Lynch's mentoring role this way:

> [She is] someone that the group and individuals can turn to from time to time when they're thinking about their own professional careers and looking for advice or feedback or reactions to things that they're doing. And I know that she has had a role in that kind of mentoring, that kind of encouragement and support to dozens of library directors in the United States and Canada. . . . I can think of no other individual who has probably influenced so many people in that way. . . . She's an extraordinary person.

Another Senior Fellow observed that Lynch has a "very unique ability" as a mentor and, if provided with the opportunity, would give "individualized attention and personal advice." Lynch knew how to deliver "straight talk." This Fellow recalled: "I had [another Senior Fellow] say to me 'Beverly sat me down and said 'Look'. . . . Often it's a 'You're selling yourself short' kind of message." According to this respondent, Lynch had offered encouragement when a particular career opportunity had not worked out, urging the respondent to remain open to other career opportunities that might present themselves.

One Fellow described Lynch this way: "She's so warm and kind. So engaged with every single one of us." After the program, this dean had consulted Lynch about a significant career move. She also recalled that Lynch would "nudge me to think about things in a different way." However, Lynch never delivered her suggestions in a directive way. Quite the contrary, the Fellow reported: "Over and over again, she'd say 'These are your 3 weeks—you need to shape them the way that you want to shape them.'"

Two Fellows praised Lynch's respect for the group's autonomy. According to one: "Beverly is an extraordinary facilitator. . . . In some ways [she] let the group help shape and determine the agenda for a lot of the open time that was organized as part of the program. . . . [T]he group got into certain discussions or issues and wanted to spend more time on them. . . . Beverly was extremely supportive and respectful in letting the group work in that way." For many, Lynch's "mentoring" role centered primarily on fostering a dynamic learning environment. "I remember being very impressed with how engaged she was with us and how provocative. She generated a lot of lively discussion," said one Fellow.

More than one respondent mentioned that Lynch's ongoing availability to program participants and her efforts to nurture and sustain community among the Fellows had helped to ensure that the benefits of the program extended far beyond the three weeks spent at UCLA. "[There is] a real effort . . . to keep the community aspect going long after your own individual class is over," said one director. Each year, participants receive an updated roster of Senior Fellows, there are biannual cocktail parties at ALA, and graduates are invited back to teach in the program. "I think all of that serves to keep people connected," this Fellow noted.

Asked about their own roles as mentors, Senior Fellows described a variety of ways, formal and informal, in which they supported the professional development of staff and colleagues. Perhaps not surprisingly, given their own experiences with Senior Fellows and other leadership development programs, a number of Fellows indicated that they had encouraged others to apply to programs of this kind. Three Fellows mentioned that they had either recommended candidates or been involved in the review process to select other Senior Fellows. One dean tells staff headed to leadership workshops:

> You're not only going to learn something. You're going to meet people, who are going to help you because they know you and want to bring something to your attention, or they may be doing a similar job, or you may just connect. This is an important thing to happen to you.

This same dean reported:

> I've had people say, "No, I don't want to go. I don't want to be an administrator." What I think they don't understand is you don't have to be an administrator to go to these things. . . . Even if you don't want to be a dean or director, it will enhance you in being a better reference person or a better cataloger. We live in an environment today where our operations are changing so dramatically and so quickly that programs like this are just a plus.

CONCLUSION

In this period of rapid change, library leaders and their professional staff need to be flexible, adaptable, and, above all, strategic in their thinking. Academic libraries operate within an increasingly integrated and interconnected environment. In this fluid setting, the old "command and control" model of leadership is no longer viable. As Senior Fellow Chris Ferguson (2003) observed, today's library leaders are placed at "the nexus, rather than the pinnacle, of change." To be effective, leaders must be willing to empower their organizational teams and to seek partnerships with individuals and groups outside of their libraries.

The Senior Fellows Program is intended to develop the capacity of library administrators to address these professional challenges and opportunities. Through a curriculum that focuses upon the broad contexts—institutional, economic, technological, and political—in which libraries operate, the program seeks to provide senior administrators with the skills and knowledge needed to think and act strategically. The fundamental purpose of the program, as articulated by Robert Hayes (1989) almost 20 years ago, is to develop a "national capability for strategic management" (p. 20). This underlying aim—to create a network of leaders able to act together on issues of collective interest—has informed much of what is distinctive about the Senior Fellows Program. The length of the program, its residential setting at UCLA, the nomination and review process by which candidates are selected, and the measure of autonomy afforded to individual cohort groups are all designed to foster a dynamic and cohesive community of participants who are prepared to engage with each other and with issues of importance to academic libraries.

As the roster of Senior Fellows participants indicates, the program has a proven track record for identifying future library leaders. The responses of the 11 library deans and directors in this study testify to its value for this group of participants. As Dartmouth College Libraries Dean Jeffrey Horrell (2001) observed about his Senior Fellows experience: "One can argue that no amount of coursework, professional reading, or 'on the job' experience completes the ongoing education of a library administrator—a network of colleagues is what ties all of that together" (p. 8).

REFERENCES

Anderson, D. J. (1984). Comparative career profiles of academic librarians: Are leaders different? *Journal of Academic Librarianship, 10*, 326–332.

Bracken, J. K. (2003). A continuing library leader education: The 2003 UCLA Senior Fellows Program [In Japanese; title and abstract in English. Japanese translation by K. Takagi]. *Journal of Information Processing and Management, 46*, 603–607.

Ferguson, C. D. (2003). Whose vision? Whose values? On leading information services in an era of persistent change. In K. Wittenborg, C. D. Ferguson, & M. A. Keller

(Eds.), *Reflecting on leadership* (pp. 16–32). Washington, DC: Council on Library and Information Resources.

Giesecke, J. (Ed.). (1994). *The dynamic library organizations in a changing environment.* New York: Haworth Press.

Grimes, D. J. (1998). Academic library centrality: User success through service, access, and tradition. *ACRL publications in librarianship ser. 50.* Chicago: Association of College and Research Libraries.

Hayes, R. M. (1989). *A long view of a broad scene: Means to prepare for strategic management of the modern large library* (Rep. No. 6049). London: British Library, Research & Development Department.

Hoffman, E. J. (1988). Career management for leaders. In A. Woodsworth & B. von Wahlde (Eds.), *Leadership for research libraries: A festschrift for Robert M. Hayes* (pp. 166–187). Metuchen, NJ: Scarecrow Press.

Horrell, J. (2001, October). Leadership development in libraries: Theory and practice. *ILA Reporter,* 6–8.

Lynch, B. P. (1994). Taking on the issues in a changing environment: The Senior Fellows Program. *Journal of Library Administration, 20*(2), 5–15.

Lynch, B. P., Murray-Rust, C., Parker, S. E., Turner, D., Walker, D. P., Wilkinson, F. C., et al. (2007). Attitudes of presidents and provosts on the university library. *College & Research Libraries, 68,* 213–227.

Williams, J. F., II. (1988). Development of leadership potential. In A. Woodsworth & B. von Wahlde (Eds.), *Leadership for research libraries: A festschrift for Robert M. Hayes* (pp. 100–125). Metuchen, NJ: Scarecrow Press.

Woodsworth, A., Allen, N., Hoadley, I., Lester, J., Molholt, P., Nitecki, D., et al. (1989). The model research library: Planning for the future. *Journal of Academic Librarianship, 15,* 132–138.

Woodsworth, A., & von Wahlde, B. (Eds.). (1988). *Leadership for research libraries: A festschrift for Robert M. Hayes.* Metuchen, NJ: Scarecrow Press.

Transition from Staff to Faculty in an Academic Library

Cheryl McCallips

INTRODUCTION

According to *Library Journal's* 2007 Placement and Salary article, "What's an MLIS Worth?," almost 37% of the 2006 graduates that responded to the survey indicated that they remained with their current employer while getting their degree (Maatta, 2007). Distance education programs and Web-based classes make that scenario more feasible than ever. As a result, it is natural for persons who really enjoy their work to desire to move into a professional position with the same library upon completing the library and information science (LIS) degree.

With the proliferation of distance education and Web-based classes, obtaining a library degree no longer demands that you move. Certainly there are benefits to being on campus with relationships that develop best face-to-face, and experience with the library school's faculty and resources, but for those who are tied to a particular geographic area, the distance education program has been an acceptable way to complete a LIS degree. Indeed, the possibility of finding an excellent library position increases if you are willing to relocate. However, with a distance education program combined with either internship opportunities or at least part-time staff work in a library, persons can gain the experience that so often is listed in the "desired qualifications" section of the job advertisement.

PERSONAL BACKGROUND

I have experienced a number of transitions in my professional career, working in public libraries, an elementary school library, and now an academic library. I began my library career in a public library in Pennsylvania as an elementary librarian. From that job, I moved within the same library to the reference/interlibrary loan librarian position, then to assistant director of the library and finally to acting director. Even without an MLIS, my abilities and efforts were acknowledged and rewarded. Positions were identified as "librarian" positions even though there was only one "professional" librarian, the library director.

When we moved to another community, I worked in a specially created position for a public library where I assessed the need and resources for funding a new building. From that role, I transitioned into a board of directors position for the same library, where I chaired the Personnel Committee.

After our next move, I worked in an elementary school library where, although my job title was library aide, I functioned as the school librarian providing library skills instruction for students, working with faculty regarding curriculum needs and special projects, as well as training the faculty as the library transitioned from card to computerized library records. During that time, I decided to pursue formal training in librarianship. Because I was unable to relocate, a distance education program provided by Clarion University in Harrisburg, Pennsylvania, was the best choice for me to begin a library science program. While continuing to work in the elementary school library, I attended weekend classes.

When we moved to State College, Pennsylvania, I was delighted to be hired as a part-time reference assistant in the Schreyer Business Library within the University Libraries at The Pennsylvania State University. It can be difficult to find the right balance of family, work, and continuing education. For me, that balance meant taking one library science class at a time. As a result, the years spent getting my MSLS spanned the years when distance education in Clarion's Library Science program transitioned from weekend classes in Harrisburg to include Web-based classes. I was very fortunate to have access to Penn State's wonderful research library to gain experience using the databases, print reference resources, and, more importantly, to be a part of a library system where I could work with nationally recognized librarians who not only know their subject area, but also understand the transition that academic libraries are experiencing right now.

After working for over a year in a part-time position, I was hired full-time in a staff position at the Business Library. The librarians were encouraging as I completed my coursework and provided opportunities to increase my professional work experience by permitting me to teach instructional sessions and provide reference service in the Smeal College of Business where we have a reference station that is staffed four afternoons each week. As part of my Clarion experience, I interned with the University Libraries' Instructional Programs and had the privilege of working with other librarians whose expertise and passions were not in a subject area but in the instructional component of librarianship. Staff at the University Libraries are encouraged to participate in committees, so by serving on various committees I got to know other people in the library as well as other aspects of the University Libraries' structure.

BECOMING FACULTY

In September 2006, I transitioned from my full-time staff position to a fixed-term librarian position within the Business Library. Because my full-time staff position was dissolved as the fixed-term position became available, there were some unique factors in the situation that I encountered. The transition away from two of my primary areas of responsibility occurred over the course of several months. I retained some of my responsibilities, including overseeing our Business Library Web page development. Additionally, as faculty, I have been charged with providing library services for the First Year Business Seminar and Business Writing classes and coordinating the instructional sessions offered to other classes that the Business Library supports. I have a specific area of collection development and participate in outreach efforts to the populations that we serve.

Because I had interned with the Instructional Programs department, worked two hours per week in the Gateway Library (an entry point for library users at the University Park campus), served on library committees, consulted with the Serials Department as I maintained the business print serials collection, and worked closely with our Information Technology department regarding Web page development issues, I felt that I had a fairly good understanding of the relationships between various library departments. Consequently, I did not ask as many questions in the fall of 2006 as I should have.

One of the immediate changes that I noticed was in the number of e-mails that I received on a daily basis. I thought I received a lot of mail as staff. However, as faculty my e-mails increased by 25%–30%. I began to realize that I did not understand the relationships and challenges that various departments within the University Libraries faced as well as I thought I did, so I began to attend more of the informational sessions beyond my area of responsibility. This new level of engagement opened up additional areas of interest, but the time necessary to participate had to be evaluated within the context of my new responsibilities.

I requested a mentor and have met with her a number of times over the past year. It is helpful to have an experienced librarian outside of the Business Library to be a sounding board and who can offer encouragement and advice. Even though publishing is not a requirement in a fixed-term position, I am interested in opportunities to publish. I am in the process of working on my first collaborative publication, and that experience allows me to work with librarians that I do not usually see on a regular basis.

Although I was an American Library Association (ALA) member before gaining faculty status, I was unable to afford the conferences. Attending ALA Midwinter 2007 in Seattle and the preconference sponsored by the Business Reference and Services Section (BRASS) was a wonderful learning experience that gave me an appreciation for the national business librarian community and the resources that are provided for those serving patrons with business needs. Now I am looking forward to contributing to those resources as a member of the BRASS Education Committee.

REFLECTION

I have been very fortunate to be able to move from a staff to a professional librarian position at Penn State. Others have been able to make that transition as well. Over the last three fiscal years, the University Libraries has had 45 professional positions advertised, and seven were filled by internal candidates (L. Powers, personal communication, October 16, 2007). While preparing to write this article, I talked with a number of persons who have worked within the Penn State University Libraries as staff members before transitioning to faculty. Some of these people are currently in tenured positions; some are in fixed-term positions. All consider their employment as staff as invaluable preparation time for their current positions. As we talked, I realized that many of the people who transitioned from staff to faculty within the University Libraries found positions with other units or other campuses instead of the unit where they were initially employed. As a result, they benefited from the knowledge they had of the University Libraries structure and resources and, at the same time, were able to start in a fresh way as librarians. For those who are still in staff positions, the lack of positive responses to applications for professional librarian positions has been discouraging. However, they are still hopeful that the experiences they have gained in their current roles will position them for an appropriate librarian position in the future. Others have found that functional specialist positions have provided professional niches that utilize additional talents and abilities. They have discovered that other areas of expertise are valued within the library community and their library school experience has given them a better understanding of the framework of the academic library.

I spoke with administrators about the transition that academic libraries are facing, especially regarding staffing issues. With the literature of the last 10 years emphasizing the aging demographics of librarians and the lack of young librarians available to step into professional positions, more attention is being given to evaluating and at times restructuring professional positions. Some of those changes were highlighted in a recent article on the library workforce. "In the past 20 years, US ARL university libraries have seen a large overall decrease in numbers of Catalogers (a 30% decline from 1985-86) and an even greater increase in Functional and Subject Specialists (a 286% increase and a 45% increase, respectively)" (Hipps, 2006). Functional specialists can fill positions in not only technical and systems services, but also in human resources, marketing, and other areas of the academic library.

Although administrators are justifiably concerned about staffing issues in libraries over the next 20 years when thousands of librarians retire, there are indicators that suggest that the expectation of LIS graduates are not being met in the entry-level positions that they anticipated during their library school experience. Statistics from ALA regarding the number of jobs advertised at ALA's midwinter and annual conferences and the number of job applicants has reversed since the 2002 annual conference in Atlanta. Now the number of job seekers has exceeded the number of jobs advertised at ALA, and overall number of jobs advertised at the conferences is much lower than in the 1990s through 2001 (ALA Placement Center Statistics, n.d.).

At the same time, *Library Journal's* Placement Surveys (published each October) indicate significant increases in the percentage of library school graduates who have found permanent professional positions after graduation and an increase in the percentage of graduates who have accepted other categories of employment within and outside of libraries. In 2003, of the graduates responding to the survey, "34% indicated that they returned to their employer as professional staff after graduation" (Maatta, 2004, p. 28). For those who are interested in transitioning to a professional position within the same library, this is an encouraging statistic.

Groves (2005) reflected on the challenges involved in relating to colleagues when one moves from a staff to a faculty position within the same organization. My experiences have been similar. I already know the people with whom I work. My colleagues already know me. Once established, social networks are difficult to change. For the most part, other library staff members have been very supportive as I moved into my faculty position. Many faculty members have congratulated me and done what they could to help me adjust to my new responsibilities. Others have continued to treat me as though there is no change in my area of responsibility. Because mixed reactions from colleagues are common, it is important to initiate changes that will be beneficial. It is also important to embrace the transition from staff to faculty as a new beginning point for professional development and creativity, not simply as an accomplished goal.

LOOKING AHEAD

As a result of my personal experience transitioning to a faculty position and the conversations that I had with others in the University Libraries, the following thoughts and suggestions have crystallized regarding continuing professional development:

Set goals: Consider your own professional development and how to creatively fulfill your faculty responsibility. Continue to learn and grow.

Stay informed: Read not only the library literature, but also when possible the literature that highlights trends in higher education.

Communicate: Talk with other librarians and others on campus, especially those whose professional interests and/or responsibilities are similar to yours or have an impact on what you do. Be part of the conversations regarding academic libraries in transition.

Reflect: How do you best serve your target population? Think about your responsibilities within your unit, how that unit operates within a department, and how that department relates to the academic library and the larger university community.

Balance: Find ways to refresh your spirit so that you can bring a positive attitude to your professional area of influence.

In *The Successful Academic Librarian,* Gregory (2005) noted an important consideration when examining any job possibility: "The match has to provide ongoing personal and professional satisfaction; the match has to be intellectually stimulating; the match has to bring enjoyment" (p. xiii). By choosing to work in an academic library during the years pursuing my MSLS degree, it was easier to gauge whether an academic position would be the right choice for me. Even though I have worked in other library settings, at this point in my life I am convinced that choosing to be an academic librarian at Penn State is the right choice for me.

REFERENCES

ALA Placement Center Statistics. (n.d.) Retrieved September 11, 2007, from http://www.ala.org/ala/hrdr/placementservice/placementcenter.htm.

Gregory, G. M. (2005). *The successful academic librarian.* Medford, NJ: Information Today.

Groves, D. (2005). Office politics: Advancing from staff to faculty within the same library. *LIScareer.com.* Retrieved July 31, 2007, from http://www.liscareer.com/graoves_politics.htm.

Hipps, K. (2006, June). Diversity in the US ARL library workforce. *ARL Bimonthly Report, 246.* Retrieved June 9, 2007, from http://www.arl.org/bm~doc/arlbr246.pdf.

Maatta, S. (2004). Jobs! (Eventually). *Library Journal, 129*(17), 28–35.

Maatta, S. (2007). What's an MLIS worth? *Library Journal, 132*(17), 30–38.

Transitions to Academic Libraries for Business Librarians and Librarians' Response to Adjunct Teaching

Christopher LeBeau

INTRODUCTION

This article is written by invitation, an invitation that asked me to cover two topics. As a librarian who transitioned from a public to an academic library, I was asked to write about such transitions. As a librarian who teaches in a MLIS program, I was asked to write about my teaching experience.

If one works long enough eventually experience and opportunity happily collide, and I found an opportunity to teach library science after years of practice. My position is a rather unique one conceived by the University of Missouri, School of Information Science and Learning Technologies (MU–SISLT). I share my position with a sister campus, the University of Missouri–Kansas City (UMKC), two hours away. I serve as a faculty member for SISLT and as a practicing business librarian for UMKC. My primary affiliation is with MU, but I work equal time for two sets of administrators and with two sets of colleagues in two different cities. This newly created job was mine to define. There were job descriptions, but no road map.

I attempt to bring together these disparate threads of transitions and adjunct teaching. This article contains personal commentary interspersed between some qualitative and quantitative survey results. Although my personal experience is a transition from public to academic library, there are as many different experiences as there are librarians. Acknowledging this, I designed a survey to discover more about library field transitions. I surveyed the same set of people to get their thoughts about teaching in MLIS programs. There is not a lot of research-based literature on work transitions between different types of libraries. Most articles are personal accounts but raise key issues nevertheless. Following a brief literature review is a summary of the survey findings.

Analyzing transitions from one library type to another is not easy work as the literature reveals. Public libraries can vary from one-room buildings serving homogeneous populations to municipal libraries serving our largest and most diverse populations. Academic libraries can reflect equal variation. To find a common transition experience would be incredible luck.

In large part, size matters. A medium-sized public library in a thriving suburb, situated near several colleges, will have more in common with a midsized university than with a rural public library. Although a corporate librarian may find cultural differences between special and academic libraries, librarians from other types of libraries may experience little difference at all.

LITERATURE REVIEW

Jennifer McCarthy (2000) wrote as a transplant from a large, metropolitan public library to a university library. She finds many "elements" of the work similar, "but the differences are profound." The most dramatic differences lie in the teaching, the librarian/patron relationships, resources, and size. Her public library "teaching" amounted to technology classes and young people's programs that assumed many off-syllabus objectives. McCarthy juxtaposed the strong librarian/patron relationship found in public libraries against the anonymity students prefer. University students' questions take on a routineness as do librarian responses. In both environments, McCarthy relied on her referral skills despite the larger collection at the university. Her experience convinces her that there is a need for better collaborations between the two types of libraries.

Susan Klopper (2006) offered an intelligent review of her transition from a major accounting firm library to an academic business library. Klopper found the two environments equally challenging, despite the high-stress corporate setting requiring long hours, teamwork, and the drive to exceed customer expectations. The appeal of the academic environment includes an emphasis on professional development, more faculty and student contact, intellectual stimulation, a greater sense of place, and more e-resources. Her corporate background helped her discover that some vendors ignore the academic market. Although she tolerates academia's lethargic pace, the academic business library still offers its opportunities and challenges. The biggest point of departure for her is the librarian's relationship to research. The corporate librarian is often required to do research while the academic librarian imparts the knowledge and research skills to users. Her other challenges include improving the information competency skills of business students and gaining recognition on campus for the knowledge and wonderful resource librarians really are.

Susan Curzon (1995) compared academic and public libraries but does not speak to the business librarianship per se. She has accumulated a wealth of experience from work as a special librarian, her directorship of a public library, and deanship of an academic library. It is Curzon's opinion that the differences between academic and public libraries should not prevent easy movement from one environment to another. For Curzon, size makes a difference. Large public libraries have reference needs similar to those of a midsized academic library. She highlighted eight main areas of service and collections where differences exist: reference, collections, access to services, library hours, librarian faculty status, bibliographic instruction, budget, and environment including governance structures. The faculty status and promotion process, continual challenges from campus faculty, and bibliographic instruction require more of a library's resources.

Ronald Edwards (2002) outlined the differences for anyone considering a job transition. For Edwards, public and academic libraries part ways with the "public librarians' long history of educational and cultural involvement" (p. 631). He portrayed the rougher environment of public libraries, subject to political stresses, heavy-handed policies from governing boards, and pressing needs of diverse communities. Like Curzon, Edwards found differences in the libraries' collections, and public libraries must contend with Internet issues unknown to academic libraries. The job application process for public libraries is form driven contrasted to the use of vitas on the academic side. Public libraries are more susceptible to economic movement, implying academic libraries are not—a questionable point. For Edwards the most noticeable difference is in the librarian's professional image, and here Edwards gives the advantage to academic librarians. Higher salaries often go along with the image.

Elisa Topper's article (2005) is a general career transition piece in a question-answer format. Topper's questioner has transitioned from business library to public library to academic library where she felt most at home. In a nutshell, the answer is "yes," transition is possible. Topper's hints on ways to accomplish transitions include taking advantage of paid residency programs, trying a part-time job in an academic library, getting a second master's degree, and increasing one's technology skills. Candidates who learn technology quickly and who are active professionally had a better chance of making the transition to academic libraries.

Scott Lanning's article (1989) is a lighthearted piece on his transition from public to academic library work. From Lanning's perspective the two types of libraries often share the same kind of patrons who pose repetitive questions. Academic libraries require less desk time, but it is the off-desk time where Lanning finds the most difference. The off-desk time in the academic library is filled with projects and research assistance that is absent from much public library work. Lanning questioned, with some odd logic, the necessity of the second master's, a common requirement for academic librarians. He concludes that the degree is unnecessary.

Ruth Pagell and Edward Lusk (2000) have undertaken a major piece of research with their comparative analysis of U.S. and international librarians, including managers and nonmanagers. They examined issues such as demographics, ethnicity, educational background, skills and competencies, hiring patterns, and professional development. A small part of their research includes career transitions to academic business librarianship. The majority of academic business librarians came from jobs within academia whereas 23% came from corporate libraries and 28% came from public libraries.[1] The researchers also examined the changes in required skills and competencies over time. The main thrust of the research was to determine the differences in the demographics of managers and non-managers, both nationally and abroad. Their survey confirmed that the U.S. managers are older, whiter, and more predominantly male than those abroad and in the nonmanager groups.

METHOD

Although my original task was to write about transitions to academic libraries, I was able to elicit information specific to academic business libraries. When possible, that specific information is included. The survey was directed to business librarians, the BUSLIB-L listserv and to the LIBREF-L listserv. Business librarians were invited to respond. To get a sufficiently large pool of respondents, generalists who spent at least 20% of their time handling business reference were included.

RESULTS

Of the 97 respondents 64 were business librarians from any type of library, and another 31 handled business reference at least 20% of the time. Further refinement yielded a group of academic librarians of whom 42 were "business librarians" and 18 were academic generalists who handled business reference at least 20% of the time. A few performed work related to business such as serving as a liaison with a higher education business school or handling business collection development (see Table 1).

TABLE 1. Survey Respondents Positions

	Business Librarians (number)		Spend 20 of Time on Business (number)		Nonbusiness Librarians (number)		Total
Total respondents	64		31		2		97
Work in academic librarians	42	65.6	18	58	1	50	61
Work in public library	8	12.5	4	13			12
Work in special libraries	10	15.6	6	19			16
Work in community college library	1	1.5	1	3			2
Other	3	4.6	2	6.5	1	50	6
		99.8		99.5			

Librarians were asked to name the type of library they were in prior to their transfer to academic libraries (see Table 2). The largest group of respondents came from public libraries. When broken down by position, the distinct public library groups fell behind the larger group of librarians that moved internally within academic institutions. The next largest group transitioned from business positions in special/corporate libraries. This group was followed by those who came straight out of library school into academic business positions.

The academic library position often requires subject knowledge, so information was obtained about the educational preparation of librarians who

TABLE 2. Transitioning to Academic Libraries What Type of Library Did ou Work in Prior to our Academic Business Library Position ($n = 51$)

Responses	Number	
Academic internal transfer	11	21.5
Public library – Generalist with 20 business	9	17.6
Special library – Business position	8	15.6
Straight from MLIS program	7	13.7
Public library – Business position	5	9.8
Special library – 20 business reference	3	5.8
Special library – no business reference	3	5.8
Public library – no business reference	2	3.9

Note 3 unusable responces.

TABLE 3. Education of Academic Business Librarians and for All Librarians Handling at Least 20   Business Reference (in all types of libraries). For Some Respondents Multiple Answers Applied, Therefore Percentages Do Not Add up to 100

Degrees	Academic Business Librarians ($n = 41$)		Librarians Who Handle at Least 20 Business Reference (all types of libraries) ($n = 33$)	
MBAs or MS in business	11	26.8	5	15
MPA	0	0	2	6
BA BS in an area of business	10	24.4	0	0
PhD	0	0	1	3
Certicate in business	0	0	1	3
Associate degree in business	1[a]	2.4	0	0
Took business courses outside of work Learned on the ob, self taught (For academic business librarians, 4 MBAs got their degrees after learning on the ob, etc)[b]	20	48.8	30	91

[a]Respondent answered two different categories.
[b]Category responses overlap some other categories.

handle business reference (see Table 3). Approximately 50% of academic business librarians had either a MBA or undergraduate degree in a business field. What is interesting is that nearly 50% of academic business librarians learned their business knowledge on the job, were self-taught, or took business courses on their own. Some later went on to get advanced degrees. Nearly all generalist librarians who field business questions fell into the self-taught, learned-on-the-job category.

Librarians were asked why they transferred to the academic business positions (see Table 4). Nearly one half expressed that they "enjoyed the academic environment." The second most popular reason was that these librarians thought they could put their knowledge to better use. Following this reason was the motivation for better pay and the need for a career change. Several reported they had been laid off from their corporate positions. Less motivating was achieving faculty status. Higher prestige fell near the bottom. A small percent responded positively to the reason, "I felt the business reference I do is more relevant to the real world." Others

TABLE 4. Transitioning to Academic Libraries Why Did ou Move from Public, Special, or School Librarianship to Academic Business Librarianship (respondents chose multiple answers) (*n* = 84)

Responses	Number	
En oy academic environment	23	47.9
Make better use of my knowledge	14	29.2
Better pay	13	27.1
Needed a career change	13	27.1
Faculty status	9	18.8
Higher prestige	7	14.6
I felt business reference I do is more relevant to the real world.	5	10.4

commented that they made the move to do research, and were motivated by the benefit of better professional development support.

So how hard is it to transfer between different types of libraries? Although Curzon (1995) believed this should be a nonissue, one hears frequently in the field that transitions are difficult due to job stereotyping. Although my first position was in a midsized public library, my real interest was academic libraries. Library school advising suggested that it was nearly impossible to get an academic library appointment without the second master's, so my MLIS program placed me into the public library track.

When I finally did apply for an academic library position, I knew my public library background was an issue. Fortunately for me, I was hired despite the concerns that a public librarian may have difficulty handling academic library work. It was a pleasure to have so many more disciplinary reference resources at my disposal, and I enjoyed information work in areas left unexplored at my public library. I have remained in academia, and over the years, I have met these stereotypical attitudes on more than one occasion. Yet only one survey respondent reported that the candidate's ability to handle the transition was questioned. Perhaps this is more of a concern expressed behind closed doors on search committees than out in the open to candidates.

At the heart of this study was the simple question, "Was it difficult to transition from another type of library to an academic library?" Of the 36 responses, 38% said *no*. Nineteen percent begged to differ, responding with *yes*. Transition difficulties can stem from internal feelings of inadequacy as well as external pressures and circumstances in the environment. Of those who found the transition difficult, the most common reason was the pressure to publish and present at conferences. Other comments mentioned the work entailed with instruction and committee assignments. Still others found the academic culture unbelievably mired in lengthy decision making, using various forms of the word "boggy." One particular comment was "we spend too much time trying to reach consensus among ourselves."

Not only are the external forces and expectations a problem in academia, but our processes and preoccupations hinder our march toward progress and productivity. This point of view has been echoed in Mark Cain's 2003 article, "The Two Cultures?" (p. 178). One respondent offered an interesting perspective on the "the two cultures" saying, "corporate libraries are cooperative internally and competitive externally, academic libraries are competitive internally and cooperative externally." Yet others reveled in the bliss of academia's less restrained atmosphere and the increased autonomy, enjoying the freedom to create and the ability to "assume responsibility for anything that sparks [one's] interest."

Because librarianship is so customer centered, transitions between libraries require skill in dealing with different types of clientele. In my own experience in public and academic settings my customers ranged from eight to 88, bringing their own distinct levels of enthusiasm, prior knowledge, and technical ability to the reference table. Serving these diverse populations requires intuition, sensitivity, emotional intelligence, people-reading skill, good listening skills, patience, and the ability to adjust responses to the audience.

Two survey questions asked respondents to characterize the differences in working with their customers and the differences in the types of questions. These responses heavily reflect business librarians' experiences.

Respondents who had spent time in the corporate sector thought that librarians did more for their clients than in other types of libraries. Their clientele admitted to being "information illiterate" and willing to pay whatever price for their information. They were intense in their needs, demanding about the research quality, and wanting immediate assistance. Corporate librarians claimed their questions were the most sophisticated. Appreciation and thanks were rare.

Public library clients were typically generalists, "seeking personal enrichment." Their questions could be quite varied. Many business questions at the public library were for the "real world," or immediate and more basic business needs, such as writing a business plan, finding competitors, or doing personal investment research. Although customers were characterized as able to look up their own information, they preferred help. One respondent felt public library customers could be "lazy" about their information needs, and were not much interested in knowing the process. Their needs ranged from immediate to not so immediate. They often were more patient about waiting for help. They were more socially and economically diverse. Public library patrons could be the most challenging in terms of social issues, including homeless patrons. Often patrons did not possess the "intellectual and emotional infrastructure to be helped." Add rowdy children into the mix, and it makes for an interesting day. Yet in helping public library patrons better their lives, at least one librarian found more altruism in the daily tasks.

Academic clientele were another sort of customer. First, "academic needs are grounded in research needs." Reference questions often were more detailed, yet at the same time there could be less variety, especially with lower level undergraduates. Undergraduates did not always come to the library prepared or with the patience to "probe" for information. They often sought the bare essentials of information necessary to complete their project. This was seen as less satisfying than questions that go beyond an assignment. Other respondents characterized academic questions as falling into two groups: short, repetitive types such as term paper formatting and how to find articles, and the "open-ended research question" that requires quite a lot of joint work with the patrons. Business questions often required 20–30 years of retrospective data that was uncommon in public or corporate work. It was expected librarians would instruct the students to do research unlike the situation with public and corporate clients. Corporate clients may have immediate needs, but somehow student deadlines for research papers were often yesterday. Finally, in academia patrons said "thank you." Personally I have been blessed countless times, and I took every one of those blessings I could get.

If corporate clients keep business librarians on the run, students "keep you thinking young." One librarian was more comfortable with the deemphasis on making money in the academic setting, and some found the special relationships with faculty very rewarding. Another respondent observed that faculty go to familiar information sources and do not scrutinize enough whereas corporations reused trusted sources with great scrutiny. One academic business librarian summarized academic work saying it "provides more intellectual challenge" than public library work.

Yet to demonstrate how subjective this exercise was, several respondents said, "The questions [in the different types of libraries] are not very different." One librarian with experience in several environments summed it up by suggesting that all patrons were "clueless of the value librarianship brings."

Another question asked how the job duties differed with the transition to academic libraries. Respondents to academic positions were very positive about their new duties. Most noticeable was the reduction of desk hours (public library with 20 hours per week; academic 10–12 hours per week) and the increase in instruction. Public library duties were perceived as more narrowly defined and lacking the richness found in the academic environment, although some public business librarians said they were enjoying creating business content for their public library Websites.

Academic librarians enjoyed collection development duties, Web page development, and they were more reliant on databases than in the corporate world. Respondents also said they had more face-to-face work in the academic library. For some the academic job entailed customer service and marketing of resources, especially on the undergraduate level. Graduate-level work consisted of more interesting projects, but public and academic librarians claimed a greater range of questions. So, there was little consensus here.

Corporate librarians indicated they had to produce more finished reports whereas academic librarians supported the research efforts of others. Those from corporate backgrounds found academia was more relaxed and less stressful. Academic liaison work was a new concept for transfers, and they noted the emphasis in service to the profession through scholarship and committee work.

Some comments reflected some of the negatives with academic business library work, notably less flexibility in the academic position. This contrasts with a previous comment about greater flexibility in academia, so environments differ. Outsiders coming into academia comment that academic librarians get hung up on details, such as cataloging issues, which would not happen in a corporate library.

One respondent raised the issue of unions, citing the fact that more public libraries were unionized than academic libraries. This would need study, but unionization can bring its attendant problems, such as poor management or barriers to innovation. I myself was a teamster in my public library days; our union meetings were often spent discussing the janitors' uniforms and the like, but I will attest that the benefits could not be beat. It must be noted that not one respondent mentioned differences with respect to benefits in different library settings. This would be an interesting source for future research.

The survey was revealing in several ways. First many librarians appear to make successful transitions, more so than expected. Very few felt their previous positions in different types of libraries were a hindrance, although this point probably needs to be explored. Second, a high number of librarians are making it into jobs where they need a lot of training to achieve an expected level of competence.

TEACHING IN LIS PROGRAMS

There is a well-known shortage of MLIS faculty, and the time may be ripe for librarians who would like to be adjunct teachers. Although I had considered teaching as a profession early in my life, I had ruled it out in favor of librarianship. Whether librarians in academia think of themselves as real teachers or not, we do a lot of teaching. Librarians feel closely allied with the teaching profession.

Adjunct teaching is another transition for business librarians seeking professional growth. The opportunity has given me a different vantage point on my academic environment. The special concerns of faculty have become much clearer. Even having lived with a professor for years, I have a new appreciation for the hours of preparation and grading, the classroom management skills, the art of teaching, the creativity, the mastery of long range planning, and the integration of technology. Teaching semester-long courses in MLIS programs requires a daily commitment and relentless pace for a 16-week stretch, unlike the one hour classes I teach as a librarian.

Wearing my librarian hat, I have had to do little staff supervision, but the management of a "classroom" of 30 students requires the same set of skills. One must lead, challenge, motivate, coach, penalize when appropriate, show empathy, and maintain boundaries and fair play in the classroom just as one would expect in the workplace. All the while the teacher is moving the class progressively toward new knowledge and insights. Much of my course delivery is done through Blackboard that levels the field between those who can command a room with their great physical presence and those who cannot. Through Blackboard, all voices have equal strength. As librarians, we hope we have made a mark on those we help. We get satisfaction out of our individual daily victories, but the influence of a teacher is of a different kind. It can last a lifetime.

Some unanticipated benefits of this joint appointment are the professional connections and new frames of reference I have made between practice and teaching. I have new ways to "connect the dots" in my library world, and I have found ways to leverage the knowledge from one job to use for the other. My greatest challenge is trying to serve all the needs of

TABLE 5. Do ou or Have ou Taught in a
Library and Information Science
Program (*n* = 89)

Responses	Number	
es	19	21.6
Thought about it, but dont	38	43.2
No, never considered it	32	36.4

my students at both institutions and to keep the job from growing into two full-time jobs.

With this as my background, I surveyed librarians about their interest in teaching. Librarians from all types of libraries have made their way into teaching in MLIS programs. The chance to share accumulated knowledge with students entering the field seems right at a certain point in one's career. Yet I have been surprised at the number of my colleagues who have had no interest in either teaching a semester-long course or in a similar joint appointment. The adjuncts I know seem to enjoy the teaching and stick with it year in and year out.

This set of questions asked whether librarians had considered teaching in MLIS programs (See Table 5). The majority of the 89 respondents were business librarians. Twenty-one percent have at some point taught for MLIS programs. Thirty-six percent said they have never considered it. Forty-three percent actually thought about teaching but never acted on it.

The survey asked why librarians do not teach. The more prevalent reason was that "no one ever asked." Nearly one third said they had no time in addition to a full-time job. Similarly another 26.5% said they did not need the extra work, they enjoyed their free time. Twenty-two percent replied they lacked proximity to a LIS program. In this day of distance education, this should be less of a problem. Seventeen percent did not feel qualified to teach, 7% were discouraged with MLIS education and 6% did not care for the pressures that come with teaching.

Those who have taught in MLIS programs seemed to enjoy several qualities and benefits (See Table 6). Most enjoyed "sharing knowledge with people entering the profession." The next most satisfying qualities were the continuous learning and an excuse to remain current in the field. Extra pay and personal satisfaction were equally important. One third said, "broadening my horizons in librarianship." Intermingling with faculty in

TABLE 6. If ou Teach or Ad unct in a LIS Program, What Do ou Like About It (*n* = 19)

Responses	Number	
Sharing my knowledge with people entering the profession	16	84.2
Learning as much as I teach	13	68.4
Being forced to stay current	13	68.4
E tra Pay	11	57.9
Personal satisfaction	11	57.9
Broadening my horizons in librarianship	7	36.8
Intermingling with faculty in a different way than Im used to	6	31.6
Prestige	2	10.5

a different way was not as important. The choice that was most surprising at a distant last was the prestige factor. Only 10.5% chose this selection. Because prestige ranked very low twice in these surveys, it could be safely concluded that people do not go into librarianship or into the teaching of librarianship for the prestige factor.

As we saw in the first survey approximately 50% of academic librarians doing business reference found the need to take courses, learn on the job, and teach themselves relevant business information. Eighty percent of librarians reported that MLIS programs needed to improve the content of business and competitive intelligence courses. Comments accompanying this question went on for several pages.

Many business librarians, or those generalists who must handle business reference, reported that few library schools offer good courses covering business sources and services. A number of responses were clearly from corporate librarians who needed more schooling in competitive intelligence, synthesizing data, and report writing. A number of schools offer competitive intelligence and knowledge management courses. However, only librarians who are very focused on this as a profession take these courses. Many librarians are not tempted to take these courses until they need them.

Some respondents complained that LIS programs were dropping more specialized courses, or that there were no faculty capable of teaching business courses. One manager complained that new hires simply did not know that a "corporate name is often different from a brand name." Respondents wanted information on sources, but as one person said, "far too much time is spent on memorizing long lists of sources that will be outdated by the time the students graduate." Several people offered that more is needed about the concepts and process of tackling business questions. "Students need to be more competent in understanding client needs." Basically, business reference courses "didn't incorporate the . . . types of in depth question I currently get on the job."

The survey results indicate a need for not only more business reference and competitive intelligence courses, but also better ones. There is a "need for librarians not to stay in their comfort zone and prepare them with content." Practicing librarians have a lot to offer regarding improvements for curriculum. In light of the scarcity of MLIS faculty prepared to teach business curriculum, perhaps one of the answers is for more qualified practitioners to think more seriously about adjuncting in MLIS programs. There is also a need for more discussion of pedagogical issues.

NOTE

1. Pagell and Lusk incorporate the study of Aubrey Kendrick from 1990 which also found the largest transition group came from academia. Pagell and Lusk's later study found more variation in the library of origin. It appeared that academic business librarians were loosening up in accepting candidates from various types of libraries.

REFERENCES

Cain, M. (2003). The two cultures? Librarians and technologists. *Journal of Academic Librarianship, 29*(3), 179–181.

Curzon, S. (1995). Difference between academic and public libraries. *The Unabashed Librarian, 97*, 17–21.

Edwards, R. G. (2002). Migrating to public librarianship: Depart on time to ensure a smooth flight. *Library Trends, 50*(4), 631–639.

Kendrick, A. (1990). The educational background and work experience of academic business librarians. *RQ, 29*, 394–397.

Klopper, S. (2006). The journey from corporate to academic librarian. *Online Magazine, 30*(5), 14–20.

Lanning, S. (1989). So what's the difference? *Public Library Quarterly, 9*(4), 47–49.

McCarthy, J. (2000). Are you sure I am only thirty miles away? *Colorado Libraries, 26*(4), 31–33.

Pagell, R. A., & Lusk, E. J. (2000). A professional photo of academic business librarians worldwide: The present picture and a future view. *Journal of Business & Finance Librarianship, 6*(1), 3–21.

Topper, E. F. (2005). Working knowledge. *American Libraries, 36*(5), 63.

Taking Business (Librarianship) Public

Mark E. Andersen

INTRODUCTION

Being a business librarian in a public library takes on many forms. A few are subject specialists who deal exclusively with business topics. These librarians are usually found in large urban public libraries where such levels of specialization are possible. However, the majority of public library business librarians are generalists who handle all subject areas but have specific responsibilities in the area of business.

Both groups are labeled as business librarians. Both are the subject experts for their institution. But how did they become business librarians?

Most graduates in library science do not plan on careers in business librarianship. Few come to library science with any background or education in business. Usually they have undergraduate degrees in English, history, art, or music but rarely do they have degrees in business. During library school, few students take a specific course on business librarianship. Often they have taken only a general reference course or a social sciences reference class, which have one component dealing with business.

Based on this information, one wonders how librarians in public libraries become business librarians. To explore this idea, I would like to explain my background and how I became a business librarian.

MY BACKGROUND

Although my own story is not typical and does not put forth a definitive career path, I think it is interesting to see that my career was not a straight path nor necessarily a conscious choice.

During high school and college, I worked as a page (shelver) in a public library branch. I enjoyed the job and the environment as well as the staff and the patrons. The staff was very good to me and tried to steer me toward librarianship, but at this point I was determined to be an accounting major. This plan was based on my abilities in math, and it seemed like a practical choice. After three years in an undergraduate program for accounting, I had a revelation that accounting might not be for me. In fact, my accounting classes were my least favorite, and each successive class was more difficult and less enjoyable. I realized that I had enjoyed my liberal arts classes most, but I was unwilling to change my major and start all over. Instead, I searched my university's other business majors and determined that marketing was the most similar to liberal arts subjects, especially psychology. This was the best way for me to utilize the business classes I had already taken, earn a useful degree, and still graduate on time.

During these undergraduate days, I was working at another library, this time in an art school. This job carried me through my college graduation as I tried to embark on my career in marketing—ideally marketing research. However, most of the jobs that I was qualified for were in sales, and I could not find the desired marketing research job. During this time, my coworkers were again encouraging me to go into the library field, but I still resisted. I enjoyed the interactions with the students, the library environment, and the search for information. However, I did not think of librarianship as a career that could support me nor did I see the challenges that this career could bring. But, after much career angst and realizing that I enjoyed library work, I decided to make myself "legal" in the library profession and pursue a library science degree.

In graduate school I was lucky enough to interview for a job at the university's Commerce Library. During the interview, I learned that having an undergraduate degree in business was very surprising and desirable. I was the successful candidate for this job. During my years in library school, a business librarianship class was only offered once but conflicted with a required class, so I did not take it. The practical experience I received at the Commerce Library would be invaluable to me later. Again, the librarians at this library were excellent role models and answered my many questions.

After graduation, my primary goal was to get back to Chicago. I was open to library jobs in any sector: public, academic, or special libraries. My first professional position was in a university library working with a social sciences bibliographer—no contact with business. After a year in this position, I accepted a job as a management reference librarian at another university. I worked in this position for about two years and during this time I experienced a crisis of faith. I liked my job, but it just did not feel right. I was not feeling fulfilled. So at this time I interviewed for a part-time job in a public library as a general reference librarian. My business background and experience in a university library were a plus, and I was hired. As I found out, most librarians shy away from business questions, so my knowledge of business was welcomed, and colleagues gladly turned business questions and business patrons over to me. It was here that I realized I enjoyed the topic of business, but that the academic setting was not for me. This was a turning point for me. I had finally figured out that I had a business mind but a liberal arts heart. Coming to terms with this was a turning point for me. I could concentrate on the business subject matter but operate in the liberal arts world of librarianship. The public library was the place I wanted to be. I loved the openness of the institution—anyone and everyone were welcome. I loved the diversity— every age, every race and ethnicity, and every socioeconomic group. As any good reference librarian, I relished the hunt for information as well as fulfillment in finding the answer. However, I also realized something else. I enjoyed the fact that I was making a difference in someone's life. Whether it was a job search, investing, or starting a new business, these reference questions had an immediate impact on people's lives. But it just was not the business questions. I enjoyed all reference questions, whether they were medical, political, or social. This is what I needed from my job and my career. A public library is where I needed and wanted to be. Subsequently I applied for a full-time position at the Chicago Public Library in the Interlibrary Loan Department and was the successful candidate. Two years later, I transferred to the Business Science Technology Division. However, for a few years I was mainly in the Science Technology section. Later, I moved back to business when the opportunity presented itself. Fourteen years later I am the Division Chief of the Business Science Technology Division.

CHALLENGES OF BEING A BUSINESS LIBARIAN

Why do so few people choose business librarianship? Why is business librarianship so much different than genealogy or art librarianship?

Traditionally, business is not a topic embraced by librarians. It has a specialized jargon, and although other subject areas have their own specialized vocabulary, business jargon tends to be especially foreign to librarians. This may be because most librarians and many other professionals have never taken a business class. They have not been exposed to these words in a formalized setting and thus feel embarrassed that they do not know their meanings. Because business patrons tend to be more demanding, this lack of knowledge can be even more intimidating. Because these terms involve the loss or gain of money, the stress and level of discomfort is raised. Most librarians tend to have liberal arts backgrounds and feel most comfortable around those topics as opposed to business ones. Additionally, many business patrons speak very authoritatively whether or not they know exactly what they are seeking. Some of these business patrons can be frustrated during the reference interview if the librarian asks too many basic questions or if the librarian seems uncertain about the subject.

Philosophically, business is also very different from traditional librarianship. Librarians value information sharing. Business patrons place great worth in keeping information to themselves—this information is their competitive edge. Thus the librarian's view of information and that of the business patron seem to be immediately at odds. However, librarians and business patrons agree on the value of information. Librarians would be wise to focus on this shared value and use this as the foundation of their business encounters.

Another source of frustration with business patrons is they are often in a hurry—time is money. They may not care how you found the information or the search strategy you used, they just want the information now. As librarians we pride ourselves in our knowledge and expertise. We also try to teach patrons to become self-sufficient. However, we know that patrons do not always want to be taught. Business patrons usually know what they want—whether or not it actually exists. And business patrons can be ruthless—if they feel that you do not know what you are talking about, they can be merciless. Therefore, a general familiarity with the topic is essential. You need to speak their language. With most patrons, we can tackle their question as a joint journey with them. In business, at least initially, the patron does not want to go on the journey to find the information. They want someone who knows the answer to their questions and where to find it. In business reference this trust between the librarian and patron is even more important than in a general reference transaction.

Another source of frustration can be the lack of colleagues or mentors. Because most librarians steer clear of business, there may be no one at your library to teach you the basics of business. However, this can be a wonderful opportunity to specialize and become a resource for the rest of your colleagues.

Librarians who want to become proficient in business usually need to look for opportunities to learn about business. General business classes are a great place to begin. They will give you the foundation of business and familiarize you with the terms and concepts. Sometimes, local library systems as well as national associations offer business workshops and seminars. Take advantage of as many of these as possible.

From the experienced librarian's point of view, I would encourage them to nudge other staff toward business topics—whether providing a business program or in the teaching of a business database. New librarians or nonbusiness librarians may need some encouragement in this area. You probably will not "convert" all of your staff or colleagues to business librarianship, but you will ease their level of comfort as well as improve the reputation of your library.

Another potential area of frustration is that in business librarianship we do not give advice in contrast to Readers' Advisory for fiction. Sometimes this is hard for patrons to grasp—some members of the public see the librarian as their own financial advisor. We must understand that these patrons do not have anywhere else to turn and may not have the resources to hire a professional advisor. This does not mean that we should give advice, but we need to understand the patron's viewpoint and provide tools for financial literacy.

These challenges do not mean that a career path in business librarianship is not worth pursuing. Even a generalist can benefit from having a business specialty or a business "minor." It just means that one must make a conscious choice about specializing in business.

IMPORTANCE OF BUSINESS LIBRARIANS

Is business librarianship a feasible career goal?

Business and its related topics such as careers, investing, real estate, management, marketing, and accounting are always in demand in a public library. During good economic times, real estate investing, and wealth management are popular topics. During economic downturns, career information and the stock market investing are likewise requested. Indeed business information is always in demand.

Therefore business topics are ideal for public library outreach. Patrons are always interested in the topics of investing, career changes, home buying, and retirement. Because most members of the public do not have access to their own financial advisors or career counselors, they come to the library. This is when the public library can indeed be the "People's University," teaching patrons to find the best information available to make their own decisions. The library's role in financial literacy is vital and one that is recognized within the library as well as by the business community. Therefore, developing a strong collection and series of programs in the area of business can position your library as an important partner in these financial literacy efforts.

In addition to the edification of individual patrons, business librarians can become valued partners of the business community. The library can provide businesses with valuable information on competitors, suppliers, and trends, as well as industry information. Many large businesses no longer have corporate libraries, and few small businesses can afford to buy the resources found in the public library. The public library is positioned to be the library for these businesses. All of these businesses have an influence on local government. Funding for public library often comes from local government, so it is important for these businesses to recognize the value of the public library. Once they benefit from the public library, they will be more receptive to funding it for everyone. They then can continue to fund many civic operations including the library. Once the business community is behind the library, they can act as an advocate for the library when tax issues or library referendums arise.

Also, in recent years, the role of the library as a tool for economic development has been seen in many cities including Chicago. When the community sees municipal investment in the form of the libraries or infrastructure, businesses, and other institutions are more willing to take a stake in the community. With this business investment, the local community and library can become more vibrant and sustainable.

It is interesting to note that so many important aspects of outreach are connected to business, and yet there are few people specializing in this area. Outreach is vital for all libraries and that includes public libraries, which rely on tax payer funds. Outreach to businesses can be an excellent way of building support for your library.

Thus, a strong business librarian is vital for the survival and well-being of the public library. Because few librarians specialize in business, business librarianship is an excellent skill to have in your professional "briefcase."

QUALITIES OF THE BEST BUSINESS LIBARIANS

The best business librarians are first and foremost excellent reference librarians. The same skills that are needed in a general reference interview can be utilized in a reference interview with a business patron.

The goal of the best library schools is to train graduates who will be able to enter into a wide array of positions in a variety of settings. Therefore, we cannot expect our new graduates to be fully trained business librarians. However, we should expect new graduates to have a strong foundation in the library field and to know the basics of searching, resources, and customer service.

The single most important trait for librarians is inquisitiveness. This applies to business librarians as well. We will never be able to know everything there is to know about business. Business is fast paced and constantly changing and evolving. However, a thirst for knowledge and a desire to learn more about a topic will always be an asset to a librarian. We must never stop learning. Reading the local newspaper is essential habit for any librarian. Today's headlines are the very topics our patrons are reading and hearing about. These topics are also the ones influencing our communities. A prepared librarian is aware of these topics and can assist patrons in finding additional information. Librarians may never fully anticipate questions, but they should have a general knowledge of the events happening around the world. When reading about current events, business is never very far away. Many mainstream topics dovetail right into business topics. Business topics are usually the top stories in the news, therefore the informed librarian already knows something about business.

Many businesses subscribe to the following philosophy: hire for attitude, train for skill. I would say that this also applies to business librarianship. Find the best and brightest librarians with the best reference, searching, and customer service skills and you can teach them the business aspects.

One does not necessarily need to have a business degree although business knowledge is extremely useful. However, a general business class at a community college would be an excellent way to become familiar with some business concepts and vocabulary.

In fact, sometimes the best business librarians are not the ones who eat, sleep, and breathe the stock market. These librarians may understand these topics and know the vocabulary, but can they explain these concepts to the public? Sometimes they are only interested in the patrons who share their depth of knowledge and care nothing about the beginning investor. In a public library you need to be able to talk to everyone from the emerging reader to the patron with a PhD.

Also, in a public library the questions can be across the board, from a very basic question to a complex inquiry. At the public library you never know what to expect. The patrons have no affiliation or common goal as they do at a university or in a special library. This is one of the challenges. As with every good reference librarian, it is not necessary to understand all the complexities of the question but where to look for this information.

Another quality needed in a successful business librarian is an appreciation for business. Business cannot be a dirty word; it is an important part of our world. Some patrons and some librarians feel this business is not a subject to be embraced and that it is beneath them—it is not intellectual, only materialistic. However, it is important to understand the role and importance of business. If the librarian feels antagonistic toward business, he or she will have hard time relating or empathizing with patrons searching for business information. Does a librarian have to love business? No. However, a respect and basic understanding is needed.

Statistics play a big role in the production and in the use of business information, therefore a basic understanding and familiarity with numbers is extremely helpful. It is extremely important for the business librarian not to be afraid of numbers.

CONCLUSION

Business librarianship is an important skill needed by every public library, and the demand for this expertise shows no sign of slowing down. Librarians who equip themselves with knowledge of business information will be able to fill a niche that is often avoided by others in the field. This business expertise will then enable their library to fulfill the needs of their individual and corporate patrons looking for this vital information.

Business librarianship in a public library has immediate benefits to patrons and therefore can provide the librarian with a great deal of satisfaction.

Professionally, business librarians will have a competitive edge when compared to those with a general background. However, there are many challenges to becoming a business librarian in a public library. Nevertheless, specializing in business librarianship for a public library is a rewarding and stimulating career move offering excellent opportunities for visibility, mobility, and satisfaction. The path to business librarianship does not come with a road map. However, those that invest in their career with a focused and conscious effort toward learning about business information will be rewarded with great personal and career dividends.

Transitioning to Corporate Librarianship

Emily Rimland
Glenn Masuchika

INTRODUCTION

U.S. News and World Report lists it as one of "The Best Careers of 2007" (2006). Kiplinger.com calls it one of seven great careers for 2007 (Nemko, 2007). What is this career? *Librarian.* CNN Money and *Parade* magazine name it as a "hot job" (Brenner, 2007; "Hot Jobs Now," 2007). What is this hot job? *Corporate librarian.*

If you are at a career crossroads, the start of a new career, or beginning a new job, you may find yourself transitioning to corporate librarianship. If you are entirely new to the profession or new to this area of the profession, this article is meant to help you find your bearings by discussing ways to enhance your education, where to look for jobs, knowing what to expect on the job, and ways to advance. The authors considered the definition of *corporate librarianship* from a broad perspective including areas such as law librarianship and knowledge management. We have interviewed a number of librarians who work in a variety of corporate library settings, and their experiences and perspectives are incorporated into this article.

LITERATURE REVIEW

The literature about beginning a career in corporate librarianship is plentiful, and many resources are found in the form of handbooks or guidebooks. Anyone thinking about beginning a career in a corporate or special library setting will appreciate the recently released *A Day In the Life: Career Options for Library and Information Science* by Shontz and Murray (2007). This book neatly categorizes the different types of library work (public, special, academic, etc.) and provides narrative accounts from professionals about a typical workday, the pros and cons of the job, and how to find and prepare for similar jobs. What makes this handbook shine is the variety of contributors—from a solo librarian in a fast-moving global financial company, to a law librarian at a large law firm, to a librarian at an Internet start-up company. It provides the nitty gritty details of the job akin to what a close personal friend could provide. Matarazzo's (1990) *Corporate Library Excellence* also does a good job of profiling corporate libraries organized by geographic region that have been selected as "outstanding" based upon certain criteria. Although the libraries featured here have surely changed, this book gives the reader the big picture of a variety of special library settings and the reasons for their selection are based on principles that are still appreciated today. *Special Librarianship As A Career* (Special Libraries Association [SLA], 1995) covers topics that are still of interest to corporate librarians such as competencies and skills, outsourcing, management, and education. The field has changed a lot, but it is worthy to note how many skills and competencies discussed in this work have not changed.

In the direction of knowledge management, there is also quite a bit of literature. For instance, "Knowledge Management for the Information Professional" (Srikantaiah & Koenig, 2000) takes a broad look at this emerging area including applications of knowledge management in libraries and information centers. *Knowledge and Special Libraries* (Matarazzo & Connolly, 1999) provides a number of contributions that address corporate libraries from a business perspective as well as an information management one.

Similar but more general in approach are other well-respected career guidebooks such as *The Librarian's Career Guidebook* by Shontz (2004), which provides advice for librarians in all stages of their careers with applicable information for any type of librarianship. *Expectations of Librarians in the 21st Century* (Bridges, 2003) also provides a number of contributions by librarians in the trenches with select articles about special libraries and other helpful articles.

TheSLA's online career section provides a large knowledge base for career information, and its flagship publication *Information Outlook* has numerous articles that would interest someone transitioning to corporate librarianship. *Online* and *Searcher* are other publications that have relevant articles on this topic from time to time.

LIBRARY SCHOOL AND POSTLIBRARY SCHOOL

As in other occupations, some librarians know from the beginning that they want to specialize in a particular area. Others may be unsure about specialization or simply "fall into" an area like corporate librarianship. If you are still in library school and think you may want to work in a corporate library setting, there are ways to customize your education to your advantage. If you are out of library school, there are some basic skills that are pertinent. Any job experience you have will be helpful, and professional development or continuing education can be used to supplement your degree.

Individuals entering or enrolled in library school who are interested in this area of librarianship may consider some options for tailoring their education to get the maximum benefit. A number of library schools offer targeted curriculums for the areas of special librarianship and knowledge management that are excellent ways to prepare for corporate librarianship. It is also common to find only a general track offered for special librarianship. However, general tracks may not always address the in-depth knowledge needed in the realm of corporate librarianship. If you find yourself in a general program, there are ways to shape your degree for a corporate library setting. In terms of course offerings, many library schools provide an overview class about special libraries, and most offer an assortment of information resource classes for specific subject areas (science, business, and law are common), which are highly recommended. If your library school participates in something like the Web-based Information Science Education (WISE) consortium, this is great way to expand and supplement your graduate school education. In this type of consortium, students are able to take courses offered at other library schools that are part of the consortium and may, therefore, have the opportunity to take more targeted classes related to corporate librarianship. In addition to specialized courses offered by library schools, it is wise to find out if you may take related courses at a business or law school and apply the credit toward your MLIS degree. Doing so will expand not only your education, but also your network of contacts, thus giving you one more "one up" in the job market.

Another way to customize the library school experience is through internships and independent study that are available to face-to-face students and distance learners alike. Internships are an invaluable way to get experience in a setting of your interest, and veteran librarians enjoy having a student intern for the extra help and for the opportunity to teach a new librarian about the profession. Additionally, if a position becomes open at the location of the internship, you might be one of the first people to find out about it. Students may learn about internship opportunities by contacting the local chapters of professional associations, asking an academic adviser, or through good old-fashioned networking. Keep in mind that if the ideal internship does not exist yet, there is nothing stopping you from creating one.

Independent or individual study courses can also offer you invaluable experience before graduation. Independent study allows students to explore a particular issue or topic that interests them by doing research, writing a report, or implementing a new program. This option is a great way to boost and deepen your knowledge on a topic, and because most independent study projects have a tangible outcome (a paper, program, data) they stand out on a résumé and are an excellent addition to a portfolio.

For graduates thinking about transitioning to corporate librarianship, obtaining your MLIS was not your last stop, and many opportunities are available. Fisher and Matarazzo's point (1993) that most library science curriculums cannot be expected to prepare graduates for every situation of the job is well taken; and in fact, much of the knowledge and skills needed to be successful in a corporate information environment are not items generally linked to library school but are instead related to communication skills and decision making. This is mirrored in the SLA competencies as well, which discusses and emphasizes personal competencies (skills, values, attitudes) as well as professional and core competencies (SLA, 2003).

It is common for information professionals who are in transition to supplement their education through continuing education and professional development. Some library schools offer certificates of advanced study (CAS) that can give professionals the opportunity for formal education in areas related to special librarianship and knowledge management. Continuing education and professional development opportunities are also available through professional associations, such as SLA. Membership in SLA not only offers excellent networking opportunities with professionals, but also provides access to resources like Click University. Click University offers self-paced training and certificate programs in a variety of areas related to corporate librarianship. Finally, volunteering and informational interviews are two more ways a graduate can get some experience and perspective about a corporate library setting.

Some corporate librarians also choose to get a second master's degree, most commonly an MBA. There are varying opinions on the value of an MBA for a librarian given the time and expense, but it is a choice that may broaden career choices. Some argue that the cost and commitment of an MBA results in a higher salary or a more rapid advancement in the company. Others lament that within the world of the corporate library, there is a limit to advancing, with many finding the library directorship the summit of their climb. An MBA can give the librarian valuable business skills including financial and managerial accounting, finance, and marketing, all of which are essential in managing a corporate library or surviving in the corporate environment, and it may allow for equal prestige among other employees that have master's degrees. Finally, further education can give librarians the necessary credentials to move up in the organization if they decide to leave the profession entirely. Whether a librarian wishes to gain another master's degree is a personal and professional choice. However many librarians do have other degrees, and a corporate librarian with an MBA is common.

SALARIES AND FINDING JOBS

As mentioned earlier, the demand for corporate librarians is hot. Librarians, including those in the corporate sector, are seeing changes that have expanded their demand and duties.

There is also some speculation that this increased demand combined with low salaries for librarians in other sectors may be pushing more job seekers to explore this area of librarianship. Although salaries do vary depending on the individual's skills and experience and the company's size and location, with more demand comes better pay. Looking broadly at special librarians such as law librarians, digital librarians, and librarians for research firms, beginning salaries came in around $47,600 for 2007 according to the American Library Association (ALA) (Carmichael, 2007). The average salary for SLA members overall in 2006 was $67,400, and *Parade* magazine lists the high end of the range for corporate librarians at $93,000 with financial service companies offering the highest salaries (Brenner, 2007; Latham, 2006). Law librarian salaries in 2007 were consistent with other areas and ranged from $40,000–$65,000 on average (The Affiliates, Robert Half International Co., 2007).

When you are looking for a job, often the hardest part is knowing where to begin. Naturally, there are a variety of sources for job postings including professional associations, newspapers, placement services, and your own contacts. Everyone has their own approach to job hunting, although most job hunters use online sources heavily. A few favorite places for online job searching for corporate library positions are given below. As with library resources, each has its own strengths, so it is a good idea to evaluate them all and decide which you like best.

- ALA Joblist: joblist.ala.org
- Information International Associates Inc.: www.iiaweb.com
- Library Associates: www.libraryassociates.com
- LISjobs.com–Jobs for Librarians and Information Professionals: www.lisjobs.com
- SLA Career Center: careercenter.sla.org
- USA JOBS: The Federal Government's Official Job site: www.usajobs.gov
- Career services Websites available via your graduate school.

When you are job searching there are a few factors to keep in mind. First, consider the idea of a temporary or contract job. Although these types of jobs may not offer the job security you may ultimately want, they often lead to full-time employment at the company or agency. If nothing else, contract work can give you a foot in the door if you are looking to transition. Another suggestion is to consider job shadowing or conducting an informational interview of a corporate librarian who works in the type of library in which you are interested. Both approaches are designed to introduce you to the job and its responsibilities, and the networking may give you a leg up on new opportunities at that company.

Once you score the interview, it is vital to prepare thoroughly by researching the company and its products and services. Employers are looking for librarians that are excellent at multitasking, tolerant of deadlines and "crunch times." They are also interested in hiring librarians who like to explore new territories and take chances, while keeping the company's bottom line in sight and aligning one's goals with those of the company's (Klopper, 2006). However, keep in mind that corporate librarianship is indeed specialized, and many employers do not expect new hires to come into the job knowing everything about the position. What is paramount is a willingness and readiness to learn new skills. The following section outlines what you might expect once hired.

A DAY IN THE LIFE OF A CORPORATE LIBRARIAN

A typical day begins as it does for many librarians: checking for e-mail or phone requests. Many of the requests are simple ready reference questions that can be answered within a few minutes. Other requests require an hour or more of searching through various databases or print sources. A few requests need clarification and may require some negotiation with the client. It is also common to receive a frantic request from someone overseas who needs a specific bit of information to close a big deal. Luckily for the librarian, there is an active library Website or intranet that houses numerous databases and targeted resources that have been collected, refined, and maintained over the years. The company Website is the primary method of communication between the library and the rest of the corporation, especially if it is a multinational corporation. Many corporate librarians are the content manager and webmaster for the company's Website or intranet. The librarian must make sure that the Website is functioning at all times, access to the company's databases is maintained, links are working, and information on the site is up-to-date and accurate.

Many corporate libraries have informational outreach programs intended to keep the community up-to-date on the business landscape. One method is to produce in-house newsletters, covering important news and providing alerts and distributing them via the company's intranet and by e-mail. These newsletters are focused only on concerns that are directly related to business and having time sensitivity. They can be about a new organizational structure of a competitor, the emergence of any newly disruptive technologies, the failure or success of a rival's products, new and potential customers, or trends of the industry. The purpose of these newsletters often falls under the category of "competitive intelligence," to know what one's competitors are doing and to alert upper management.

After the daily tasks are finished, the day may be peppered with meetings with other members of the library staff or the company. Changes to funding for electronic or print sources are a priority because they directly affect what is available to the librarians and which areas of the corporation will be affected. Brainstorming often takes place about how to maintain relationships with the various parts of the organization, whether it is new services for departments the library faithfully serves or to forge new relationships. New projects or initiatives the library will undertake and who will take charge of them are discussed. Some projects are limited by the contracts received from the corporation or by the time allotted. Here coordination is paramount as librarians may be working simultaneously on two or more different yet overlapping projects. Librarians and staff give status reports on other ongoing projects and, if need be, resources are reallocated to achieve the desired outcomes. Last, yet very important, projects to advertise the library's services are considered. It is important to constantly remind the entire organization how the library can help all units succeed in their appointed business areas especially for international corporations. Outside of these activities, corporate libraries do a variety of other tasks. Some corporate libraries have the ability to directly bill clients for work performed. This is often found in law libraries where the library has a line item on a customer's bill for information services rendered. If a library has permission to bill, time and charges for a specific contract are recorded in financial log books and are often examined by the corporation's accountants.

At least once a week, there is usually some kind of disruptive occurrence that affects a project's completion. No matter how stressful, the very nature of the corporation's library is to solve informational dilemmas—the issue must be taken up immediately, and if need be, by the entire staff. Examples are searching for critical, missing information to complete a contract minutes before a deadline or retrieving a critical article and delivering it to a vice president preparing for a stockholders meeting that begins in 30 minutes. Although such occurrences are often stressful, they can get your adrenaline pumping and are good opportunities to once again prove the value of the library to the decision makers in the corporation. Successful delivery by the library often leads to forging a bond between the library and the grateful party. The day ends with checking for any last-minute information crises to be solved.

Depending on the company, there may be travel involved with the job, especially in a multinational corporation. The reasons for travel may be to take part in company meetings, workshops, or retreats, to provide bibliographic instruction to other branches, or for professional development. These are some things that you might expect in a typical day in a corporate information center. In addition to practical matters, there are some philosophical differences that make corporate librarianship special.

WHAT'S DIFFERENT ABOUT CORPORATE LIBRARIANSHIP?

Corporate librarians share many characteristics with other types of librarians. They enter the profession for the same reasons as all librarians: an interest in information; how that information is stored, retrieved, and delivered; and a proclivity to help others access information to meet their needs. All librarians attend a recognized graduate program and receive a master's degree in library and information studies. They assess the needs of their designated community and either build or sustain a collection according to the perceived needs of the community. When information is delivered and satisfies the community's needs, the librarian's goal has been reached. In most cases, it is at this point that the similarities between corporate librarians and other types of librarians end.

Although all librarians provide those items described above, two differences between corporate librarians are the overarching goals for providing the information and the corporate librarian's audience. For example, public and academic librarians focus on forming an educated populace that can think critically. They seek to provide untainted and free-flowing information, so patrons can make choices based on the given information. To this end, the librarian is a major player in the preservation and promotion of democracy and works to better society.

In contrast, a corporate librarian's scope is narrower and does not focus on wide-reaching societal goals. The corporate librarian's focus is primarily the business, and it is common for the mantra of the corporate librarian in a publicly held company to be "increase the shareholder's value." The corporate librarian, a member of the corporation, has a simple goal which is to contribute to keeping the company "in the black."

These differences in philosophies determine the activities of each type of librarian. Public and academic librarians place a greater emphasis on instruction and learning. In public and academic settings, librarians help patrons who enter the portals of their library and are teachers to whomever seeks information. They show students how to get to what they want and to critically evaluate what they find. Corporate librarians in general do not have primary teaching assignments and may do little or no instruction, but rather large amounts of reference and collection development, depending on the position.

The corporate librarian, similar to other librarians, strives to meet its community's needs; however, their environments are often different. In the corporate world, it is often the attitude that the librarian is an active member in the corporation no less than the engineer who designs the products or the marketer who sell the products. Here the librarian takes a proactive role and proves daily to upper management that their work adds value to the corporation by directly impacting the bottom line. Like all employees in the company, one must constantly prove one's worth by performing duties directly involved with the corporation's success. It is an exhilarating environment, testing oneself against one's peers, always cognizant that you are having a direct effect on the outcome of a company's project, product, or campaign. It is difficult and even presumptuous to judge each type of librarianship by the criteria of the other. It is simply one profession in two different worlds, each serving their clients as their environments demand.

CHALLENGES FOR TRANSITIONING

As librarians know, the perception of a librarian as someone who sits at a desk in the library and can point to the works of Jane Austen by memory is an old and inaccurate one. But nowhere is this stereotype dashed more assertively than in the corporate world. The corporate world of timetables and ledgers, where wrong decisions can result in company losses, and information must sometimes be provided in minutes, is frightening to some and invigorating to others. For those who wish to enter the corporate world of information retrieval and delivery, there are challenges to keep in mind.

Primarily, it is wise to acknowledge that there is a change in philosophy. Corporate librarians should remember the fact that their position and the library's existence is based on the perceived value it adds to the corporation and the climate of the company's management. Although it is rare for libraries at educational institutions to close or librarians to be fired for anything less than gross malfeasance or criminal indictment, the closing or restructuring of corporate libraries can occur without much warning. There is little to defend against seemingly irrational decisions made by a new vice president who believes he or she is saving money by dissolving the library. Thus the world of corporate libraries is tenuous and on par with everything else in the corporation. But there are reasons to stay positive. In the *2006 SLA Salary Survey* nearly 75% of organizations that have outsourced information functions had no reduction in library or information center staff. Additionally, slightly more than one half of respondents were expected to increase their library or information center budgets in 2007 (Latham, 2006).

However, there are strategies for maintaining relevance and staying abreast of changes within the company. First and foremost, corporate librarians should be proactive. Become a full participant in the corporation and accept nothing less than the same status as the other workers in the hive. By assisting other branches of the corporation, alliances can be created. In times of cutbacks, these alliances can speak volumes for the library and librarians. A strong advocate in upper management is a shield, however the library must also support the advocate's positions and opinions. These strategies are based on the fact that the library creates more wealth than it costs to maintain and, in the end, increases the shareholder's value.

The ability to keep a pulse on the business landscape and obtain the skills to make deals is not a skill generally taught in library school. For the librarian wanting to enter the corporate world, it is important to know how "businesspeople" think and what language they speak. Although there are differing opinions about the value of an MBA for librarians, formal knowledge and education in business is helpful. No matter your take on this debate, most agree that the case methods used in MBA programs can give librarians a good idea of how corporations operate and provide a strong preparation for entrance into a business setting. Thus the corporate librarian needs to become a chess player, knowledgeable about who has power, how to wield one's own power, and the best move for a given situation.

The discussion of skills and knowledge necessary to be a corporate librarian is often focused on the general business environment. Of equal or greater importance is knowledge of the corporation's products and the industry in general. There is a misconception that business is business, that it does not matter if a company is producing widgets, nuclear power plants, or winning lawsuits. Fully embracing the philosophy that the engineers worry about the manufacturing details, the marketers about the customers, and the librarians deal with the information concerning these fields is not recommended. There is no greater danger of irrelevance to the corporation than by taking this attitude. Just as it is important to prepare for an interview at a particular company by studying the company's products beforehand, the librarian must also constantly be aware of the products of their corporation. Whether it is finding accurate specifications and standards for a military aircraft for an engineer, or providing a marketer with a recent list of potential customers in a foreign country, or gathering competitive intelligence for the CEO, alliances with coworkers are directly based on what a librarian can contribute to the process. Corporate librarians are in the unique position of interacting with many different employees and departments and have the ability to understand the grander schemes and direction of the corporation. Thus there are many opportunities to network and assess the community's needs within the company.

Another challenge that faces corporate librarians is the practice of moving information professionals out of the library or information center and into other departments within the company. In the *SLA 2006 Salary Survey*, 58% of information professionals reported working outside the library or information center (Latham, 2006). Such lateral or upward movements are thus common in corporations as many positions are filled from within their ranks. Librarians who work in corporate information centers are often favored as good candidates by departments who seek people immediately knowledgeable about the corporation's objectives and goals and who already understand the politics of the organization. Librarians can successfully transfer into such positions as market analysts and forecasters, mergers and acquisitions specialists, competitive intelligence officers, or any field directly concerning the gathering, synthesizing, and disseminating of information within a corporation. One could even think of working as a corporate librarian as a good starting place for those who want to move up the corporate ladder.

Some corporate librarians have expressed that professional associations are not seen as a priority by their employers, and therefore involvement on company time may be limited. However, professional associations are a good way to network with peers about resources and strategies relevant to challenges that corporate librarians face. Professional associations are also important for seeking ways to advance in a corporate librarian career.

STRATEGIES FOR ADVANCING IN CORPORATE LIBRARIANSHIP

Corporate settings offer unique adventures and challenges that keep librarians on their toes. As in other areas of librarianship, the ability to adapt to rapid change is imperative, and even more so for advancing in a corporate setting. Corporations are known for being fast paced but compounding the change is the speed at which libraries are changing. As Stephen Abram (2007) reminded us, "the dinosaurs didn't go extinct because the climate changed. They disappeared because they couldn't adapt to the changes happening around them" (p. 36). Along with the ability to adapt, comes "a greater degree of experimentation and risk taking than has been the case in the past" (Plutchak, 2005, p. 23). Because of rapidly changing environments, librarians need to rethink where to invest their time and try new things to find the best, most efficient, or most popular technique for clients. It may be designing a new program without knowing that it will be a success, or discontinuing a print resource that the library always had but no longer seems fiscally warranted. Last, embedding ourselves in the areas where users need us will be vital to success. By attending meetings, visiting departments, and providing programming, librarians can not only remind coworkers of what libraries have to offer, but also can also keep a pulse on the information needs of the company. As Plutchak (2005) stated, "We can get people to think about librarians in new ways by acting in new ways." (p. 27).

It is a great time to be a corporate librarian. The job market is good, the image is "hot," and there are many unique and challenging environments out there for individuals who seek this kind of stimulating work. By doing your homework, taking advantage of specialized courses or professional development, and remaining flexible and adaptable, you can make a successful transition into the world of corporate librarianship.

REFERENCES

Abram, S. (2007). The future of reference in special libraries is what information pros can make it. *Information Outlook, 11*(10), 35–37.

The Affiliates, Robert Half International Co. (2007). *2007 salary guide*. Retrieved October 5, 2007, from http://www.careerjournal.com/salaryhiring/industries/law/20070116-law-tab.html.

Brenner, L. (2007). How did you do? *Parade Magazine.* Retrieved November 25, 2007, from http://www.parade.com/articles/editions/2007/edition_04-15-2007/WPE_lead.

Bridges, K. (2003). *Expectations of librarians in the 21st century.* Westport, CT: Greenwood Press.

Carmichael, A. (2007). The changing role of library science. *Wall Street Journal Online.* Retrieved October 5, 2007, from http://www.careerjournal.com/salaryhiring/industries/librarians/20070103-carmichael.html.

Fisher, W., & Matarazzo, J. (1993). Professional development for special librarians: Formal education and continuing education for excellence. *Library Trends, 42*(2), 290–303.

Hot jobs now. (2003). *CNN Money.* Retrieved October 26, 2007, from http://money.cnn.com/2003/08/28/pf/saving/hotjobsnow/index.htm.

Klopper, S. M. (2006). The journey from corporate to academic librarian. *Online, 30*(5), 14–20. Retrieved November 4, 2007 from EbscoHost.

Latham, J. R. (2006). Member salaries continue to outpace inflation. *Information Outlook, 10*(11), 52. Retrieved November 27, 2007, from ProQuest Direct.

Matarazzo, J. (1990). *Corporate library excellence.* Washington, DC: Special Libraries Association.

Matarazzo, James M., & Suzanne D. Connolly, eds. (1999). *Knowledge and special libraries.* Boston: Butterworth-Heinemann.

Nemko, M. (2007). 7 great careers for 2007. *Kiplinger.com.* Retrieved November 21, 2007, from http://www.kiplinger.com/columns/onthejob/archive/2007/job0402.html.

Plutchak, T. S. (2005). If you're flexible, adaptable, and willing to take risks. *Information Outlook, 9*(5), 23–29. Retrieved November 27, 2007, from ProQuest Direct.

Shontz, P. K. (2004). *The librarian's career guidebook.* Lanham, MD: Scarecrow Press.

Shontz, P., & Murray, R. A. (2007). *A day in the life: Career options in library and information science.* Westport, CT: Libraries Unlimited.

Special Libraries Association. (1995). *Special librarianship as a career: An SLA information kit.* Washington, DC: Author.

Special Libraries Association. (2003). *Competencies for information professionals of the 21st century.* Retrieved November 27, 2007, from http://www.sla.org/content/learn/comp2003/index.cfm.

Srikantaiah, Taverekere & Michael E. D. Koenig, eds. (2000). *Knowledge management for the information professional.* Medford, NJ: Published for the American Society for Information Science by Information Today.

Successful Mentoring Programs: Examples from Within and Without the Academy

Bonnie A. Osif

INTRODUCTION

There are numerous definitions of *mentoring*, most with relatively subtle differences. Each article in this issue of *Journal of Business & Finance Librarianship* could cite a different and correct definition. In her book on coaching, Metz (2001) provided one clear and detailed definition that is worth consideration:

Mentoring is guidance from someone who has gone before. A mentor has first-hand knowledge and experience in a career path that the player wants to pursue. For example, a librarian may be a mentor for someone who aspires to become a librarian, or a person who has climbed the corporate ladder may be a mentor of a middle manager. The mentor role assumes that the mentor has experience, knowledge, and contacts that can help a particular individual achieve a specific goal. (p. 8)

Several words stand out from this definition—guidance, knowledge, experience, and contacts—all of these are essential to quality mentoring. Willingness to help and the desire to see the mentee succeed are two traits that could be added to this list.

There are many examples of good mentoring programs, and most share some common characteristics. In addition, many programs have some distinguishing aspects that address individual needs or situations. For example, faculty status and rank issues differ from one university to another, evaluation criteria vary, and career path options vary among institutions and individuals. Mentees have strengths and weaknesses that need to be addressed within the context of the individual demands of their libraries. So, though mentoring programs normally will have some variation from institution to institution, the programs will add another layer of variation when addressing individual needs. For these reasons, there is probably no single program that fits all situations. However, a review of successful programs can provide guidance in planning and ideas to incorporate into either a new mentoring programs or to revise existing programs. A review in academic libraries and several other organizations can provide a snapshot of successful mentoring programs and some unique features worth considering.

MENTORING IN UNIVERSITY LIBRARIES

The University of Delaware has had a set of guidelines and procedures for a mentoring program in place since 1997. The goal of the program is to "provide professionals with peer counselors and role models to supplement the relationships within reporting lines . . . enhance the professional atmosphere within the library, and to encourage all professionals to create and participate in career enrichment activities" (Wittkopf, 1999, p. 24). The program is voluntary for mentors and mentees. There are three mentoring programs at Delaware: orientation for new library professionals, promotion for those interested in advancement, and, professional for those interested in changing their career emphasis, job enhancement, or development of skills needed for administrative or specialty positions.

Orientation mentoring is a six-month, structured program that acquaints the new professional to the university and the geographic area and introduces the organization and mission of the library, their specific library department and its relationships and interactions with other departments, career issues including committees, organizational issues, and professional issues such as professional organizations and scholarly research opportunities. Mentors volunteer to serve. It is recommended that they have two or more years at the University Library, have good knowledge of the Library and the University, be aware of the issues facing new librarians, be willing to follow the mentoring checklist, meet at least monthly with the mentee, and provide feedback to the Mentoring Program Coordinator (MPC) who administers the program for the Libraries. There is a checklist to assist the mentor and an evaluation form for mentee feedback to the MPC.

Promotion mentoring is a six- to 12-month process directly focused on dossier preparation and professional activities. Mentors are of the same or higher level of responsibility and may not be direct supervisors. They also should have been promoted or have served on the promotion committee and have a clear understanding of the promotion process. The goal is to assist the mentee with promotion and in focusing their professional activities appropriately to fulfill the promotion criteria at Delaware. Dossier preparation and advice in professional activities are a major focus. To assist the mentees in the process, knowledge of university and professional organizations and publishing opportunities is important. Evaluation of the mentoring process is provided to the MPC.

The third type of mentoring is professional, which has a goal of career enrichment or diversification and advancement into management or specialty areas. It is the most flexible, least formal of the three types of mentoring options. The length of the relationship is flexible based on an individual's specific needs. This program is designed for the middle- and upper-level librarian. Mentors are considered experts in their fields and can be selected from any level in the library but may not be a direct supervisor. The mentor works with the mentee to determine the best ways to address individual goals for advancement and provides appropriate assistance. As with the other mentoring types, there is an evaluation form.

Overseeing the three mentoring tracks is a MPC. A member of the University of Delaware Library Assembly of Professional Staff, the MPC is elected for a twoyear term. MPC responsibilities include promotion of the mentoring program, organizing the mentor/mentee matches, inviting new staff to participate, mediation of problems, management of records, evaluation of the mentor/mentee pairings, and recommending changes when needed.

The University Libraries at The Pennsylvania State University comprise the main library and four branch libraries at the University Park campus as well as libraries at 20 campuses, a technology school, a medical school, and two law school locations. Providing mentoring opportunities in this complex environment requires a clear set of policies and procedures. The program is voluntary, but most new librarians participate as mentees, and many senior librarians volunteer as mentors. Some of the major tasks of the mentor are to acclimate the new librarian to the Libraries and to the Penn State corporate culture, to the promotion and tenure process, and to professional development opportunities. Because librarians at Penn State are hired on the faculty tenure track, it is important to get new librarians active in appropriate professional activities locally and nationally and to have them begin to consider the focus of their research agenda within a relatively short time after they arrive at the Libraries. The initial mentoring assignment is made by the deans and lasts for the first review period, approximately two years. At that time the mentee can request another mentor or choose to continue with the assigned mentor. Most often a change will be made for research or professional reasons so the mentee can select someone whose research agenda and professional organizational focus are similar. In addition to the official promotion and tenure mentorship program, there can be additional, specialized mentoring. For example, librarians can ask for mentoring in instruction, collection development, reference, technology, or other areas that they wish to improve, adding another mentor for guidance in these areas.

Mentors are expected to meet with their mentees on a regular basis. A monthly meeting for two hours is the normal recommendation although the mentoring pair can select the best meeting schedule for their needs. During these meetings it is expected that the mentor will act as a sounding board for difficulties, an encourager, answer questions and suggest committees, publishing opportunities, workshops, and other activities that will enhance the mentee's skills and develop the dossier. Mentors are also encouraged to meet with the mentee's supervisor to discuss progress, but confidentiality is always stressed. One of the most important ground rules is to "espouse a positive attitude and be supportive of the new faculty member and of Penn State and the Libraries" (The Pennsylvania State University, 2007). Although the promotion and tenure process is rigorous, it is one that is very attainable and an honestly supportive attitude is important.

The University Libraries has developed a Website with links to "Ground Rules for Mentors," "Suggestions for a Successful Mentoring Program," a description of the program, and a short bibliography. In addition to the Website, the libraries host a promotion and tenure workshop annually and mentoring workshops periodically. These support the activities of the mentee and the mentor and help keep the dispersed library faculty up-to-date on the promotion and tenure process, provides tips for success, and offers a venue to ask questions and share concerns.

Although the first page of the Library Advisory Website at the University of Washington is humorous with a photograph of an overwhelmed librarian trapped by stacks of books, the resources that support the program are clear and serious. The Website includes information for the advisors and the advisees, forms, calendars, and the Libraries' Librarian Personnel Code that outlines the ranks, promotion process, and more. "The Library Advisory Program is designed to assist in the advancement of the University Libraries' mission to recruit and develop a quality staff and to contribute to the library profession" (University of Washington, 2007a). The advice to the advisors and advisees is similar to that of the other universities (consult with supervisors, serve as a resource, communicate projects and interests, etc.); however, one of the strengths of the site is the short list of very specific bibliographic resources. For example, the bibliography on the advisee site is for mentees, not about being a mentor or mentoring in general. In addition, there is a very useful, albeit short FAQ.

Washington also appoints two advisors for each new librarian. Normally, one is from the new librarian's area of expertise and the other from outside that area. This arrangement continues for one year, at which time the mentoring team can continue or make changes in membership. The advising continues until the new librarian has earned continuing or permanent appointment. An evaluation process is required by the Personal Code and is conducted every three years.

The University of Utah has a slightly different take on the purpose of their mentoring program. That purpose according to their Website, is to "help librarians achieve their potential, concurrently making them more marketable. Make the Retention, Promotion and Continuing Appointment (RPCA) process more meaningful. Encourage librarians to conduct research, initiate projects, and publish accounts of their work. Integrate the librarian into the library and the university" (University of Utah, 2007). Although three and one half of these aspects are routine, the marketability aspect is different. They support the goals with a very well thought out, clearly defined mentoring program.

Although it functions like most other mentoring programs, the University of Utah excels in their documentation that is very clearly written and provides practical guidance to the mentors in understanding their role in the process. The Website states "mentoring should provide a safe, protected environment in which one can learn." Several other Web pages provide valuable information that is not routinely seen in other programs. The first link is to a "New Ideas Forum" that allows the sharing of library technologies, services and methods, as well as a venue to post problems to solicit ideas, solutions, and input. Forums are held once a month. The second interesting Website is a "New Librarian FAQ," an excellent review of the things everyone assumes are known but are not. New people often are hesitant to ask, therefore making it difficult to find the answers. Although this is not unique to the University of Utah, the placement of the FAQ with the mentoring information and the detail of the site stand out. Overall, the information on the Website is an excellent resource for the mentoring program.

Yale University Library's mentoring program began after focus groups revealed that there was "a good deal of anxiety about the promotion process and general professional development issues" (Yale University Library, 2007) that could be alleviated by a mentoring program and the advice and perspectives that mentors could share with new librarians. Although the rest of their documentation is similar to many other programs, they have one intriguing difference—in addition to a mentoring program for new librarians, they have "Mentoring for Future Librarians" that is open to Yale Library staff or students who are or will be studying for their library degrees. This extra aspect of the program is worth consideration as there are many who work in a library who could benefit from a mentoring relationship, as well as the mentors learning all that is new and innovative from those they mentor. In addition, there is the satisfaction in having a role in encouraging and guiding the next generation of professionals.

Another model is the one used at California State University Long Beach (CSULB) that has a Resource Team that meets once a month for a librarian's first six months (H. Ramachadran, personal communication, October 19, 2007). Their role is to provide guidance and advice during the transition to a new job. At one time CSULB used one-to-one mentoring but found it had mixed results so they moved to the team approach with better results.

The Louisiana State University (LSU) Library began a pilot mentoring program in 1998. "The primary goal of the LSU Libraries program was to assist tenure-track librarians in participating successfully in professional service, and in identifying research arenas in the field of librarianship that are appropriate for the individual"(Kuyper-Rushing, 2001, p. 442). A three-member mentoring committee paired mentors and mentees. As in most programs, the mentor could not be a supervisor of the mentee. The Libraries sponsored a daylong workshop held by a consultant from outside the LSU Library. After a year, evaluation of the program included separate meetings with mentors and mentees to discuss progress and perceptions. One important result of these discussions was the assignment of a peer mentor for the first several months of a new librarian's appointment. This served to help acquaint the new librarians to the LSU Libraries as well as to give them time and opportunity to meet potential mentors and improve the success rate in forming mentor/mentee pairs. Two other features that are not routine in other programs is the use of written reports from the mentee to the coordinator of the mentoring committee and periodic meetings of members of the mentoring partnerships that may be called by the coordinator if deemed necessary.

Colorado State University (CSU) formerly had a program that used peer mentoring, as well as the formal mentoring process (Level & Mach, 2005). The formal mentoring program operates similar to that of other programs, although the supervisor can be the mentor. However, they also had developed a peer mentoring program that, though it has not had formal evaluation, received very good feedback. The basic premise of peer mentoring is the pairing or grouping of people at relatively the same level to share experiences, ideas, and information, rather than to pair an experienced, promoted, or tenured person with relative newcomers to help them through the process. The group or pair helps each other through the process. Level and Mach concluded that both models have benefits and can coexist. Recent informationindicates that the peer mentoring program is not currently in use at CSU (A. Level, personal communication, October 27, 2007).

MENTORING OUTSIDE THE UNIVERSITY

Although not a university, the National Academies is one of the premier educational institutions in the United States with a well-designed mentoring program. The National Academy of Science, the National Academy of Engineering, the National Research Council, and the National Institute of Medicine constitute the National Academies. Their Website states the Academies are the "advisors to the nation on science, engineering, and medicine"(National Academies, 2007a) fulfilling these roles by bringing together appropriate experts to "serve *pro bono* to address critical national issues and give advice to the federal government and the public."(National Academies, 2007b) Its 1,100 employees provide the organization, resources, and technical support for the numerous experts who work on the panels and studies overseen by the Academies. The reports from the Academies provide information to the government and the public.

The National Academies has a mentoring program that normally begins within the first two weeks of an employee's hiring. Mentoring is available to all staff members who are new to the Academies. According to their documentation "except in unusual circumstances, participation in the program is required" (J. Richardson, personal communication, October 5, 2007). The coordinator of the program provides a list of possible mentors to the supervisor or director of the new employee who then selects a suitable person. The names of the mentor and new employee are sent to the Staff Development Program (SDP), which monitors the mentoring process. The formal mentoring program lasts one year, but a longer, informal relationship is encouraged.

Mentors share the same work unit with their mentee but may not work on the same projects, be the mentee's supervisor, or part of the same subunit. Although not supervisors, the mentors can assist as teachers of resources, processes, and procedures at the Academies and as guides to the corporate culture. A *mentor* is described as one who is a respected role model, skilled in the type of work he or she is mentoring, committed to working with new employees, has good communication and interpersonal skills, and has a clear understanding of the mission and operation of the Academies.

The goal of the program is to "foster learning, increase communications, provide guidance and timely advice, and broaden leadership skills for mentors and mentorees." It has the "ultimate goal (of) developing and retaining staff and increasing both the ability of staff members to do their work and their job satisfaction."

There are clearly articulated responsibilities for the mentor. These include a minimum number of meetings per month at which time they should discuss the mentee's work and provide suggestions and resources for continued growth and improvement. "Mentors should use the relationship with their mentorees to encourage learning and personal growth and build the competence and self-confidence of their mentorees.

They should encourage professional behavior, teach by example, and share experiences and insights that will help their mentorees succeed" (J. Richardson, personal communication, October 5, 2007). The mentee has the obligation to be an active participant in the process: asking questions, sharing information to solicit appropriate feedback and suggestions, and following the advice of their mentor.

The mentor/mentee relationship is confidential and can only be shared with others with the agreement of both parties. Assessment is done every three months using guidelines from the SDP. At the close of the formal mentoring year both parties review their experiences in the mentoring program for SDP. One of the interesting features of the program is the accounting of time spent in the program. Due to the administrative structure at the Academies, time spent in the mentoring process must be charged to cost centers. Funding for 12 hours per year actually is provided by SDP for the process. This specific level of accounting and the actual computation of a cost to the mentoring process may be instrumental in the success of the program. Time, money, and effort are documented, and valid assessment is required per the National Academies' mentoring guidelines.

MENTORING OUTSIDE THE ACADEMY

The nonacademic world has a number of programs that could provide useful framework or ideas for implementation in the academic world. Megginson, Clutterbuck, Garvey, Stokes and Garret-Harris' second edition of their *Mentoring in Action* (2006) provided numerous, short case studies of mentoring programs in situations as varied as domestic abuse centers, facilities for juvenile offenders, engineering firms, and a number of businesses. The book is international in scope. Several scenarios have special pertinence in the library. In one case study, participants Allen and Hinchcliffe recount a mentoring relationship that spans more than two decades in the corporate world. It began as a traditional mentoring situation and morphed into a peer mentoring situation as Allen moved through the ranks. Communication is stressed in this very personal account of the longitudinal development of the mentoring process. Discussion of projects and corporate culture is supplemented by discussion of a variety of topics to promote success. This relationship evolved into a mutually beneficial one that adjusted as there were changes in the positions and responsibilities of the two participants. They noted that they see mentoring as an integral part of the job and not an add-on task and that, for them, friendship is another important part of mentoring.

Another useful example from *Mentoring in Action* is the chapter on e-mentoring and the relationship that developed between a student, Kate Kennett, and one of the leading experts in mentoring, David Clutterbuck. Kennett wrote, "After two years, I am left with an invaluable trail of ideas, advice and questions that are transferable to enable effective thinking in many different situations" (p. 216). Noting that there is less scope for development of thoughts and definition of an issue or problem with e-mentoring, she stressed the need to communicate clearly. Negative aspects of electronic communication are that the important nonverbal aspect of face-to-face communication is missing, there is the possibility of some loss of information or meaning in the written messages, and finally, the readers cannot see each other in action at work. However, offsetting these negatives is the benefit of having the advice in writing. Kennett concluded, "On balance, the experience of e-mentoring is something I would probably recommend as a valuable adjunct to face-to-face mentoring, rather than a replacement for it. I would qualify this by saying both that this is a personal judgment and that, where choice is limited, e-mentoring could definitely 'stand alone' as a form of mentoring" (p. 217). This case study is very intriguing with real potential, especially for people with very specialized positions in the library. E-mentoring with a specialist at a distant institution could be combined with traditional mentoring from a librarian in the local library to address the corporate culture aspect of the job. In this arrangement local information and subject or task specification could be addressed. In the concluding chapter of the book, the authors noted, "E-mentoring now stands in its own right as a different kind of development process from face-to-face mentoring. We envisage that this trend will continue"(p. 255). Benefits include not being dependent on time or location, providing time between question and response for reflection, and providing a permanent record. Overall, the case studies in *Mentoring in Action* provide background for the development or the improvement of mentoring programs in libraries.

Giving us another example of a mentoring program (this time in banking), Garvey and Galloway's article (2002) notes several interesting features that could be incorporated into a library program. Halifax plc merged with the Bank of Scotland, becoming one of the largest banks in Britain. A program for new managers was developed to "help them make the transition from trainee to manager." One of the features of the program that is not noted in other mentoring programs is a questionnaire for mentors and mentees with the purpose to "help the mentors orientate their thoughts toward the skills, attitudes, knowledge and behaviours they are offering to the relationship. The second is to help with the matching purpose" (p. 272). The bank also developed separate workshops for mentors and mentees. Both of these ideas could be incorporated in a library mentoring program. Granted this program began when there were a significant number of new hires so there is not the staggered influx of new employees over the year, a common occurrence in libraries. Still, accommodations could be made for the workshops (minisessions with a mentoring coordinator is one possibility) at different times during the year. The idea of a questionnaire to match candidates could be a relatively easy task with the distinct possibility of improving the mentee/mentor pairings. Although the context is very different, the practicality and usefulness of these program features makes translation to a library setting worthwhile.

Blue Cross and Blue Shield Association (BCBSA) provides another example of mentoring in the corporate world. An article in *PR Newswire* (2007) notes that BCBSA was recognized by *BusinessWeek* and American Association for Retired Persons (AARP) for their mentoring program. Although much is similar to other successful programs (training for mentors and mentees, a handbook, periodic meetings, and the use of a written application that allows matching of mentoring pairs with similar interests and backgrounds), several features of their program are especially notable and may account, at least partially, for their award. These include a signed formal contract by the mentoring team with an agreement to work together for at least one year, quarterly evaluations, a celebration at the conclusion of the mentoring year, continual evaluation and adjustments in the program, and the extension of the mentoring program to those transitioning to new jobs within the company. Another change under consideration is the inclusion of retirees as mentors (P. Cholette, personal communication, October 19, 2007). This last proposal has very intriguing implications for libraries.

ASPECTS OF SUCCESSFUL MENTORING PROGRAMS

There are many similarities in mentoring programs. With rare exceptions, mentors are not direct supervisors of the mentee, volunteer for the task, and have significant experience in the organization, and the mentoring program provides some type of guidance to the participants.

However, differences abound. Length of the programs varies from little more than an orientation through the complete promotion and tenure process, and possibly beyond. Although most have one mentor per mentee, some have several mentors and may even include peer mentoring. Evaluation can range from very casual to formal written reports. Even the terminology varies from *mentee* to *mentoree* to *protégée*.

It is clear that there is no one magic mentoring program that is appropriate for all libraries. Corporate cultures vary. Requirements for retention or promotion and tenure vary and, in some cases, are not controlled by the library but by the organization as a whole. Interpretations and emphasis on evaluation criteria can vary, not only by organization, but also within an organization over time. These variations are clear in the different manners the reviewed organizations have used to address their mentoring programs. Another factor that must be considered is that individuals are different and a program that is perfect for one librarian may need to be adjusted to address the characteristics and needs of another librarian.

Beyond the need to provide guidance for the specific requirements for success there is another reason to promote mentoring in a library that may be overlooked. In most academic fields, the new faculty member has been through the intense mentoring or advising that is inherent in the doctoral process. They have witnessed, if not participated in, the promotion and tenure process, they have had faculty work with them closely on their research, possibly their teaching, and can usually call upon their advisors when they have questions about their career. Few librarians have had that level of advising before they enter the profession, so mentoring is an important aspect of career development.

In an article on the evaluation of two mentoring programs for new librarians, Hallam and Newton-Smith (2006) stated, "Mentoring relationships represent a form of continuing professional development that has the advantage of being supportive of an individual's learning needs and that "socializes" a person into a profession . . . A mentoring program encapsulates the significance of continuing professional development for both mentors and mentees alike" (p. 155). They noted it is a supportive, learning, sharing relationship. It is also important to note that participants, the mentor as well as the mentee, benefit from a good mentoring program and relationship. Although programs must be tailored to local demands and corporate culture, a well-planned, competently administered, and evaluated mentoring program is essential to recruit and retain a quality library staff. Excellent programs exist to provide guidance in this process.

REFERENCES

Blue Cross and Blue Shield Association Nationally recognized by BusinessWeek and AARP for creating a unique workplace environment for new and mature employees (2007, September 25). *PR Newswire*. Retrieved October 26, 2007, from ProQuest Database.

Garvey, B., & Galloway, K. (2002). Mentoring at the Halifax plc (HBOS)—a small beginning in a large organisation. *Career Development International, 7*(5), 271–278.

Hallam, G., & Newton-Smith, C. (2006). Mentoring for new library and information professions. *Library Management, 27*(3), 154–167.

Kayper-Rushing, Lois. (2001). A Formal mentoring program in a university library: components of a successful experiment. *The Journal of Academic Librarianship 27*(6), 440–446.

Level, A.V., & Mach, M. (2005). Peer mentoring: One institution's approach to mentoring academic librarians. *Library Management, 26*(6/7), 301–310.

Megginson, D., Clutterbuck, D., Garvey, B., Stokes, P., & Garrett-Harris, R. (2006). *Mentoring in action* (2nd ed.). London: Kogan Paul.

Metz, R. (2001). *Coaching in the library*. Chicago: American Library Association.

National Academies. (2007a). Retrieved October 26, 2007, from http://www.nas.edu

National Academies. (2007b). Retrieved October 26, 2007, from http://www.nas.edu/about

The Pennsylvania State University, University Libraries. (2007, October 8). *University Libraries faculty mentoring program: Ground rules*. Retrieved October 26, 2007, from http://www.libraries.psu.edu/admin/mentoring/

University of Utah, J. Willard Marriott Library. (2007, March 22). *Program mission*. Retrieved October 26, 2007, from http://www.lib.utah.edu/mentor/mission.html

University of Washington. (n.d.-a). *Library Advisory Program*. Retrieved October 26, 2007, from http://staffweb.lib.washington.edu/Lap/lap.html

University of Washington. (n.d.-b). *Librarian Advisory Program: If only Harry had an advisor*. Retrieved October 26, 2007, from http://staffweb.lib.washington.edu/Lap/default.html

Wittkopf, B. (1999). *Mentoring programs in ARL libraries: Spec Kit 239*. Washington, DC: Association of Research Libraries.

Yale University Library. (2007, February 26). *SCOPA mentoring program for Yale University*. Retrieved October 26, 2007, from http://www.library.yale.edu/scopa/mentoring/background.html

The Mentoring Role of Professional Associations

Diane Zabel

INTRODUCTION

Mentoring is an important socializing process for the library profession. The huge professional changing of the guard (as a result of retirements) gives mentoring even more urgency. Lynch, Tordella, and Godfrey (2005) wrote on the "surge in retirements in the near future," noting that "the decade beginning in 2010 will see 45% of today's librarians reach 65" (p. 28). These researchers predicted that retirements will peak between 2015 and 2019. Given these projections, librarianship will experience a significant loss of seasoned professionals in the coming decade. Mentoring can help develop new leaders for the profession. Although mentoring may involve ad hoc arrangements between individuals, professional associations play an important role in facilitating mentoring.

Professional associations can help new members of the profession connect with more experienced professionals. These mentors can offer practical on-the-job advice, career guidance, and the opportunity to network. At the same time, mentors can find it rewarding and rejuvenating to work with mentees who bring a fresh perspective to professional issues.

Professional associations are keenly interested in mentoring for a variety of reasons. First, mentoring can be used to "sell" membership in an association. The ability to find a mentor in an association can be marketed as a benefit. Additionally, mentoring is a critical component of succession planning for any association. It is the role of current leaders in an association to cultivate future leaders, and mentoring can be used as a strategy for growing leaders.

I served as the 2005–2006 President of the Reference and User Services Association (RUSA), a division of the American Library Association (ALA). During my tenure I was acutely aware of my mentoring responsibilities (even though RUSA had no formal mentoring program in place) and the need to get other RUSA leaders and members actively involved in mentoring less experienced members. Although my RUSA colleagues and I were mentoring individuals to assume greater responsibilities within the Association, we were also by extension developing leaders for the profession. While RUSA President I attended an excellent training session on association leadership sponsored by the American Society of Association Executives and The Center for Association Leadership. One of the themes of this symposium was that all professional associations need to rethink how they reach prospective members, and all need to pay attention to succession planning. I was one of three librarians attending this workshop with more than 125 participants, and it was eye opening to learn that RUSA's (and the ALA's) concerns were very similar to those of associations for physicians, lawyers, manufacturers, and other professional groups.

I predict that the role of RUSA and other ALA divisions will become even more important in the socialization of the new type of individuals entering our profession. James G. Neal (2006), Vice President for Information Services and University Librarian at Columbia University, wrote about the new "feral professionals" in the academic library, professionals hired without the traditional master's degree in library and information science (p. 42). Professional library associations will play a role in conveying our profession's core values to this new generation of professionals holding advanced degrees in other disciplines, or who are hired because of their expertise in areas such as technology and facilities management. Wilder (2007) calculated that by using Neal's examples of feral job categories, "people in nontraditional positions accounted for 23 percent of the professionals at research libraries in 2005, compared to just 7 percent in 1985" (p. C1).

LITERATURE REVIEW

Much of the literature on the topic of mentoring for library professionals consists of case studies describing mentoring programs in academic libraries or articles advocating mentoring as a professional development tool. Osif's (2008) review of mentoring programs (in academic and nonacademic settings) identifies some model programs and best practices. This article is an extension of Osif's (2006, 2007) reviews of the mentoring literature that are invaluable in updating the extensive bibliography contained in Wittkopf's (1999) survey of mentoring programs in large academic libraries.

In contrast, the literature on the mentoring role of library associations is sparse. Much of the literature consists of brief articles (in some cases, little more than announcements) describing mentoring initiatives within ALA divisions and round tables. An exception is Fennewald and Stachacz's (2005) detailed report on one division chapter's mentoring program linking academic library practitioners with library school students. Other articles have taken the form of personal reminiscences. Hardesty (1997) reflected on his role in the College Library Directors Mentor Program, a project developed by the College Libraries Section of the Association of College and Research Libraries (ACRL). Golian-Liu (2003) shared her perspectives on how the mentoring she received through the ACRL/Harvard Leadership Institute enriched her career.

Recent articles ("New Emerging Leaders Sought," 2007; Paul, 2007) have focused on the ALA Emerging Leaders program, an initiative developed by 2006–2007 ALA President Leslie Burger. The goal of this program is to provide new entrants to the profession opportunities for involvement in ALA. Participants in 2007 worked in virtual project groups, directed by mentors. Emerging Leaders also met face-to-face at the ALA Midwinter Meeting and Annual Conference. Given the success of the pilot, this program has been renewed for 2008. Visit http://wikis.ala.org/emergingleaders/index.php/Main_Page for a description of 2007 and 2008 projects.

Other library-related professional associations have reported on mentoring activities. McGreevy (2001) and Leavitt (2007) profiled successful mentor and mentee pairings facilitated by the Business & Finance (B & F) Division of the Special Libraries Association (SLA). This division initiated a mentoring program in 1999 (Chindlund & Kirkwood, 1999; Kochoff, 1999). Jones-Quartey (2000) reflected on the mentoring she received as a participant in the SLA Diversity Leadership Program. Houdek (1999) compiled the recollections of almost 30 law librarians regarding their mentors, including descriptions of mentoring relationships fostered by the American Association of Law Librarians (AALL). Levor and Cranford (2000) recounted their experiences as participants in the AALL Mentor Project. Sarah G. Holterhoff, 2006–2007 AALL President, (2007) wrote on the relationship between mentoring and leadership and chronicles the history of the AALL Mentor Project, an initiative developed more than two decades ago. Law librarian Joan S. Howland (2002) explored more fully the connection between leadership and mentorship.

Research literature on the mentoring role of professional associations is limited. Although a few articles have examined the mentoring practices of the Australian Library and Information Association, the focus of this article is U.S.-based library associations. Lenzini's (2002) survey of five professional associations found that four out of the five (ALA, SLA, AALL, and the Medical Library Association [MLA]) are concerned about the aging of the library profession. Although no details are provided, she commented that mentoring is a common strategy for member recruitment. Mason and Wetherbee (2004) compared and contrasted 31 library leadership programs (including workshops and residential programs), noting that many of the programs use mentors. Golden (2005) discussed the multifaceted approach (the Sunshine State Library Leadership Institute, a pilot mentoring program, and symposiums for middle-level managers) used by the Florida State Library and Archives to recruit, retain, and advance library professionals. Kwasik and Fulda's (2006) survey involving members of a chapter of the MLA found that though members were aware of mentoring resources and services, participation rates need to be increased. Davidson and Middleton's (2006) survey involving science and technology librarians also found less-than-desirable participation rates in mentoring programs sponsored by professional associations. However, these librarians value their association memberships, particularly those in subject-oriented organizations. The authors concluded that "professional associations play a valuable role in mentoring members" (p. 218). However, they made an interesting observation: "Although professional associations tout professional development and mentoring as critical benefits for their members, very little research assesses the actual value members find in these programs" (p. 206). Finally, mentoring is a topic of interest to associations serving a wide variety of professions. Although the literature is scant, I found references to mentoring activities in associations serving engineers, scientists, nurses, health care executives, female executives in the foodservice industry, and African American corporate executives. However, these articles are descriptive and anecdotal rather than research based.

METHOD

This article reports on interviews with 21 leaders in 15 professional organizations related to librarianship. Participants included leaders in 10 ALA divisions, two ALA round tables, three national library-related associations, and two state library associations. Telephone interviews, typically 45 to 60 minutes in length, were conducted March through November 2007. The objective was to obtain detailed information about the organization's existing or planned mentoring programs. In addition, open-ended questions gave participants an opportunity to talk about their experiences as a mentor and mentee, and to share their insights on the attributes of a good mentor.

FINDINGS

Mentoring Activities in ALA

Although the American Association of School Librarians (AASL) has no formal mentoring program, it recently established the New Member Mentoring Committee (C. Phillip, interview, April 18, 2007). I followed up with an e-mail exchange with the chair of this committee. She provided the following information about AASL's mentoring plans:

> We decided to concentrate our efforts on an event. We are planning at the upcoming AASL conference to pair "newbies" with mentors. Currently our plan involves using persons in leadership positions as mentors. We are looking at this as a "one shot" opportunity, but the paired members could continue the relationship if they wished. We felt that New Members Round Table (NMRT) did an excellent job of helping new members, and we should promote their activities more. We felt the biggest area of AASL weakness was making new members

feel welcome and seeing ways they could become more active. [There are] things that AASL already does at each conference. We have a program called Calibrate Conference. This program, aimed at new conference goers, is well attended by newbies and leadership. We also put a lot of new people on committees. Working on committees is one of the best ways to become involved and get to know members. (F. Roscello, personal communication, May 7, 2007)

The ACRL has a long history of mentoring at division and section levels (P. Snelson, interview, May 16, 2007). The division sponsors the Dr. E. J. Josey Spectrum Scholar Mentor Program, a program designed to encourage culturally diverse library school students and recent graduates to pursue careers in academic librarianship. Four ACRL sections (Education & Behavioral Sciences Section [EBSS], Literatures in English Section [LES], Rare Books and Manuscripts Section [RBM], and Science & Technology Section [STS]) have fully developed mentoring programs. Details about these programs and online application forms can be found on each section's Website, easily accessible from ACRL's home-page: http://www.ala.org/ala/acrl/aboutacrl/acrlsections/sections.cfm.

Mentoring efforts within the Association for Library Collections & Technical Services (ALCTS) have been concentrated in the Cataloging & Classification Section's CETRC Mentoring Program, a formal mentoring program established in 1996 to mentor new catalogers and students interested in the field of cataloging (B. Johnson, interview, March 2, 2007; D. Miller, interview, May 9, 2007; P. Williams, interview, May 24, 2007). Applications are submitted online. CETRC committee members are responsible for pairing mentors and mentees. This committee has given careful thought to the mentoring process. A set of guidelines outlines expectations for participants (mentors, mentees, and liaisons whose role is to facilitate the mentoring relationship). A formal evaluation is conducted at the end of the year. Although the program is structured, discussions between mentor and mentee are often informal. For details about this program visit the section's Website, accessible from the ALCTS homepage (http://www.ala.org/ala/alcts/alcts.cfm).

ALCTS strives to develop members in other ways (B. Johnson, interview, March 2, 2007). Intern positions on committees provide opportunities for new members. ALCTS also sponsors a number of annual events: ALCTS 1001, a forum designed to help librarians new to the division; a new leaders orientation (though targeted to ALCTS chairs anyone may attend); an orientation for ALCTS Board members; and a volunteer forum.

The Association for Library Service to Children (ALSC) does not have a mentoring program but "talks about it all the time" and "it's something we want to get started with" (K. Horning, interview, April 16, 2007). ALSC views mentoring as a critical activity, recognizing that it could be used to attract new members and to reenergize experienced members.

The Association of Specialized and Cooperative Library Agencies (ASCLA) also has no formal mentoring program (M. Irwin, interview, April 16, 2007). However, Marilyn Irwin, 2006–2007 ASCLA President, hopes that given its relatively small size, it is easy to develop mentoring relationships in ASCLA. She explained the importance of this informal mentoring: "Because members often have isolated professional roles, they often have no one to go to. ASCLA serves as a mentoring center."

The Library Administration and Management Association's (LAMA) Leaders of the Pack was a funded three year project (2003–2004 to 2006–2007) that provided new library professionals interested in administration and management with a senior mentor (A. Lapsley, interview, May 1, 2007). Participants in this program also received travel support, free LAMA membership, free registration to ALA conferences, and were guaranteed appointment to a LAMA committee. Because funding has ended for this program, LAMA has formed a mentoring committee to study other options. This committee is being chaired by Janine Golden, a nationally recognized expert on mentoring. According to Andrea Lapsley, 2006–2007 LAMA President, "LAMA recognizes how important mentoring is" and "LAMA's membership have indicated that they want both formal and informal mentoring programs."

The Library and Information Technology Association (LITA) is investigating how to augment the excellent mentoring already available through ALA's New Members Round Table (B. Postlethwaite, interview, May 3, 2007). Bonnie Postlethwaite, 2006–2007 LITA President, explained that LITA is somewhat different from the other ALA divisions as it has a fair number of members who are not librarians. Consequently, any mentoring that LITA develops must be tailored to meet their needs.

Although the Public Library Association (PLA) does not currently have a formal mentoring program (outside of the mentoring provided at its National Conference for new members/attendees), informal mentoring occurs in PLA committees (S. Hildreth, interview, June 4, 2007). Susan Hildreth, 2006–2007 PLA President, informed me that PLA is implementing structural changes to create an association where members are organized by communities of practice. This restructuring should enhance opportunities for virtual participation and mentoring.

The RUSA has no division-wide mentoring program. Although some sections have experimented with mentoring over the years, none of these initiatives has been sustained. Instead, RUSA "keeps trying to do mentoring in small ways" through orientations such as RUSA 1001 and a volunteer forum (D. Shonrock, interview, May 1, 2007). However, this is about to change because one of the 2008 Emerging Leaders projects is the development of a mentoring plan for RUSA.

The Young Adult Library Services Association (YALSA) established a mentoring program in 2004 and is in the process of evaluating it (J. Nelson, interview, April 26, 2007). The goal of this program is to retain members and develop future YALSA leaders. According to Judy Nelson, 2006–2007 YALSA President, "YALSA's challenge is that we have a large number of student members—perhaps the highest percentage of any ALA division." She went on to say that, "More individuals are looking for mentoring than we have individuals who can provide mentoring." YALSA is currently surveying student members to identify what these members need.

Although the Library Instruction Round Table (LIRT) has no formal mentoring program, it has created a task force on mentoring (V. Bowman, interview, April 19, 2007). According to Vibiana Bowman, 2006–2007 LIRT President, "LIRT realizes that mentoring is an important way to bring people into the organization." She acknowledged that "Although we have a big membership, we keep drawing upon the same people." Recognizing this issue, LIRT is "trying to grow our leadership." Although LIRT has no formal program, informal mentoring occurs within the organization. LIRT also uses its newsletter as a recruiting tool. Bowman's philosophy is that organizations need to use multiple approaches when mentoring members. She emphasized that it is not just library school students who could use mentoring, noting that librarianship attracts many career changers. Additionally, she views LIRT as playing an important role in socializing those librarians who have no background in instruction, commenting that "lots of librarians are not knowledgeable about developing a lesson plan or writing curriculum."

ALA's New Members Round Table (NMRT) has made mentoring a priority. NMRT has two formal programs: conference mentoring (which matches up experienced conference attendees with new members in order to make the ALA Annual Conference less intimidating) and career mentoring (a year-long program that pairs up a new librarian with an experienced librarian (C. Renfro, interview, April 23, 2007). There is an online application for both (http://www.ala.org/ala/nmrt/comm/mentoringcommittee. htm). Crystal Renfro, 2006–2007 Mentoring Co-Chair, calculated that 91 mentor/mentee pairs have participated in the conference mentoring (during the 2004, 2005, and 2006 Annual Conferences) and 80 pairs have participated in career mentoring since the pilot was launched in 2005. Renfro provided the following details about the career mentoring program: "The program tries to target librarians in their first jobs. In order to facilitate discussion between mentor and mentees, monthly discussion topics are developed. These have ranged from networking to planning for promotion and tenure. While these are just ideas to get started, the emphasis is on practical topics."

Mentors and mentees are matched based on interests, type of library, type of position, and geographic location. The ideal arrangement is one where mentor and mentee meet at conferences. Mentors are recruited by announcements on discussion lists. Individuals who have served previously as mentors are invited to participate again. According to Renfro, mentors are encouraged to be positive, and mentors and mentees are encouraged to share as much as they feel comfortable with. Although there are generally no problems, individuals will be reassigned if there are conflicts. Feedback is collected at the end of the program. Mentors and mentees are surveyed, and the instrument includes opportunities for comments.

Although Renfro was not sure if NMRT's mentoring programs have been promoted as a member benefit, she feels that the programs have been "fairly well received" and that mentoring "is critical in order to build future leaders within the library profession." She summed up the value of NMRT's career mentoring program in the following way: "It allows new librarians to freely ask questions that they worry might be regarded as stupid in other venues. It also allows you to be more open than you might be with colleagues at work. It also gives you a broader perspective."

Mentoring Activities in Other Library-Related Associations

The AALL has a well-established Mentor Project that pairs up new law librarians with experienced law librarians using information obtained from the online application form (S. Holterhoff, interview, May 29, 2007). Feedback is collected annually by surveying participants. Many mentoring relationships continue beyond a year. Although AALL provides detailed tips for mentoring (available at http://www.aallnet.org/), the program allows for considerable flexibility. Although Sally Holterhoff, 2006–2007 AALL President, was not sure how many people have participated in the Mentor Project, interest has been strong. Mentors provide practical advice and career guidance. Holterhoff also hopes that they "model behavior" for beginning law librarians. In addition to this program, AALL's Quick-Mentor Service provides short-term professional guidance to members. AALL also hosts The Conference of Newer Law Librarians (CONELL), an event held in conjunction with the AALL Annual Meeting. This purpose of CONELL is to welcome new members and to acquaint them to the association.

The MLA has a mentoring database that lists members by subject and geographic location (J. Shipman, interview, May 31, 2007). This mentoring database allows members to network, learn about a specific type of work, and to share expertise. No one is responsible for pairing members up; instead, the database facilitates networking. MLA has several other programs for new members: a "colleague connection" that pairs up new conference goers with experienced people, a new members breakfast, and a special interest group for new members. In addition, MLA has done some programming for new members. Finally, MLA has a formal mentoring program in place for those seeking certification in the Academy of Health Information Professionals program.

The SLA offers formal and informal mentoring (R. Vargha, interview, May 23, 2007). Much of the mentoring occurs within SLA's divisions. Of particular interest to business librarians is the mentoring offered by SLA's B & F Division. In a follow-up interview with the chair of the B & F Division's newly reformed Mentoring Committee, I found that there are plans to market mentoring as a benefit, especially because "new members want to see value" (L. Leavitt, interview, November 26, 2007).

Two State Models

In conversation with association leaders, the programs of two state library associations were mentioned more than once as mentoring models: the Connecticut Library Association (CLA) and the New Jersey Library Association (NJLA). The CLA's mentoring program has been evolving for the past seven years. Kathleen Lescoe, Mentoring Committee Chair, recalled that "Initially, it was an opportunity for seasoned librarians to explore other options—to breathe new life into a career. However, it has evolved into seasoned librarians helping new professionals" (interview, November 14, 2007). This formal program pairs people up using a mentor/protégé profile.

The process for the New Jersey Library Association is also a formal one (T. Dawes, interview, May 16, 2007). Two cochairs match up pairs using a detailed application form (available at http://www.njla.org/) that includes questions about academic background, years in the profession, career goals, and expectations of the program. The Association also has well-developed and detailed mentoring guidelines. Mentoring relationships are viewed annually. Although the process is formal, the mentoring that occurs is more likely to be informal.

MENTOR ATTRIBUTES

Several leaders commented on the valuable "reverse mentoring" or "mutual mentoring" that has occurred in their own mentoring relationships. Others spoke eloquently about how they (and other association leaders) provided leadership by simply being a mentor. Participants also provided insights about who makes a good mentor. I asked the following question: "In your opinion, what characteristics make a good mentor? The traits most frequently listed were the following: a good listener, a good communicator, willing to give their time when needed, experienced in the field, knowledgeable about the internal politics of the organization, open minded, frank, patient, caring, encouraging, positive, willing to share opportunities, sympathetic yet able to direct, willing to share their successes and failures, and able to see things through the eyes of a beginning professional.

When asked about barriers to being a mentor, association leaders were overwhelmingly positive. Most responded that time is the only barrier. Although many expressed the opinion that face-to-face mentoring is preferable, most acknowledged that mentoring at a distance can work thanks to technology and some extra effort by mentor and mentee (with perhaps some prodding by a liaison responsible for checking on progress).

CONCLUSION

Although mentoring may involve ad hoc arrangements between individuals, interviews with leaders in library organizations confirm that professional associations play an important role in facilitating mentoring. Those mentoring programs that have been sustained over time are more likely to have a formal structure in place. However, the mentoring that occurs is often informal. Professional associations are interested in mentoring for several reasons. Mentoring can be used to promote membership in an organization. However, most of the associations I surveyed failed to adequately market mentoring as a benefit. Mentoring is a critical component of succession planning for any organization. Almost all of the association leaders that I interviewed were concerned about growing leaders. Several admitted that is was often easier to call upon the regular cadre of experienced members than develop a new generation of leaders. On the other hand, several association leaders made the development of new leaders a top priority and recognized that mentoring is a critical component of leadership development.

REFERENCES

Chindlund, J. F., & Kirkwood, H. P., Jr. (1999, Fall). Business & Finance Division mentoring initiative—lifelong learning. *Business & Finance Bulletin, 112*, 21–23.

Davidson, J. R., & Middleton, C. A. (2006). Networking, networking, networking: The role of professional association memberships in mentoring and retention of science librarians. *Science & Technology Libraries, 27*(1/2), 203–224.

Fennewald, J., & Stachacz, J. (2005, February). Recruiting students to careers in academic Libraries: One chapter's approach. *C & RL News, 66*(2), 120–122.

Golden, J. (2005). Leadership development and staff recruitment—Florida style. *Florida Libraries, 48*(2), 17–20.

Golian-Lui, L. M. (2003). Fostering librarian leadership through mentoring. *Adult Learning, 14*(1), 26–28.

Hardesty, L. (1997). College Library Directors Mentor Program: "Passing it on": A personal reflection. *Journal of Academic Librarianship, 23*, 281–290.

Holterhoff, S. (2007, June). What I know now—thoughts on mentoring and leadership. *AALL Spectrum*. Retrieved December 19, 2007, from http://www.aallnet.org/products/pub_sp0706/pub_sp0706_Pres.pdf

Houdek, F. G. (1999). "Meet my mentor": A collection of personal reminiscences. *Law Library Journal, 91*(1), 177–255.

Howland, J. S. (2002). The leader as mentor. In H. E. Cihak & J. S. Howland (Eds.), *Leadership roles for librarians* (pp. 155–168). Buffalo, NY: William S. Hein & Co.

Jones-Quartey, T. (2000). Mentoring—personal reflections of a special librarian. *Information Outlook, 4*(7), 26–30.

Kochoff, S. (1999, Spring). The Division's mentoring initiative: Sharing knowledge to advance your career. *Business & Finance Division Bulletin, 111*, 9–10.

Kwasik, H., & Fulda, P. O. (2006). Strengthening professionals: A chapter-level formative evaluation of the Medical Library Association mentoring initiative. *Journal of the Medical Library Association, 94*(1), 19–29.

Leavitt, L. (2007, Fall). Mentoring milestones. *The Bulletin: The Newsletter of the Business and Finance Division, 136*, 7–8.

Lenzini, R. T. (2002, July/August). The graying of the library profession: A survey of our professional associations and their responses. *Searcher, 10*(7), 88–97.

Levor, R., & Cranford, J. (2000, April). AALL Mentoring Program: How it really works. *AALL Spectrum*. Retrieved December 19, 2007, from http://www.aallnet.org/products/pub_sp0004/pub_sp0004_Mentoring.pdf.

Lynch, M. J., Tordella, S., & Godfrey, T. (2005, January). Retirement and recruitment: A deeper look. *American Libraries, 36*(1), 28.

Mason, F. M., & Wetherbee, L. V. (2004). Learning to lead: An analysis of current training programs for library leadership. *Library Trends, 53*(1), 187–217.

McGreevy, B. (2001, Spring). Mentoring magic: One spark can ignite an entire career. *Business & Finance Division Bulletin, 117*, 8–9.

Neal, J. G. (2006, February 15). Raised by wolves. *Library Journal, 131*(3), 42–44.

New emerging leaders sought. (2007, August). *American Libraries, 38*(7), 13.

Osif, B. A. (2006). Mentoring, Part 1. *Library Administration & Management, 20*(4), 209–213.

Osif, B. A. (2007). Mentoring, Part 2. *Library Administration & Management, 21*(1), 44–48.

Osif, B. A. (2008). Successful mentoring programs: Examples from within and without the academy. *Journal of Business & Finance Librarianship, 13*(3).

Paul, C. (2007, June/July). Emerging Leaders fire up the profession. *American Libraries, 38*(6), 120.

Wilder, S. (2007, February 23). The new library professional. *Chronicle of Higher Education, 53*, C1, C4.

Wittkopf, B. (1999). *Mentoring in ARL libraries: Spec Kit 239*. Washington, DC: Association of Research Libraries.

Keeping Up With Business Reference

Celia Ross

INTRODUCTION

Congratulations! You have managed to find some time in between meetings, a reference desk shift or two, phone calls, e-mails, projects, and more meetings to sit back, relax, and read this article and learn about some resources and strategies that will help you stay current in the business reference field. Ironically, after reading this article, you may have even more information sources to try to stay on top of. To that end, there will be a few time management tips included to help you manage information overload. A caveat, though, before you read any further. It is best to stop right now and acknowledge to yourself that you will never keep up on everything. Accepting this fact is the first step in keeping up. That said, this article focuses less on time management strategies and highlight instead the many useful resources available that, when integrated in whatever way works best in your repertoire of business reference tools, will help you stay informed and keep current.

CHALLENGES AND STRATEGIES

Time Management

Managing your day-to-day tasks, along with the inevitable projects that come up, can leave you with little time left over, if any at all, for "keeping up" on new business reference developments. After accepting that you'll never truly keep up on everything, the next step in "keeping up" (with anything) is to evaluate your time management skills and look for areas of improvement. The key to a successful evaluation is to give yourself an honest appraisal. Are you constantly multitasking and feel like you never can get anything substantial done towards any of your many projects? Learn to prioritize. Are you easily distracted? Learn to let the phone ring. Leave your e-mail unlogged-into for an hour or find other ways to work uninterrupted. Do you take on too much, knowing your project plate is already full? Learn to say no gracefully. True—this is all easier said than done—but even small steps may lead to improvements over time.

You will also want to review where your time is currently being spent. Are there things you could be turning over to a student worker? Or not doing at all? Or doing more efficiently? Taking the time to review your personal habits and your work priorities may help you in the long run to streamline your workflow overall. If personal reflection and self-improvement are not your forte, enlist the assistance of a trusted supervisor or colleague. They may be able to see gaps and overlaps in areas of priority for you that are not as obvious from your entrenched perspective. There is also a vast array of literature related to time management and organizing that may also be worth investigating. Browse the shelves at your local public library or bookstore and see which titles appeal to you.

Taking the time to learn new time-saving technologies and tricks can also be worthwhile in the long run for some people. Some of the resources pointed to in this article will provide update options that you can harness if you are up to speed on RSS feed readers, e-alerts, and related tools. Bloglines (http://www. bloglines.com) and Google Reader (http://www.google.com/reader) are two free, online feed aggregators. Set up an account and start tracking some of the sites referred to in this article which have RSS feeds.

Continually Hone Your Searching Skills

Great business librarians have great information searching skills. These skills are not innate, nor are they permanent. To stay sharp, skills need to be used regularly and updated over time. Keep up with your favorite databases by signing up for e-mail alerts or taking advantage of online training opportunities. Vendors often make trainers available to individuals or groups for tailored instruction. Haven't been in your reference stacks in ages? Make a trip and flip through some print sources to remind yourself of what can be found in there. Remember that searching skills go beyond the scope of traditional print and online business sources. The broad nature of business means that information can be found on it virtually anywhere, so keep up on Internet search strategies and general newspaper and other databases as well. The following Websites and publications may also provide some useful searching tips:

Mary Ellen Bates is a solo business researcher who publishes a monthly *InfoTip* newsletter (http://www.batesinfo.com/tip.html) that offers a mix of time management ideas, database reviews, and searching tips. Although not specifically business focused, Bates' work as an independent researcher has given her a lot of great ideas on how to efficiently sift through piles of business haystacks.

Information Today publishes a number of titles related to advanced Internet searching and business reference. Their Supersearchers series (http://www. infotoday.com/supersearchers/) features interviews with top searchers on topics from starting your own research company to global business searching to competitive intelligence research. In addition to books, they publish journals such as *Online Magazine* (http://www. info-today.com/online/default.shtml) and *Searcher* (http://www.infotoday.com/searcher/default.asp).

Marylaine Block is a member of the Supersearching elite (see above). Her ExLibris Website (http://marylaine.com/exlibris/index.html) offers helpful insights into all kinds of things, including the occasional business research development. This is not a flashy site, but do not let the rudimentary Web design throw you off. In addition to her "Rules of Information" and interviews with "Internet Gurus," she passes along search tips, favorite sites and "neat new stuff" found that month.

Google and Beyond

Explore beyond the basic Google (http://www.google.com) search and take advantage of some of the advanced search features offered, such as limiting to certain domains, finding sites that link to a site you are interested in, or limiting by file extensions. Or try your search across some of the other Google products such as Google Scholar, Google Books, and Google Patents. You may be surprised by what kinds of clues and other data you can turn up. Google also offers a librarian newsletter (http://librariancentral.blogspot.com/) that provides all kinds of tips and updates related to Google. The librarian newsletter is currently on hiatus (as of June 2007), but the site points to additional Google resources that you can peruse in the meantime, including the official Google blog (http://googleblog.blogspot.com/) and their "Inside Google Book Search" blog (http://booksearch.blogspot.com/).

That said, as great a search tool as Google is, it is not the only game in town. Explore beyond Google and do not limit yourself to just one search engine. Ask.com (formerly Ask Jeeves) has some handy recommendations for broadening and narrowing your searches and other unique ways of presenting search results. Clusty (http://clusty.com) is another "clustering" search engine worth experimenting with. Also consider trying a business-specific search engine like Business.com or browse the Internet Public Library's Business & Economics directory (http://www.ipl.org/div/subject/browse/bus00.00.00/) or use Marketresearch.com to browse through thousands of industry reports.

Broadening your Internet search strategies to include advanced Google searching and resources beyond Google will not only help you to keep your searching skills sharper, you may just turn up new information since no single search engine (not even Google) crawls everything. To keep up on the business of search engines and stay current on these tools of the trade use Search Engine Watch (http://searchenginewatch.com/).

OTHER RESOURCES FOR KEEPING UP

Resources that cover new developments and other news related to business reference abound. In fact, you are reading one right now. Professional journals can be an excellent source of current information on the field. Here are just a few.

Professional Literature

As you probably already realize, the *Journal of Business & Finance Librarianship* (*JBFL*) (http://www.haworthpress.com/web/JBFL/) is a fantastic source of reviews of business reference resources, including books and databases, and other useful articles related to business research geared primarily to the academic librarian. *JBFL* also periodically publishes special theme issues (such as the one this article appears in) that dive more in-depth into a particular aspect of business reference. Another professional journal, *Business Information Alert* (http://www.alertpub.com/hpbia.html), includes articles on business topics and lots of reviews on business books and other resources. Both journals are available either indexed or full-text through a few different databases. And, because it is unlikely that there will ever be a moratorium called ceasing all new publishing of journal articles until we can catch up on our reading, you may want to consider taking advantage of some of the new alert services available in many of the databases or on publisher Websites to be informed when new issues are published (see the above mention of feed readers, too, for help in this area). Another good way to keep up on what is being published is to subscribe to the Informed Librarian (http://www.informedlibrarian.com/) that compiles the tables of contents for over 300 library- and business-related and other journal titles, including *JBFL* and *Business Information Alert*. Although you can access some of the content of the Informed Librarian for free, full access requires a nominal subscription fee.

Colleagues and Peer Groups

Your business reference colleagues and other groups of information professional peers are other potential resources in the fight for keeping up and staying current. The BUSLIB e-mail group (http://list1.ucc.nau.edu /archives/buslib-l.html) has saved its readers countless hours of searching. Sign up for the BUSLIB digest and see the kinds of questions that are asked, and answered, by other helpful business librarians. Once you have signed up, you can also search the archives to see if you can find any helpful pointers. The BUSLIB group is an excellent place to turn to when you are faced with a business stumper question or when you just want to "lurk" and keep up on what other business librarians are asking about.

Another growing group of business peers can be found through the Business Librarians Ning site (http://businesslibrarians.ning.com/). If you have not seen Ning yet, check it out. This particular Ning social network group is a place where you can meet and learn from other business librarians. You can get tips on purchases, programs, and all kinds of other ideas as you build your network of business librarian colleagues and hone your Library 2.0 skills all at the same time.

Business school library sites and other business-related library Websites are often overlooked and yet are invaluable sources of information and inspiration. Harvard's Baker Library (http://www.library. hbs.edu/) offers a "new books at the Baker Library" section. Use this to keep up on what they are collecting. The Baker site also contains some great business guides and other tips that you can turn to for help when you need it. The Lippincott Library @ Wharton site (http://www.library.upenn.edu/ lippincott/) features a "Business FAQ" (http://faq.library.upenn.edu/ recordList?library=lippincott) section that answers common questions by topic and provides useful starting points for business research. The FAQ feature is part of a collaborative pilot between a number of different business school libraries and is intended to draw upon the specialized expertise available at each institution. Currently Wharton manages the software, and each school involved hosts their own FAQ server. Similarly, the Massachusetts Institute of Technology Libraries' Subject Guides (http://libraries.mit.edu/help/subjects.html) provide some excellent starting points on reference sources and strategies for researching topics related to business and economics. Bizlink (http://www.bizlink.org/) from The Public Library of Charlotte and Mecklenburg County is a good place to turn to when you are tired of being pointed to fee-based resources that you do not subscribe to.

Michigan's Kresge Business Administration Library (http://www.bus. umich.edu/KresgeLibrary/) points to some useful database instruction handouts and also has a version of the Business FAQ called Find.It.Fast! The Library of Congress Business Reference Service (http://www.loc.gov/rr/business/) publishes a Business & Economics Research Advisor series. The most recently published issue covers industry research. The Librarians Index to the Internet (LII) business section (http://www.lii.org/search/file/busfinjobs) is a helpful directory pointing to various business related links all over the Internet. Business is only one of many topics covered by the LII team. Another useful directory is provided by the Internet Public Library (http://www.ipl.org). Their business subject collection is another good source for browsing useful sites at the top level and keeping up on what is out there. Georgetown's Business Intelligence Center has pulled together a number of useful help sheets (http://www.library.georgetown.edu/bic/help.htm) that serve as a collection of links to "cheat sheets" for business databases. This is a good place to turn to if you are trying to figure out a tricky database and do not want to recreate the wheel.

For an interesting use of the Wiki format to present and organize business information resources, turn to the Biz Wiki from Ohio University (http://www.library.ohiou.edu/subjects/bizwiki/index.php/Main_Page).

Finally, a few nonbusiness library sites are worth highlighting. SpecialIssues.com's "Lists of Lists" (LOL) site can provide clues of all kinds that can speed up your business searching and point you towards industry-specific journals and special issues with ranked lists and other information. The LOL portion of SpecialIssues.com is offered free as a service to the Internet community. Some of the content of LOL is provided by ResourceShelf (http://www.resourceshelf.com/), a site that is added to daily and highlights new or updated Web based resources. Although ResourceShelf does have a Business & Economics category, they cover a wide range of topics that can help you to stay current on all kinds of new reports and other Web resource news. ResourceShelf's sister site, DocuTicker (http://www.docuticker.com/), specifically highlights new full-text reports from government agencies and other public interest groups. To keep up on ResourceShelf and DocuTicker themselves, be sure to subscribe to their feeds or e-mail alerts.

Professional Development

Taking the time to get involved with professional associations and attend conferences and other professional development workshops related to business are great ways to help yourself stay current. The Business Reference and Services Section (BRASS) of the Reference and User Services Association (RUSA) sponsors a forum and a program, among other events, at every annual meeting of the American Library Association. The BRASS Website (http://www.ala.org/ala/rusa/rusaourassoc/rusasections/brass/brass.htm) has a number of helpful links to not only the Best of the Best Business Web Sites and the Core Competencies for Business Reference, but also to handouts and presentations. The Special Library

Association (SLA) has some Divisions geared towards the business librarian, including the SOLO Division (for solo researchers), the Advertising & Marketing Division and the Business & Finance Division (http://www.sla.org/content/community/units/divs/division.cfm). Many states have local groups as well, for example SLA Business & Finance Illinois. The Society of Competitive Intelligence Professionals (http://www.scip.org/) is another organization that offers training and publications and other resources. And, mentioned earlier in referring to their publishing arm, Information Today hosts a number of conferences that often focus on business-specific research strategies as well as Internet searching skills in general, including Internet Librarian (http://www.infotoday.com/il2007/default.shtml) and Web Search University (http://www.websearchu.com/).

Becoming an active member of any of these groups or exploring some of these professional development opportunities is a great way to expand your business reference support network as well as to hone your skills and keep up with the changing business reference landscape.

CONCLUSION

The paradox presented by this article is that it has likely added to the list of things you feel you need to keep up on. Remember the original caveat, though, and do not let yourself fall into the "keeping up=constant frenzy" trap. This article highlights a number of resources and strategies that can be useful to you in keeping up and staying informed on business reference topics. Choose one or two that caught your eye, but do not plan on following up on all of them at once. Spend some time to save some time and allow a small amount of room in your schedule for "keeping up" in whatever way works best for you. Put it on your calendar and treat it as an appointment you can't break. This is the same advice you will hear from fitness trainers trying to get you to stop skipping your workouts. Consider the time part of your business reference fitness plan and start keeping up and staying informed today.

Networking Strategies for Business and Economics Librarians

Bobray Bordelon

INTRODUCTION

Business and economics librarians have always been in demand. The language of business is in many ways similar to a foreign language. It seems every time a patron approaches the reference desk with a business or statistical question, the business librarian is summoned. Although being always on call may have seemed to be a burden at times, this should now be viewed as an opportunity. At a time when so many librarians are throwing up their hands in despair as to why patrons are not coming into the library, business librarians continue to be in demand. We can not rest upon our laurels if we expect to continue to be in demand. Just as most researchers have bypassed the librarian for literature searches as the interfaces and availability of electronic full texts have improved, the business librarian who thinks that his or her command of the language of business is enough will soon be of little use.

How does one continue to have that competitive edge? A key strategy is networking. Networking is a two-way relationship. Just as you expect to obtain valuable information, the other contact expects the same from you. Networking can be with other business librarians, with other librarians or information professionals, or with our communities and clientele. It can be face-to-face, virtual, or ideally a combination of the two.

LITERATURE REVIEW

No literature focusing specifically on networking strategies for business librarians was found. Articles tend to describe networking for the profession as a whole and often take a humorous approach. The basic strategies outlined in Cohen (2006), Crosby (2000), Gordon (2004), and Pearle (2001) are useful in any field of librarianship.

PROFESSIONAL ASSOCIATIONS
FOR BUSINESS LIBRARIANS

The form of networking that often first comes to mind is through the professional associations for business librarians. In the United States, the major ones are (1) the Business Reference and Services Section (BRASS) of the Reference and User Services Association (RUSA) of the American Library Association (ALA) and (2) the Business and Finance Division of the Special Libraries Association (SLA).

Although the majority of BRASS membership is either in academic or public libraries, corporate librarians and vendors also play a vital role. The group meets twice a year at its Midwinter Meeting and the Annual Conference. Discussion Groups take place at both meetings. At Midwinter, a Publisher's Forum is held where publishers are invited based on a theme, and the audience is allowed to pose questions to the vendors. At Annual, a half-day program provides an in-depth look at a particular topic with experts as speakers. The detailed handouts are often referred to many years after the program and are typically archived on the BRASS Website (www.ala.org/rusa/brass). The Academic and Public Library committees take turns hosting a forum. There are many opportunities for members to become more involved through a wide array of committees, some of which have virtual members. For many the highlights of each ALA meeting are the social activities. Welcoming receptions and a Monday night dinner allow members to catch up and make new friends and contacts. The BRASS Website includes many other educational materials. The contacts made through BRASS often allow one to quickly turn to a library that has the needed resource, an expert in the field, or a place to go when evaluating a possible new product.

The part of SLA most associated with business is the Business and Finance Division. However, there are other specialized divisions to consider such as the Advertising and Marketing Division, Insurance Employee Benefits Division, and the Labor Section of the Social Science Division. Divisions focusing on specific industries such as petroleum and energy resources, pharmaceutical and health technology, and transportation provide a rich array of experts. SLA hosts an annual conference each June. Regional chapters hosts frequent meetings. Membership is a mixture of corporate librarians, academic librarians, and a few public librarians. The Business and Finance Division has a College & University Business Libraries Section. A Website (http://www.slabf.org) includes many of the past presentations, and access is open to all regardless whether or not one is a member. Other parts of the site such as the resource Wiki are open to members only. SLA is famous for its lavish receptions and attracting many specialized vendors that go beyond the academic and public library market. The rich membership of corporate librarians from many settings allows academic and public librarians to expand their network beyond their traditional circles.

In addition to the divisions and sections of SLA that are specifically related to business or specific industries, one should always try to meet members from other divisions. Business and economics cross over into most disciplines. Almost any area is a possibility for one interested in developing or business or considering the economic aspects. Likewise in ALA, many useful contacts can me made in other parts of the organization. Some are obvious such as the American Federation of Labor/Congress of Industrial Organizations (AFL-CIO) – ALA Library Service to Labor Groups which is part of RUSA. Others are less obvious but play a vital role such as the Government Documents Round Table (GODORT) and the Map and Geography Roundtable (MAGERT). Governmental agencies and organizations such as the Department of Commerce, the Treasury Department, the Federal Reserve System, the Organization for Economic Cooperation and Development (OECD), the International Monetary Fund, and the World Bank are all closely tracked by members of GODORT. With geographic information systems playing a larger role in business decision making, MAGERT is the place for geographic information systems (GIS) experts.

RELATED LIBRARY ASSOCIATIONS

Although ALA and SLA have an incredible amount to offer and are typically the first places one thinks of joining for networking opportunities, other related library organizations can offer a fresh perspective as well as specialized knowledge. ALA and SLA are very large organizations, and even their divisions can be overwhelming at first due to their size and offerings. Much of business and economics is based on data and statistics. There are several organizations that focus on data. Some of the better known are the International Association for Social Science Information Service and Technology (IASSIST) and the Association of Public Data Users (APDU).

IASSIST describes itself as "an international organization of professionals working in and with information technology and data services to support research and teaching in the social sciences. Its 300 members are from a variety of workplaces, including data archives, statistical agencies, research centers, libraries, academic departments, government departments, and non-profit organizations." (http://www.iassistdata.org) The international membership allows one to network around the world. With an increasing emphasis on global trade, it is important to have contacts outside of one's home nation. IASSIST holds an annual conference that alternates between locations in the United States, Canada, and Europe. Even if one never attends the conferences, many join the organization to gain access to its listserv that provides a rich knowledgebase of international experts. Many of the presentations from conferences are available for free on its Website: http://www.iassistdata.org.

APDU describes itself as "national network that links users, producers and disseminators of government statistical data." The focus is on U.S. governmental data. It hosts an annual conference and also puts many of its presentations on its Website: http://www.apdu.org.

RELATED SUBJECT ASSOCIATIONS

Most will probably not have the opportunity or the funding to belong to much less attend meetings of related subject associations such as the

American Economic Association (http://www.vanderbilt.edu/AEA/), the American Marketing Association (http://www.marketingpower.com), American Management Association (http://www.amanet.org), or the American Finance Association (http://www.afajof.org/). However, if the organization is in one's city or region, one may want to consider attending a meeting. In academia, these professional associations are typically the ones that faculty join and where they present papers. The vendors are often targeted to the professionals and can provide key insight into the larger discipline. Most important, key contacts can be made.

NETWORKING WITH ONE'S USER BASE

Although the outside organizations can provide the knowledge and contacts needed to serve our clienteles, it is equally important that we remain a vital part of the lives of our patrons. If working with an academic community, it is crucial to maintain close ties with the chairs of the departments along with the associated faculty. Welcome new faculty, as they are often the most enthusiastic to take advantage of library services. Senior faculty can make the difference between obtaining funding for a much needed database and having to rely on one's own budget. Keep track of departing faculty with whom you had a close working relationship. They can also help expand your network of contacts. They can sometimes alert you to new resources they find helpful at their new institution which could in turn benefit your existing researchers.

Use the alumni directories and keep track of students you worked closely with. As alumni find careers in investment banks, businesses, and research organizations, remind them gently of the help you once provided and you will often find they can open up doors that were previously closed to you. Even if they are not the one at the organization with the answer, calling someone you know will always get better results than contacting a stranger. An inside contact can put you in touch with the right person.

If in a public library, get to know the local business owners. Invite the editors of the local business section of the paper to coffee or lunch. The newspaper writers and editors have detailed knowledge of your local community and can often provide information that may be not readily available. Attend Chamber of Commerce meetings. Invite members of the business community to your library and show them what you have to offer and you will often find they have much to offer in return.

Librarians in all settings should get to know the staff at their state data center. State data centers can provide detailed knowledge of one's state economy and can often help with hard-to-answer statistical questions. The Census Bureau describes state data centers as "a cooperative program between the states and the Census Bureau that was created in 1978 to make data available locally to the public through a network of state agencies, universities, libraries, and regional and local governments. The Business and Industry Data Center Program (BIDC) was added in 1988 to meet the needs of local business communities for economic data" . A listing of state data centers in your area can be found at http://www.census.gov/sdc/www/.

LIBRARY SCHOOL ALUMNI

Although many library schools have closed over time or now offer distance education programs, the alumni from your library school can be a prime source. Like any educational setting, library schools create a sense of place and a commonality among its alumni. Graduating classes or surrounding classes often form close ties. Few professions provide as many opportunities to stay connected as librarianship. Whether it be through reunions at ALA conferences, listservs, or blogs set up by your alumni association, or e-mail, reconnect with your former classmates. Some are doing precisely what you do. Others are vendors, indexers, or in other areas that can be of great use to you. Likewise, the professors from your library school can be a key source for providing the next generation of business librarians to your organization. When looking for a new business librarian, contact the business reference professor and find out who is on or about to enter the job market that is their shining star.

VIRTUAL NETWORKING

Virtual networking can also prove to be invaluable. BUSLIB-L is a listserv where business librarians post reference questions, product ideas, and conference announcements. Joining is free, and one can either get the day's postings in a daily digest or receive each question as posted. The list is moderated so that one is not flooded with irrelevant postings or spam. It is a great means of discovering experts in niche fields, and professional relationships are often formed as a result of the list. It is always fun to meet someone in person after years of corresponding only via e-mail. Many of us also maintain a strong list of contacts that we communicate with via e-mail or chat. In some cases, the relationship is completely virtual, but one that provides useful information. Online social networks are becoming increasingly common and may take the form of blogs or services such as Facebook and del.icio.us.

BRINGING IT ALL TOGETHER

There are many ways to network, and each has its own advantages. No one has the time to do all of them, so the key is to find the right mix for you and to try not to rely only on a few forms. Particularly with professional associations, it is easy to become very comfortable with one's colleagues and to become established in the hierarchy of the organization. Burnout is also a common occurrence for those that do become heavily involved. It is important to take a break every now and then or become less involved in the form of networking one is most accustomed to allow new opportunities. When one returns to one's comfort zone, one will often discover new faces and chances to succeed as well as be able to bring in fresh perspectives from the outside. Look for opportunities to attend events. If not able to attend national conferences, look at what your state or metropolitan area has to offer. Large metropolitan areas often have specialized formal or informal networks that can provide local ties. Look for grants or scholarships to attend conferences. ALA and SLA offer many funding opportunities. Go to the meetings, discussion groups, programs, and forums, but also take the time to get to know the person sitting next to you. Join the group lunches that often form after a discussion. Go to the parties and get to know your colleagues in a different setting. You may find that not only do your colleagues have much to offer in terms of knowledge but they may also become good friends!

REFERENCES

Cohen, S. M. (2006, January/February). Anyone can take a reservation. *Public Libraries,*
   45, 29–31.
Crosby, J. (2000, August). Networking the right way. *Information Outlook, 4*, 12.
Gordon, R. S. (2004, April 15). Is association membership worth it? *Library Journal, 129*,
   56.
Pearle, L. (2001, September/October). Eyes on the stars, ears to the ground. *Knowledge
   Quest, 30*, 41–42.

Burnout Strategies for Librarians

Kevin Harwell

INTRODUCTION

Chronic exposure to stress in the workplace can lead to emotional, social, and mental exhaustion. Personal resources are used up or "burned out." One has difficulty feeling positive emotions. Patrons become queries instead of human beings. The easy, directional queries become annoyances. The challenging ones may trigger feelings of dread.

A few years ago, I experienced burnout. I was chronically tired and sleeping poorly, but demands of work and family prohibited me from taking a meaningful break. The thought of walking into the library had an unpleasant effect on me. I found that intellectually challenging questions were draining rather than energizing as they had been earlier in my career. I was weary of the repetitive, routine queries. My attitude toward patrons, in particular, alarmed me and was in direct opposition to the ideals that had brought me to this profession in the first place. I had an adequate notion of how I had arrived at this state of mind. The real challenge was in determining how to get past it and return to a state of connectedness and productivity.

WHAT IS BURNOUT?

"Job burnout is a psychological syndrome that involves a prolonged response to stressors in the workplace. Specifically, it involves the chronic strain that results from an incongruence, or misfit, between the worker and the job" (Maslach, 2003, p. 189). The cumulative effect of chronic exposure to job related stress can take its toll. Without adequate replenishment of mental and emotional resources, the tension, fatigue, repetitive tasks, and other stressors can wear us down. Exhaustion is a key component of burnout, but there are additional components that characterize it as a syndrome distinctive from other disorders. Christina Maslach and a host of other researchers have developed a clinical conceptualization of burnout based on more than 30 years of investigation. Accordingly, burnout is a patterned response to chronic job stress characterized by three dimensions of response: "overwhelming exhaustion, feelings of cynicism and detachment from the job, and a sense of ineffectiveness and lack of accomplishment" (Maslach, Schaufeli, & Leiter, 2001, p. 399).

Cynicism and *detachment* are often referred to as depersonalization or dehumanization. Service employees may regard the customer as an object rather than as a human being (Maslach et al., 2001). In the library, patrons might be regarded as queries, questions, or cases, rather than people. Library employees may frequently retreat to an office or cubicle to avoid others. They may habitually offer a plastered-on smile rather than a genuine interaction. If a worker habitually treats patrons with callousness, makes derogatory remarks, or deals with situations strictly "by the book" rather than tailoring effective solutions for patrons, this may be an indication of depersonalization (Cordes & Dougherty, 1993).

Sometimes we create distance between ourselves and patrons for appropriate reasons. We place limits on our involvement with patrons in keeping with professional standards for specialized information service such as legal, medical, and business information (Reference and Adult Services Association, 2007). Responding to requests in these subject areas often requires the establishment of special client–provider relationships that are beyond the mission of the library. We also distance ourselves from some patrons to stay focused on our responsibilities. Getting too involved in the patron's issues can create shortages for other patrons and other duties. Distancing ourselves becomes problematic when a library employee is chronically unable to provide quality service to patrons within the expectations of the profession and the library. This is a key distinction in cases of burnout.

A tendency to evaluate oneself negatively is the third key characteristic (Cordes & Dougherty, 1993). This characteristic is sometimes referred to as inefficacy or diminished personal accomplishment. Findings of Maslach et al. (2001) suggest that, "a work situation with chronic, overwhelming demands that contribute to exhaustion or cynicism is likely to erode one's sense of effectiveness. Further, exhaustion or depersonalization interferes with effectiveness: It is difficult to gain a sense of accomplishment when feeling exhausted or when helping people toward whom one is indifferent" (p. 403).

Certain job characteristics are known to be related to burnout. These include the following: high workload; time pressure; conflicting demands on the job; lack of adequate information to do the job well; lack of social support, especially from supervisors; and lack of feedback. Individuals who have little influence on decision making tend to experience burnout more often than those who have more influence. Individuals experience burnout in the context of work. It differs in this respect from depression, which encompasses many areas of a person's life. Individuals who are prone to depression are more likely to experience burnout than others are, but burnout also visits many who are not depressed (Maslach et al., 2001).

CONTRIBUTING FACTORS

Burnout is rooted in the relationship between the worker and the job and work environment. Recent investigations have evaluated mismatches between people and their jobs, sometimes referred to as "job-person fit." Maslach et al. (2001) offer six conditions relating to job-person fit that contribute to burnout, involving workload, control, rewards, community, fairness, and values. Each of these conditions is manifest along a continuum of possibilities.

- People's workload can be excessive or sustainable. If excessive, they may feel that they are overloaded. They may lack basic skills, sufficient time, or important resources to complete assigned tasks effectively.

- They may sense a lack of control of key processes, resources, or choices needed for success.
- Financial, social, or intrinsic rewards and recognitions may be insufficient to keep them motivated.
- The work community may be nonsupportive. A supportive community reaffirms a person's membership in the organization or work unit through appropriate emotional exchanges with coworkers and supervisors. Supportive colleagues assist each other. They share values. Organizations in which there is chronic, unresolved conflict, isolation, frustration, or hostility are not supportive.
- Fairness, as a condition relating to respect and self-worth, is lacking in inequitable workload or pay situations, places where cheating for resources or attention is allowed, or where evaluations are not handled appropriately.
- Values relate to ethics, aspirations, and the mission of the organization and are expressed in official policy and statements, but validated in actual practice.

These researchers also note important contrasts between burnout and job engagement. Whereas burnout is characterized as a combination of job-related exhaustion, cynicism, and inefficacy, job engagement exhibits itself as positive energy, involvement and personal effectiveness. Also, in work situations where the six conditions of job-person fit fall on the positive, desirable side, there is more job engagement and job satisfaction and less burnout (Maslach et al., 2001).

Some sources of library stress are shared with other professions. Many of these relate directly to the potential mismatch conditions. They include budget cuts, frequent technological changes, increased competition for fewer positions, heavy workloads, bureaucratic inertia, red tape, poor management and supervision, low pay, sex discrimination, obnoxious customers or patrons, lack of private work space or office, few opportunities to participate in goal setting or decision making, shifting priorities, lack of closure on ongoing projects, few opportunities for advancement, and working nights and weekends (Caputo, 1991).

CONSEQUENCES OF BURNOUT

Research has found significant consequences of burnout for individuals, families and employers. Maslach and Jackson (1981) reported,

Research on this syndrome ... suggests that burnout can lead to a deterioration in the quality of care or service that is provided by the staff. It appears to be a factor in job turnover, absenteeism, and low morale. Furthermore, burnout seems to be correlated with various self-reported indices of personal distress, including physical exhaustion, insomnia, increased use of alcohol and drugs, and marital and family problems. (p. 100)

Cordes and Dougherty (1993) offered a rather detailed accounting of the consequences of burnout, concluding:

Thus as the scant but growing body of evidence illustrates, the consequences of burnout have some very real physical, emotional, interpersonal, attitudinal, and behavioral implications. Not only does the individual suffer, but the employee's family and friends, the organization, and the people with whom the employee interacts during the work day all bear the costs of this organizational problem. (pp. 639–640)

MEASURING BURNOUT:
THE MASLACH BURNOUT INVENTORY (MBI)

The Maslach Burnout Inventory (MBI) is a survey developed to measure the incidence of burnout in individuals. The survey offers statements relative to the three dimensions of burnout. Respondents rate each statement on a scale in terms of how often the statement is true. The survey yields numerical scores for the three dimensions, which are compared to normative score ranges representing low, average, and high ranges. High scores in the dimensions of emotional exhaustion and depersonalization, especially when combined with a low score in personal efficacy, indicate the presence of burnout. Users of the survey should keep in mind that the MBI is best used as an indicator of whether someone is experiencing burnout. It is not a psychological assessment or diagnostic tool. A complementary "Staff Survey" instrument exists for organizations to use in conjunction with the MBI to aid in developing intervention strategies for the work groups (Maslach & Jackson, 1981; Maslach & Leiter, 1997).

BURNOUT INCIDENCE IN LIBRARIES

A number of studies have set out to assess and document the incidence of burnout among library employees. The conclusions have been variable. Fisher commented on this issue in 1990:

> Empirical investigations are severely outnumbered by ideological proclamations from the believers. The faithful are of one voice: library life is stressful and significant numbers of librarians are burning out. They do not often make direct comparisons with other professions, but when they do it is to show that librarianship is at least as stressful as other callings. They do not have to prove any of this, they *know* it is true. (p. 229)

Fisher could only find a handful of empirical studies of burnout in libraries and could not conclude that burnout was widespread in libraries. Caputo (1991) and Ray (2002) found numerous empirical investigations of burnout in libraries. Nearly all of the investigations show that some librarians experience burnout. Whether the percentages of librarians are high or low for any given time frame, type of library, demographic, or other variable is worthy of further study at another time. The significant issue for this discussion is that it happens at least some of the time to some library staff. For the librarian who experiences burnout, or the library which has even a small percentage of burned-out staff, burnout is a significant issue with personal and workplace consequences.

Those who would claim that librarianship is at least as stressful as other callings may have difficulty arguing their perspective with law enforcement personnel, emergency room staff, rescue workers, and others who work with high levels of human contact in intensely emotional conditions. Nonetheless, library work involves specific stressors found in few other work environments. These include dealing with stereotypes about librarians; timely response to reference inquiries; censorship issues; professionals having to perform clerical tasks; equipment problems, including computer and network problems; theft and mutilation of library materials; insufficient notice for required collection acquisitions; temporary reassignment of duties; and limited authorization in collections decisions (Caputo, 1991).

Some library work functions lack stimulation and challenge. Some involve repetitive tasks, such as multiple sessions of library instruction, and librarians often do not see the results of their efforts. Patrons often regard their library tasks negatively, such as writing a research paper, and share that negativity with staff. A divergence often exists between patron expectations and the availability of information resources or library services. Stakeholders outside the library often misunderstand the role of librarians in the community, corporation, or university and are unaware of their professional or faculty credentials (Sheesley, 2001).

PERSONAL EXPERIENCE

In my career, I have encountered numerous library deanships, difficult managers, temporary administrators, a rigorous tenure process, disappointing budgets, prolonged staff vacancies, redrawn mission statements, restructured organizations, innumerable changes in policies and practices, explicit position changes, and dozens of implicit changes in my day-to-day responsibilities. I have faced conflicting expectations from faculty, students, friends, and members of the larger community. I have learned a new focus to my work at least four times, starting with government documents, then patents and trademarks, law, and my current work, which is business and economics.

My experience with burnout happened in response to a sequence of three major events. Three years after I joined the library faculty at Penn State, my wife and I became parents to our second child, who has a number of serious disabilities. Adapting to this new reality required much time and adjustment. Feelings associated with the initial shock did not taper off until many months after I returned to work. My library administration gave me flexibility to accommodate medical appointments and to meet extra family demands. The university also provided extra time to meet specific timetable obligations with respect to tenure. For a long time, my job performance was not optimal or consistent, nor was coming to work particularly enjoyable. I was challenged to find a new balance—one that I had when I enjoyed coming to work.

The second event was completion of the six-year tenure process. The process was stressful in and of itself. Although the extra time I was allowed was very much appreciated, it was a temporary grace. The tenure track did not go away. It just waited for me for a short, specified period of time. I still had to meet the requirements for librarianship, research, and service. Meanwhile, I was a part of a family adjusting to my young son's needs through long nights with little sleep, medical appointments, meetings with early intervention specialists that resulted in few opportunities to work on library projects during evenings and weekends.

Earning tenure was a big boost, but time for celebration and rest was very brief because the third big stressful event was just starting. The library broke ground on a three-year renovation and expansion of our physical plant without interruption of service while dust, noise, and major changes were happening all around us. This project also involved moving every book and every person's work area at least once.

The renovations also involved a major reorganization of reference departments. Government Documents and Maps spun off the Maps Library and assimilated part of General Reference to become the Social Sciences Library. General Reference then became the Business Library after having spun off history materials to the Arts and Humanities Library. Lack of office space meant that numerous key librarian and staff vacancies were left unfilled. Departmental tensions and interdepartmental tensions ran very high. Personality conflicts, especially, seemed to be at an all-time high.

Ongoing family care needs coupled with the struggle for tenure and the constant upheaval associated with library renovations left me exhausted over a long period of time. I frequently complained about work when I arrived home each evening, and I had trouble sleeping. At work, I had difficulty engaging students and faculty in reference, consultation, and instruction. Measured against the time and energy I was expending for my job, I often felt that my accomplishments were very limited.

IMPLICATIONS FOR COPING
WITH EMPLOYEE BURNOUT

Empirical research about the effectiveness of interventions for burnout has been inconclusive. That is not to say that interventions do not work. Rather, limitations in study design, in the form of inadequate control groups and a lack of longitudinal studies, have resulted in varied responses to interventions. Theoretically, the workplace that endeavors to support the positive measures of job-person fit—seeking ways to match employees with equitable balance in workload, choice and control, recognitions and rewards, supportive community, fairness and justice, and values—may improve job engagement and job satisfaction (Maslach et al., 2001).

One way to consider contributing factors for burnout is in terms of job demands and job resources. Job demands contribute to exhaustion. They include physical workload, poor environmental conditions, demanding clients, time pressure, unfavorable shift-work schedules, and work–home interference. Job resources are identified as performance feedback, rewards, job security, participation in decision making, and support from supervisors. When job resources are thought to be inadequate, the employee experiences the burnout dimension of depersonalization (Demerouti et al., 2001). In case studies where job demands were high, but job resources were also high, employees did not experience high levels of burnout (Bakker, Demerouti, & Euwema, 2005).

High demands alone do not necessarily result in burnout. If the employee has access to sufficient physical and social resources, burnout can be avoided. Recent studies seeking positive psychological constructs suggest that although burnout and job engagement are best measured on different scales, one is the antithesis of the other. Burnout seems to be best measured in terms of exhaustion and depersonalization. The positive dimension of personal efficacy seems to be a better measure related to the experience of job engagement, along with employee vigor, dedication to the organization, and absorption in one's work (Schaufeli & Bakker, 2004). Movement in the direction away from burnout and toward job engagement may be accomplished by managing job demands and job rewards. The six dimensions of job-person fit mentioned earlier may be helpful. If working conditions need to be modified so that employees' experience of burnout can be minimized or managed, perhaps some combination of the following actions would be helpful such as a more sustainable workload, better employee control of processes and resources, improved reward systems, a more supportive work community, stronger sense of fairness, and a reassessment of applied values.

The suggestions above are largely institutional recommendations. Individuals can also take steps to maintain or increase personal resources to help cope with job demands. These would include keeping a healthy lifestyle with proper rest, exercise, and diet. Friends and family can provide important social supports that help meet nonwork demands, which may boost personal resources available for meeting job demands. Vacations, weekends, and holidays can be used to get one's mind off of work, engage in interesting "change of pace" activities, and recharge personal resources. Many people short-change themselves by working longer than necessary hours and workweeks, and not taking earned time off.

PERSONAL COPING STRATEGIES

A significant resource that helped my wife and I was flexible scheduling. We were fortunate and grateful to be able to work schedules that minimized daily transitions between school and after school care for my son who was disabled. This has worked much better for us than other flexibility options, such as telecommuting, which others find beneficial. Frequent days with long hours and nonstandard schedules were quite taxing, as was "tag-team" parenting. However, the odd work schedules were more than compensated by the relief of providing my son with a consistent daily schedule.

The stressful time during library renovation created an opportunity to assert some control over my library career. I petitioned for a transfer from the government documents unit to the newly formed business library. I was eager to move to a new department with new people and a new subject area with which to work. The change also brought new challenges: getting to know an entirely different staff, learning new information resources, and developing relationships with different academic departments. The change has been very good. Our newly renovated facility is a great improvement over the tired and inflexible surroundings we had before the renovation, and I enjoy working with my business colleagues.

Involvement in family, community organizations, church, and other connections are important for many reasons. These activities and communities have great meaning and value. They have also been instrumental for managing stress. I appreciate having friends who share ideals in a context that does not involve performance goals. Activities with family and friends help me to maintain a healthy perspective about my accomplishments at home and at work. It is not unusual to leave my work week in a funk and spend time with family or serving the community in some way, only to return to work on Monday morning refreshed and ready to focus.

CONCLUSION

A good way to manage burnout may be to seek working conditions that enhance job and personal resources for an optimal fit to meet job demands. Much depends on the organization's culture, policies, and practices. Management of personal resources can also better prepare an individual to face the stresses that lead to burnout. An individual's capacity in this regard can vary from person to person and from time to time. A welcome and emerging body of research is looking at factors that contribute to job engagement. New measurement tools are being created and tested for the validity of the responses they elicit. Researchers are seeking a convenient method for assessing employee vigor, dedication to the organization, and absorption in one's work, in much the same way that the MBI measures exhaustion, depersonalization, and personal efficacy (Demerouti et al., 2001).

I have a great job as a librarian, but some days are better than others. Unfortunately, not all days are completely wonderful. On one day, someone needs a journal subscription I will not be able to acquire until next fiscal year, or later. On another day, I miss a meeting due to a schedule conflict and pay for it with a new, unexpected assignment. Sometimes, my students tone me out as I teach them about properly citing their sources. However, on a really great day, I look forward to coming to work. I help patrons find information, collaborate with faculty about their research or their courses, and guide students in their discovery of useful resources. I also work on meaningful collections projects, create useful user guides, and strategize with colleagues about future initiatives for my unit and my library. Once in a while, I get so involved in a project that the passage of time goes nearly unnoticed.

REFERENCES

Bakker, A. B., Demerouti, E., & Euwema, M. C. (2005). Job resources buffer the impact of job demands on burnout. *Journal of Occupational Health Psychology, 10*(2), 170–180. Retrieved November 13, 2007, from PsychARTICLES.

Caputo, J. S. (1991). *Stress and burnout in library service*. Phoenix, AZ: Oryx Press.

Cordes, C. L., & Dougherty, T. W. (1993). A review and integration of research on job burnout. *Academy of Management Review, 18*(4), 621–656. Retrieved October 5, 2007, from ABI/Inform on ProQuest.

Demerouti, E., Bakker, A. B., Nachreiner, F., & Schaufeli, W. B. (2001). The job demands-resources model of burnout. *Journal of Applied Psychology, 86*(3), 499–512. Retrieved November 13, 2007, from PsychARTICLES.

Fisher, D. P. (1990). Are librarians burning out? *Journal of Librarianship, 22*(4) 216–235.

Maslach, C. (2003). Job burnout: new directions in research and intervention. *Current Directions in Psychological Science, 12*(2) 189–192. Retrieved October 5, 2007, from Blackwell Synergy.

Maslach, C., & Jackson, W. E. (1981). The measurement of experienced burnout. *Journal of Occupational Behaviour, 2*, 99–113. Retrieved October 5, 2007, from ProQuest Research Library.

Maslach, C., & Leiter, M. P. (1997). *The truth about burnout: How organizations cause personal stress and what to do about it*. San Francisco: Jossey-Bass.

Maslach, C., Schaufeli, W. B., & Leiter, M. P. (2001). Job burnout. *Annual Review of Psychology, 52*, 397–422. Retrieved October 5, 2007, from ProQuest Research Library.

Ray, B. (2002). *An assessment of burnout in academic librarians in America using the Maslach Burnout Inventory (The MBI)*. Unpublished doctoral dissertation, Rutgers, The State University of New Jersey, New Brunswick.

Reference and Adult Services Association, American Library Association. (2007). *Guidelines for medical, legal, and business responses.* Retrieved October 26, 2007, from http://www.ala.org/ala/rusa/rusaprotools/referenceguide/guidelinesmedical.cfm

Schaufeli, W. B., & Bakker, A. B. (2004). Job demands, job resources, and their relationship with burnout and engagement: a multi-sample study. *Journal of Organizational Behavior, 25,* 293–315. Retrieved November 15, 2007, from PsychARTICLES.

Sheesley, D. (2001). Burnout and the academic teaching librarian: An examination of the problem and suggested solutions. *Journal of Academic Librarianship, 27*(6), 447–451. Retrieved October 5, 2007, from ProQuest Research Library.

The Career Choices of Business Librarians: A Survey and Discussion

Todd M. Hines
Amia L. Baker

INTRODUCTION

Before becoming business librarians, each of us had prior careers, one as a paralegal and the other as an accountant as well as a paralegal. This does not seem to be an unusual anecdote, as many librarians have written over the years about changing careers to become professional librarians. However, even though there have been several surveys of business librarians looking at aspects of their career choices—primarily their educational background—we found that very little information appears to have been collected about the prior work history of current business librarians. In addition, most of the earlier career surveys have concentrated on academic business librarians, excluding other types of business librarians such as those who work in corporate/special libraries. Therefore a survey was undertaken that attempted to reach a large variety of business librarians to find out about their career choices, including prior work history, time in the profession, and level of satisfaction with their business librarian career choice.

METHOD

We developed a survey instrument to collect data about the career choices of business librarians that asked participants to respond to questions regarding their employment history. For those people who indicated they had careers prior to becoming librarians, we inquired about the reasons that they chose librarianship as a second career. All participants were then asked why they chose to specialize in business librarianship. Finally, the survey asked participants to rate their level of satisfaction with their choice of business librarianship as a career.

To reach a large number of business librarians, announcements about the survey were posted on BUSLIB-L and SLABF-L, two popular business librarian listservs. We were able to reach a diverse population of business librarians using this method because of the wide distribution of the two listservs. Subscribers to the listservs hail from countries all over the world and perform business research in different types of organizations, including librarians in academia, corporate/special, public, governmental, law, and medical libraries. Although the subscribers of these listservs work in many fields, the invitation to take the survey specifically requested that business librarians participate in the survey. The online survey was made available through http://www.surveymonkey.com over two weeks in August 2007, during which time a total of 289 people completed the survey.

SURVEY RESULTS

Current Employment

We first wanted to find out what types of librarians were taking the survey, so all respondents were asked to identify where they currently

TABLE 1. Type of Librarian ob Setting
Where ou Currently Work

Current ob Setting	Number	Percent
Corporate special	150	51.9
Academic library	95	32.9
Othernot categorized	11	3.8
Public library	11	3.8
Othergo vernment nonprot	10	3.5
Information broker	5	1.7
Otherla w r m	5	1.7
No answer	2	0.7
Total	289	

work. As shown in Table 1, a majority of the respondents (51.9%) are currently employed in corporate/special libraries. Overall, almost 85% of the respondents indicated that they were presently employed in either corporate/special libraries (150 responses) or academic libraries (95 responses). The majority of the previous business librarian career surveys located by us—namely Kendrick (1990), Pagell and Lusk (2000), and Winston (1997)—surveyed only current academic business librarians. An online career survey conducted by Houdyshell, Robles, and Hua (1999) and published in the trade periodical *Information Outlook* did have a respondent pool similar to ours. Special librarians made up their largest group and along with academic librarians represented around 75% of their respondents. Unfortunately, they did not ask many specific questions about prior careers, so not many comparisons can be made to their data.

Business Librarianship—Years Experience

The survey also asked for the total number of years worked as a business librarian. As illustrated in Table 2, the years worked as a business librarian were fairly evenly distributed. A slight majority had 10 years or fewer experience as business librarians, but a substantial number, around 43%, had more than 10 years of business librarian experience. Kendrick (1990) asked the same question, but in that survey a much larger proportion of the librarians, around 80%, had fewer than 10 years experience in business librarianship. One possible explanation of this difference could be that our survey was not limited to academic business librarians. Regardless, the important aspect is that the current survey findings represent the career choices of neophyte and very experienced business librarians.

TABLE 2.   ears Worked as Business
Librarian

ears	Number	Percent
0–5	89	30.8
6–10	73	25.3
11–15	49	16.9
16–20	32	11.1
Over 20	42	14.5
No answer	4	1.4
Total	289	

Previous Careers

It is widely accepted that librarianship is a profession that attracts many second-career individuals.[1] However, it does not appear that anyone has previously collected information about what percent of business librarians entered the profession after working in another career or careers. Winston's (1997) doctoral research, which focused only on academic business librarians, touched on a portion of this, but the results were limited to those with previous business careers and library experience, excluding other types of prior work experience.

Among librarians responding to our survey, a majority entered the field of librarianship after having worked full-time in another career. As summarized in Table 3, 180 of the 289 (62.28%) respondents indicated that they held at least one full-time position prior to becoming a professional librarian. Still for a substantial number, 109 people (37.72%), librarianship was their first career. The next three sections focus on the previous full-time jobs held by the 180 respondents who indicated they had previous careers/jobs before becoming a professional librarian.

TABLE 3. Worked Full Time in Another
  ob Career Prior to Entering Professional
Librarianship

Answer	Number	Percent
es	180	62.3
No	109	37.7
Total	289	

Previous Careers—Types of Jobs

The respondents who indicated they had previous careers were asked to list all of their full-time jobs prior to becoming a professional librarian. As this was an open-ended question, respondents could provide as little or as much information as they desired. Some respondents chose to list each job title they held along with the number of years of employment, while other people were more general, simply indicating that they held several jobs in a particular field. Because of this variation in reporting, we were unable to determine an accurate range, median, and mode for the number of jobs that the respondents held prior to becoming a business librarian.

As one might expect, an examination of the previous jobs held by the 180 business librarians yielded a vast array of occupations. Some of the more unique jobs people reported included being the CEO of a consulting firm, a flight attendant, an army musician, a dancer, a computer programmer for the FBI, an artist in a match factory, and a quality control chemist at a winery. Many other colleagues held positions directly related to business: accountant, human resources manager, market researcher, and equity research assistant.

Because respondents were allowed to list all of their prior careers, this question generated a rather long list of careers in diverse fields. Prior jobs/careers were categorized into broad job families, with a distinction being made between paraprofessional and professional business jobs. The main distinction being that jobs that do not require a four-year degree (such as an accounting clerk) were considered paraprofessional, while jobs requiring a degree (such as a CPA accounting position) were classified as professional. Table 4 summarizes the 24 most popular jobs/careers listed. Specifically, any career mentioned by more than three respondents was included in Table 4. Not surprisingly, the most common type of previous job experience shared among this group of people was as a library paraprofessional, with 28 people having worked in these positions before becoming a professional librarian. Beyond that common link, other popular jobs and fields included administrative assistant, teaching, publishing, computer-related occupations, retail sales, and finance careers.

As mentioned previously, we were not able to identify other surveys that have done this type of comprehensive look at the previous jobs held by business librarians. There have been several surveys of students in library school that asked about prior careers. White and Macklin (1970) found that about 72% of the respondents' prior nonlibrary jobs were either in K-12 teaching or administrative assistant positions. Heim and Moen

TABLE 4. Most Popular obs Held Prior to Becoming a Professional Librarian

Prior ob Career	Number	Rank	of Total Respondents[a]
Library–paraprofessional	28	1	15.6
Administrative assistant	25	2	13.9
TeacherPre–K 12	24	3	13.3
Publishing editing proofreading	21	4	11.7
Marketing public relations advertisingprof essional	19	5	10.6
Computer occupationsprof essional	10	6	5.6
Retail & retail sales, e cluding booksellers	10	6	5.6
Finance relatedprof essional	9	8	5.0
University college staff (nonlibrary)	8	9	4.4
Library positionprof essional	7	10	3.9
Medicalpar aprofessional	7	10	3.9
Paralegal	7	10	3.9
Researcher research analyst	7	10	3.9
Accountant CPA	6	14	3.3
Art theatre operations	6	14	3.3
Customer service representative	6	14	3.3
Not for prot sector	6	14	3.3
Ofce manager	6	14	3.3
Accountingpar aprofessional	5	19	2.8
Restaurant wait staff	5	19	2.8
Retailbookseller	5	19	2.8
Television, radio, Improduction & writing	5	19	2.8
Social work	4	23	2.2
ournalism	3	24	1.7
Research assistant	3	24	1.7
Salesprof essional	3	24	1.7

$N = 180$.
[a]The number of responses does not sum to 180, and the percentage of total respondents does not equal 100 because respondents were allowed to choose multiple prior obs. Top 24 answers are presented.

(1989) found that a lower percentage had worked in these two professions, but they still represented a majority, 50.9% of previous jobs.

There is a bit of an "apples-to-oranges" comparison with the previous studies mentioned, as they appear to have allowed only one prelibrarian occupation to be listed, whereas this survey allowed all previous careers to be listed. Even taking this into account, our survey takers, composed of people who work as business librarians, were not as likely to concentrate in the two professions of K-12 teaching and administrative assistant positions. We had 25 respondents who indicated they had a prior career in teaching and 24 who had worked full-time in administrative assistant careers. Of the 180 respondents who indicated a prior career, this represents less than 30%, a lower percentage than found in the other two studies.

Not surprisingly, it also appears that our survey had a higher percentage of people who worked in business-related careers prior to entering librarianship. It is difficult to determine exactly how the surveys of White and Macklin (1970) and Heim and Moen (1989) classified business versus non-business careers for the respondents with prior careers, but it is estimated that White and Macklin had 5% with prior business careers, whereas 20.5% in Heim and Moen had previous business-related employment. They do not mention whether these figures differentiate between paraprofessional and professional business occupations, but they appear to include both. Winston (1997) reported that 18.1% of the academic business librarians in his survey held business positions before becoming librarians. However, he only collected information about prior business or library-related careers, so it is not possible to determine what percentage of his total respondents had prior careers. Also, nearly one fourth of the people he classified as having previous business careers are listed as working secretarial jobs or an undifferentiated category called "Other." Unfortunately, because of these collection and categorization decisions, it does not appear feasible to compare his results to the other surveys.

Because our respondents could list all their prelibrarianship jobs, it was possible that the same person could have had multiple business careers (e.g., in marketing and in finance). To account for this, we examined our source data to determine how many of the 180 respondents who indicated a prior career had a previous business occupation. To compare our results to White and Macklin and Heim and Moen, we left out a number of jobs that might be considered business careers but appear to have been excluded in the previous studies. These include jobs in editing/publishing, arts careers, journalism, as well as film, television, and radio careers. Even with these exclusions about 51% of our respondents with prior careers had previous experience in para- or professional business jobs. It does not seem surprising that business librarians would have a much higher percentage of prior business career experience than the librarian profession as a whole.

Previous Careers—Years Worked

Next, the survey asked people who had previous careers to indicate how many years they worked prior to becoming a professional librarian. A summary of the data is presented in Table 5. Around 40% worked fewer

TABLE 5. Total ears Worked Full Time in Prior Career(s)

ears	Number	Percent
0–2	32	17.8
3–5	43	23.9
6–10	52	28.9
11–20	43	23.9
Over 20	9	5.0
No answer	1	0.5
Total	180	

than six years in any prior career(s), but a majority of the respondents, about 60%, worked more than six years, with 5% working more than 20 years in other careers before they entered librarianship. It does not appear that this type of information has been collected by any of the previously published library science career surveys.

Previous Careers—Factors Influencing Career Change

So, why choose librarianship? We wanted to know why people who were already working in a career opted to change occupations to become a professional librarian. In our survey, those who indicated that they had worked in a prior career were asked about the factors that influenced their decision to become librarians. Respondents could select multiple answers from a list of possible factors or they could choose to write in their own response. The information is summarized in Table 6, with the 10 most popular answers presented. Over one half of the 180 survey takers who worked in a prior career listed at least two factors as having influenced their decision. "Job functions" was chosen by 96 (53.3%) and "love of field" by 91 (50.6%). Note that because more than one answer was permitted there were more than 180 total responses.

Previous articles have looked at the factors that influence people to choose librarianship careers. In 1980, Dale asked a group of women librarians with doctorate degrees why they chose librarianship. She found that respondents to her survey listed "love of books and libraries" as the most important factor in their decision. "Love of field" and "love of books" were also ranked highly by business librarians in our survey. However, in a study by Ard et al. (2006), graduate students in library science did not consider these two factors to be strong motivations for their career choice but did

TABLE 6. Factors That Inuenced Decision to Change ob Career and Become a Librarian

Factor	No. of Responses	Rank	of Total Respondents[a]
ob functions	96	1	53.3
Love of eld	91	2	50.6
Love of books	62	3	34.4
Recommendation of mentor, professor, coworker, or friend	58	4	32.2
Compensation	44	5	24.4
Increased marketability	43	6	23.9
Love of research	22	7	12.2
Clientele	12	8	6.7
Prestige	10	9	5.6
Previous library work e perience	8	10	4.4

$N = 180$.
[a]The number of responses does not sum to 180 and the percentage of total respondents does not equal 100 because respondents were allowed to choose multiple factors. Top 10 answers are presented.

list job functions as an important factor. This finding suggests that there may be a generational difference developing in the values held by graduate students just entering the field versus librarians with years of experience.

Librarianship Career—Age Started

Having focused entirely on the business librarians with previous careers up to this point, the direction of our survey then shifted to capture the career experiences of all respondents since becoming professional librarians. Our survey asked all 289 respondents to indicate at what age they first became a librarian. As one might expect, the results confirmed that the overwhelming majority of people entered the profession between the ages of 20–39, with 59% in their twenties and 30% in their thirties (Table 7). Business librarians do not seem to differ much as a group in the age they began their professional careers compared to the profession as a whole. Luzius (2005) found that 50% of the Association of Research Libraries (ARL) academic librarians he surveyed began their career in their twenties and 31% in their thirties. It is interesting to note that even though a majority of the respondents to our survey (180 out of 289) had a previous career, around 90% of people in our survey still began their librarianship careers before age 40. It was extremely rare for the business librarians who took our survey to have started their library careers after their 30s.

TABLE 7. Age When Started Professional
Librarianship Career

Age	Number	Percent
20–29	171	59.2
30–39	86	29.7
40–49	25	8.7
50–59	6	2.1
60+	0	0.0
No answer	1	0.3
Total	289	

Business Librarianship Career—Age Started

In 1990, Kendrick found that most business librarians started their career in some other type of professional librarian position and then moved to business librarianship later in their career. Because of Kendrick's findings, we asked our respondents to indicate at what age they first chose to specialize in business librarianship. These results are presented in Table 8. As with the previous question, it is interesting to note that a large percentage (77.5%) started before age 40. The previous table showed that only around 11% started their librarianship careers after age 40, whereas Table 8 shows that around 21% (18.3% + 2.8%) of all respondents became business librarians after they were age 40 years. This supports Kendrick's findings that an appreciable number worked in other areas of librarianship before becoming business librarians.

TABLE 8. Age Respondent Became a Business
Librarian

Age	Number	Percent
20–29	126	43.6
30–39	98	33.9
40–49	53	18.3
50–59	8	2.8
60+	0	0.0
No answer	4	1.4
Total	289	

TABLE 9. Reason for Specializing in Business Librarianship

Reason	Number	Rank	of Total Respondents[a]
Interested in business as a sub ect	141	1	48.8
Only position available at time	59	2	20.4
Previous education and or e perience in business or business library	44	3	15.2
Compensation	22	4	7.6
Best good position available	20	5	6.9
Field is challenging e citing full of variety	19	6	6.6
No one else on staff was willing to do it	9	7	3.1

$N = 289$.
[a]The number of responses does not sum to 289 and the percentage of total respondents does not equal 100 because respondents were allowed to choose multiple reasons. Top 7 answers are presented.

Reasons for Becoming Business Librarians

The motivations for becoming a business librarian can be as varied as the librarians who accept these jobs. When asked what factors influenced their decision to specialize in business librarianship, 48.8% of respondents indicated that they were interested in business as a subject (Table 9). However, just over 20% reported taking the job because it was the only position available at the time. Previous education and/or experience in business or a business library factored into the decision for 15.2% of respondents. Compared to Kendrick's study (1990) of academic business librarians that also asked why librarians chose to specialize in business, it seems that more people today chose business librarianship because they are interested in business as a subject. Only about 36% of respondents in Kendrick's study chose business librarianship because they were interested in business as a subject. Also, exactly one half of Kendrick's survey takers said they became a business librarian primarily because it was the only position available at the time. Fewer people in our survey stated that a factor that led them to become a business librarian was because no one else on their staff was willing to do it. About 3% in this survey selected that as a factor in their decision versus 11.7% of respondents in Kendrick's study.

Career Satisfaction

Table 10 presents the level of satisfaction with their business librarian careers. As a group, the business librarians surveyed appear to be quite satisfied with their career choices. Only 1.4% of the respondents are slightly

TABLE 10. Level of Satisfaction with Business Librarianship Career Choice

Satisfaction Level	Number	Percent
Very satised	225	77.8
Slightly satised	48	16.6
Slightly dissatised	4	1.4
Very dissatised	0	0.0
No answer	12	4.2
Total	289	

dissatisfied, and no one indicated he or she was very dissatisfied. Deeming and Chelin (2001) asked a similar question to people who had changed careers to become librarians (they did not limit their sample to business librarians). Interestingly in their survey, while a large majority (around 90%) indicated they were at least slightly satisfied with their career change to librarianship, they had a much higher percentage (around 10%) that indicated a level of dissatisfaction. Although not large, this is a much higher level than was found in the current survey of business librarians.

CONCLUSION

Although not all business librarians follow the same career path into business librarianship, we do seem to share some common traits. According to our survey, a majority of business librarians worked in at least one other career prior to becoming a librarian, and of those who had prior careers a large percentage worked in some type of business field. The business librarians in our survey showed a tendency to enter the field at the same age as the general population of librarians and brought with them many years of prior work experience. Future studies may want to identify the transferable skills that business librarians feel they gained in their previous jobs that have helped them as subject specialists. A comparison of skill sets with business librarians without prior career experience might also provide valuable insight into the educational needs of future business librarians.

Many articles have discussed the need for business librarians to exhibit an understanding of business terminology and theory. Our survey found that over one half of the current business librarians have at least some type of prior work experience in a business field before becoming librarians.

Perhaps business librarians are bringing a great deal of business knowledge with them into the field and therefore do not require additional educational degrees or courses in business to be an effective business librarian. Future studies may want to investigate the depth of business knowledge that business librarians are bringing with them into the field, regardless of their educational background.

Business librarians in our survey profess having a high level of satisfaction with their choice of business librarianship as a career. This is encouraging news as the library profession as a whole is expected to experience high rates of retirement in the next few years. This may lead one to believe that we are unlikely to experience additional attrition related to career dissatisfaction, which could lead to an even greater shortage of business librarians.

Finally, it seems that librarians in corporate/special libraries are an underrepresented group in research studies focusing on the career choices of business librarians, whereas academic business librarians have been repeatedly studied. With the ease in communication today among business librarians, we believe that it is now easier than ever to conduct research that includes these groups to get a broader picture of the career choices of business librarians. Specifically, researchers may want to examine if corporate/special business librarians have similar backgrounds to academic business librarians and look at the factors that influence business librarians to choose the type of environment in which they work.

NOTE

1. See, for example, the quote to this effect from Denise M. Davis who was then Director of the American Library Association's Office for Research and Statistics in a 2004 report, *Library Retirements–What can we expect?* at http://www.ala.org/ala/ors/reports/LISGradsPositionsAndRetirements_rev1.pdf (Retrieved July 26, 2007).

REFERENCES

Ard, A., Clemmons, S., Morgan, N., Sessions, P., Spencer, B., Tidwell, T., et al. (2006). Why library and information science? Results of a career survey of MLIS students along with implications for reference librarians and recruitment. *Reference and User Services Quarterly, 45*, 242–246.

Dale, D. C. (1980). *Career patterns of women librarians with doctorates* (Occasional Papers No. 147). Champaign: University of Illinois at Urbana-Champaign, Graduate School of Library Science.

Deeming, C. D., & Chelin, J. (2001). Make your own luck: a study of people changing career into librarianship. *New Library World, 102,* 18–20.

Heim, K. M., & Moen, W. E. (1989). *Occupational entry: Library and information science students' attitudes, demographics and aspirations survey.* Chicago: American Library Association, Office for Library Personnel Resources.

Houdyshell, M., Robles, P. A., & Hua, Y. (1999, July 3). What were you thinking? If you could choose librarianship again, would you? *Information Outlook, 3,* 19–23.

Kendrick, A. (1990). The educational background and work experience of academic business librarians. *RQ, 29,* 397–399.

Luzius, J. R. (2005). The career choice of academic librarians: A study of motivational factors and demographics. (Doctoral dissertation, Auburn University, 2005). *Dissertation Abstracts International, 66,* 1297.

Pagell, R. A., & Lusk, E. J. (2000). A professional photo of academic business librarians worldwide: The present picture and future view. *Journal of Business & Finance Librarianship, 6*(1), 4–10.

White, R. F., & Macklin, D. B. (1970). *Education, careers, and professionalization in librarianship and information science.* Washington, DC: U.S. Office of Education, Bureau of Research.

Winston, M. (1997). The recruitment, education and careers of academic business librarians (Doctoral dissertation, University of Pittsburgh, 1997). *Dissertation Abstracts International, 58,* 1971.

The MBA
and Academic Business Librarians:
More than Graduate Education
for Subject Specialists

Glenn S. McGuigan

INTRODUCTION

In this article, the author contends that the MBA degree provides a valuable credential for academic business librarians by increasing subject knowledge and nurturing the development of interpersonal skills. The author offers commentary on the topic as one who pursued and obtained the degree part-time, while serving as an academic business librarian.

LITERATURE REVIEW

Within the literature of library and information science (LIS), researchers have examined academic business librarians' possession of the MBA degree and skill sets in business. Concerning the number of academic business librarians who hold MBA degrees, Kendrick (1990) found that only 18.5% held that degree or a master's degree in economics, and similarly Winton's survey (1997) found that only 18.1% of respondents held the MBA degree. Pagell and Lusk (2000) found that 23.5% of the group sampled possessed the MBA or economics degree. Similarly, Liu and Allen (2001) found that 23.8% of academic business librarians possessed an MBA or master's degree in economics. In viewing these results over approximately 15 years, one can see that, regardless of the study, fewer than one in four academic business librarians have an MBA in addition to a master degree in LIS. Although investigating the number of academic business librarians who hold the MBA degree, the literature of LIS has not attempted to empirically show a relationship specifically between librarians with the MBA degree and the provision of effective information services in business. Studies have shown however that there is a relationship between subject knowledge and effective information retrieval (Fidel, 1991; Hsieh-Yee, 1993).

Research studies in LIS have explored the labor market for qualified academic business librarians. O'Connor and Marien (2002) examined the problems of recruiting quality business librarians, finding that a staggering 70% of employers were disappointed with applicant pools, with applicants averaging just 7.7 minimally qualified candidates per position. Revealing an extremely tight labor market for qualified business librarians, the authors concluded that the poor availability was due to the small quantity of candidates, the overall quality of candidates, and the qualifications of candidates regarding experience. They pointed out that respondents to their study often cited a low supply of business librarians and high competition in the public and private sectors as reasons for being unable to find qualified applicants, rather than the issue of salary (in which only 27% reported low salary as a primary factor). The authors noted the dire consequences of the current situation concerning unqualified business librarians. "Those organizations that cannot afford to offer competitive salaries may find themselves without a qualified business librarian or information professional. Costs associated with unfilled positions or positions filled by under qualified professionals have not been quantified in this case, but have obvious service repercussions" (p. 74). Those service repercussions should be a serious concern for the profession and for those institutions that have not been able to place qualified academic business librarians in vacant positions.

White (1999), in a content analysis of academic subject specialist positions in the United States from 1990 to 1998, found that of the 103 business subject specialist positions ads, 63 listed some type of additional education desired, with 24 stating MBA/second masters; 13 with academic background/coursework; 11 with degree (not specified); seven with undergraduate degree or MBA; six with degree or experience; and two with second masters or PhD. Of these positions, he found that approximately 8% required an MBA or second master's degree. Although desiring additional educational experience, employers appear flexible regarding the type of educational background for potential employees for the positions. White (2004) also undertook a content analysis of business information courses in LIS programs. He found that courses are not uniform and contain significant differences in content, including subject focus, assignments, materials, and other characteristics. For example, of the general topics covered in business information courses, he found 36 different areas, in which almost one half were listed in only one or two course syllabi. White's study has begun the process of investigating the business curriculum within LIS programs and examining core competencies required for business librarians. This study raises the question of whether LIS programs are adequately preparing students for careers in business librarianship.

James (1989) identified eight areas that she refers to as "basic management skills" for business librarians (or "business information professionals" as she refers to them) that include the types of skills that one would ideally obtain through an MBA program. These skills include (1) understanding and appreciation of organizational structures; (2) financial budgeting and accounting; (3) personnel: selection, management, and development; (4) negotiating; (5) planning; (6) internal data management; (7) time management; and (8) communications and marketing. Although not addressing specifically MBA programs, her listing of managerial skills for business librarians reinforces the value of MBA programs to academic business librarians because many of these topics are rarely covered in depth within the LIS curriculum. Even putting aside the more business-oriented skills such as financial budgeting and personnel selection, LIS programs could benefit students in general by stressing some of these skills often featured in courses within MBA programs. As Winston (1997) found, however, less than one third of academic business librarians polled had completed a course in business and/or economics.

QUALITIES OF MBA GRADUATES

As a terminal degree (like the MLS), the MBA provides students with an introduction to the various disciplines of their applied professional fields within the context of theory and application (possessing all of the contradictions inherent in such a relationship). In studying these disciplines of business, diverse elements of learning within the curriculum of MBA programs contribute to enhancing skills of academic business librarians. Factors contributing to this enhancement of skills include a formal introduction to theories and applications of business, improved communications skills, and team-building skills. References to the literature of business and business education reinforce these points.

For the purposes of academic business librarians, the curriculum within an MBA program should provide an introduction to various areas of specialized knowledge and enhance their abilities to engage effectively in their responsibilities as subject specialists. As related by the Education Committee of the Business Reference & Services Section (BRASS, 2006), core competencies for business knowledge include (but are not necessarily limited to) accounting, advertising and marketing, banking, company and industry research, insurance, international business, investment and finance, jobs and human resources, small business, and taxation. These subject areas would be addressed by most MBA programs that may categorize fields of study in the areas of accounting, finance, management, marketing, operations management, and increasingly, information systems. Familiarity with studying these topics within a classroom setting should strengthen the subject specialist's abilities in assisting students who are doing research for these very same courses.

Although there have been many critics who have questioned the value of MBA programs to business students, most notably by the strategy and management theorist Mintzberg (2003) and also in a frequently cited study by Pfeffer and Fong (2002), one can easily find research studies that support the value of obtaining an MBA. One such study done by Hunton, Stone, and Wier (2005) indicates that performance evaluations of accountants with MBA degrees are generally higher than those without the degree. These results suggested that the degrees increased specific types of knowledge and enhanced the ability to learn. Hay's (2006) exploratory study found that MBA programs were highly beneficial to managers and identified the following three learning outcomes: (1) broadened perspectives, (2) an enhanced sense of self, and (3) tools, techniques, and theories. Although there will always be criticisms of MBA programs as being purveyors of managerial theory divorced from real-life business practice, which is documented and analyzed by Spender (2007), these programs communicate a body of knowledge critical to the subject specialist who serves as a liaison to those programs. Studying in an MBA program provides the future or current academic business reference librarian with a formal introduction to the theories and applications of business practices that should prepare them to conduct their work effectively and efficiently.

MBA programs focus upon enhancing communication skills and communication strategies of business students. Resulting from a study of management communication in MBA programs, Knight (1999) found that classes that serve as "core requirements" of these programs emphasize more than just effective writing and speaking, but rather address advanced communication strategies, with a focus on elements of persuasion (p. 18).

> Almost all required courses focus on communication strategy and include far more than just skill acquisition. The communication competencies stressed in core courses assume that students have come to business school to learn how to become successful managers, and that developing strong communication skills is one part of that process and not a set of techniques that should have been mastered earlier. (p. 19)

Referring to this advanced level of literacy that encompasses communication in the academic and work environments, Forman (1999) used the term "managerial literacy" to describe this set of communication skills that include the skills in effective oral and written communication, persuasion, and information technology (p. 10). She discussed the importance of managerial literacy within the curriculum of MBA students.

> Ideally, instruction in managerial literacy occurs in both the core classes and in separate classes that can extend communication issues described here and address others. In fact, most schools that offer instruction in management communication do so in separate courses. These courses go beyond attention to basic skills, such as grammar and style, to include topics such as group writing and presentations, graphical presentation of complex quantitative data, argumentation, cross-cultural communication, media relations, corporate advocacy, and rhetorical and communications theory. (p. 15)

These skill sets described by Forman, requiring effective critical thinking and decision-making processes, would contribute to professional effectiveness of any academic librarian, whether a reference librarian or a library director. Regardless of the role of an academic librarian with the MBA degree, this acquisition of managerial literacy may contribute to the overall success of the organization because graduates should be able to effectively communicate, persuade, and utilize information technology.

These effective communication skills are not only beneficial to the academic business librarians themselves or to the libraries where they work, but also strengthen the relationship between the business faculty and the liaison librarians. Enhanced by effective communication, a strong relationship between academic business librarians and the business faculty is a mutually beneficial one that will serve the missions of the library and the business school. Bergevin and Winston (1998) commented on the importance of effective communication between these parties.

> Communication between business faculty and business librarians is necessary if a business school is to fulfill it mission. The communication process is facilitated if both parties understand the organizational culture, professional orientation, processes and economic factors which drive the other.. . . the interaction must be one of continuous, open communication designed to meet the mission of the business school and the mission of the library. Both business librarians and business faculty must view each other as educational partners in the continuous improvement process, and, thus, find ways to initiate and perpetuate ongoing and substantive communication. (p. 31)

The communication skills developed through the experience of the MBA curriculum provide the academic business librarian with tools to effectively engage in outreach to the business faculty. The academic business librarian's possession of the MBA may also enhance his or her standing in the eyes of the business faculty, a potential leveling of the playing field in the librarian's relations with business faculty.

The experience of working in groups as an MBA student may strengthen the abilities of graduates to work in teams within the workplace.

> Whether case-based or not in their instruction, business schools usually emphasize team building and group work in the service of producing persuasive discourse. In other words, students are required to produce group-written documents and group presentations. The

challenges of these communications are considerable, especially because they involve group process and presentation or writing strategies and techniques. (Forman, 1999, p. 11)

The need to produce group work within the curriculum provides experiences for the MBA student to create "deliverables" that require group
interaction and cooperation. Because much of the work in academic libraries and within colleges and universities requires committee or team
interaction, the experience of MBA graduates in doing regular group work
may be beneficial to the institutions of these academic business librarians.

The "soft skills" of teamwork and interpersonal communication are skill
sets that have become acknowledged amongst business schools as being
necessary to produce well-rounded graduates. As related in an article in the
Wall Street Journal, MBA programs are increasingly focusing upon these
"soft" or "people skills," in these business programs that have typically
focused upon "hard" skills such accounting or finance. This curricular
change is a result of the needs of the marketplace. "The schools are responding to employers' growing interest in soft skills. Executive suites
are increasingly composed of managers running far-flung operations who
must attract and retain knowledgeable workers" (Dvorak, 2007, p. B3). As
mentioned previously in regard to Hay's (2006) work, MBA programs can
also instill in students other qualities, such as a broadened perspective and
enhanced self-esteem that will benefit their organizations.

PURSUIT OF THE MBA: AUTHOR'S EXPERIENCE

Like many colleagues within the profession, I ventured into the role of
academic business librarian without an undergraduate degree in business
or an MBA. Prior to being hired as a business reference librarian, however,
I had already started attending an MBA program part-time while serving as
a reference librarian at Penn State Abington, taking classes offered by the
nearby campus of Penn State Great Valley. During that period, I completed
three courses and then transferred to the MBA program at Penn State
Harrisburg, where I had been hired as a business reference librarian. I then
completed the next 14 classes at the Harrisburg campus. Taking one class
per semester (including through the summer), I began the MBA program
in the spring of 2000 and completed it in the fall of 2005.

The Penn State Harrisburg School of Business is accredited by the Association to Advance Collegiate Schools of Business (AACSB). The AACSB

is the most significant agency that evaluates collegiate schools of business (Lawrence & Dangerfield, 2001). According to the organization, this accreditation represents "the highest standard of achievement for business schools worldwide" (AACSB International Website, 2007). Therefore an MBA degree from an accredited school indicates a standard of excellence and provides a stronger credential than a degree from a nonaccredited institution.

I found studying in an AACSB-accredited MBA program to be challenging and exciting. As with many students enrolled in a rigorous MBA program without an undergraduate degree in business (I held a BA in English and a minor in Italian), I was required to take all of the "business core requirements" in addition to the regular MBA classes, along with the math prerequisite. Although not having the academic background in business, the experience of studying English and a foreign language as an undergraduate student provided me with strong writing skills that proved very beneficial when composing the many papers that were demanded of students in the program. The interaction with business information, in the form of readings and assignments, reinforced and strengthened my abilities in utilizing business resources within the library environment. Although I was challenged by the rigor of the program, every semester became a new and exciting learning experience.

The MBA program at Penn State Harrisburg included three tiers of business courses: core requirements (18 credits), breadth courses (18 credits), and elective courses (12 credits). In addition, there was a mathematics prerequisite requirement of advanced algebra/calculus that students were required to complete if they did not have the proficiency. Table 1 shows the course numbers and titles within the MBA program at Penn State Harrisburg as the curriculum existed at that time (it has since been reconfigured but still comprises the same number of credit hours). I included the elective courses that I chose to take within the program and also the courses that I transferred to Penn State Harrisburg that served as equivalent courses or electives, totaling 17 classes.

As Forman (1999) related concerning the importance of group work and communication in MBA programs, I found this to be true in my experience as an MBA student. More than one half of the classes I took demanded some kind of group project or presentation that required regular meetings outside of class, including classes such as Business Research Methods, Business in a Global Society, and Strategic Management. In addition to addressing the project at hand utilizing the knowledge that we were acquiring in class, these group assignments also necessitated cooperation and

TABLE 1. Classes Taken between Spring, 2000 and Fall, 2005 Within the MBA Program at Penn State Harrisburg (including the courses transferred from Penn State Great Valley that served as equivalent courses or electives[a])

Business Core Requirements (18 credits)	Breadth Courses (18 credits)	Elective Courses (12 credits)
BUS 501 – Statistical Analysis	BUS 502 – Business Research Methods	B A 517 – Communication Skills in Mgmt[a]
ECNMS 510 – Managerial Economics	BUS 584 – Business in a Global Society	BUS 596 – Independent Study
MGMT 501 – Organizational Behavior*	BUS 588 – Strategic Management	MGMT 505 – Managing Human Resources
MNGMT 522 – Operations and Supply Chain Mgmt	FINAN 521 – Corporate Finance	PADM 500 – Public Organization and Mngmt
MRKT 520 – Marketing Management	MIS 531 – Management Information Systems*	Prerequisite (3 credits)
P ACC 501 – Financial Statement Analysis	P ACC 540 – Managerial Accounting	QUANT 310 – Advanced Algebra & Calculus

[a]*Note:* The three courses transferred from Penn State Great Valley were considered to be equivalent in quality to those offered at Penn State Harrisburg.

communication between the students to produce a successful outcome. This included such matters as scheduling meetings, assigning tasks, refining the presentation or project, and meeting deadlines. Considering the diverse nature of MBA students, it often required an array of interpersonal skills such as cooperation, negotiation, and persuasion, to result in a successful outcome.

USE OF THE MBA IN THE ACADEMIC LIBRARY SETTING: AUTHOR'S EXPERIENCE

For many generalist reference librarians, encounters with patrons seeking business information are frequent. As information assistant during my internship while pursuing graduate studies in LIS, and in my earlier positions prior to becoming a business librarian, I was surprised by the number of business reference questions that I encountered at the reference desk. As opposed to many librarians, I actually delighted in the business reference questions and found these questions to be interesting to research and satisfying to answer. Unlike some other types of reference questions that appeared to remain open ended even after a thorough probing of the subject in a reference encounter, I noted that many of these questions required a clear and defined answer (such as specific company or financial information, etc). These reference transactions were generally very clear-cut in terms of the information need and were often concluded with great mutual satisfaction at the retrieval of the needed data. As time goes on, I have found that many business research questions, notably those within management and marketing, are not as unambiguous and tangible as those business questions initially seemed to be. Nevertheless, the universe of business information continues to be intriguing to me and provides great personal fulfillment. It is very satisfying to identify and locate these pieces of business data or knowledge, whether in the format of numeric data, such as a historical stock price, or in the form of textual data, such as information on a company's management strategy.

As one who studies business topics as academic disciplines and engages in reference and instruction regarding these subjects, the concept of business information literacy has become a personal mission. Regarding the connection between information literacy and business, I found that the structures of business information are important to clarify with patrons when approaching the identification, evaluation, and use of the information. As related by Edwards and Fiscella (1996), the structures of business information are in the forms of textual/bibliographic, numeric data/statistical, or directory information. By understanding the nature and the structure of business information, as well as by increasing their familiarity with the resources through formal study, the business librarian is able to encourage the critical analysis and use of the information by library patrons. For many of us in the profession, this becomes a highly satisfying experience.

No one can doubt that for academic librarians who serve as subject specialists, an advanced degree in their subject area can only further enhance their expertise in, and knowledge of, the subject areas for which they are responsible. "Subject expertise is an important factor in determining the quality of information services offered by business librarians in academic libraries" (Liu & Allen, 2001, p. 561). This applies not only to reference of course, but also to instruction, collection development, service, and research activities related to librarianship. The low number of academic business librarians with formal graduate (or undergraduate) business education is a result of market forces that pull those with business degrees into higher paying jobs within the private sector. As Liu and Allen (2001) explained, the vast difference in salaries between academic business librarians and those in the private sector with an MBA "reflect the fact that librarianship is not in a very advantageous competitive position when compared with business jobs. Accordingly, it is not surprising that relatively few academic business librarians have business degrees" (p. 559). Therefore, unless a drastic change takes place, the environment of a labor shortage for qualified, academic business librarians will continue.

The question arises therefore whether an MBA or graduate degree in another business-related field is necessary to be an effective business librarian. As in the world of business or in librarianship itself, it is not possible to equate success, efficacy, or knowledge with certain credentials or degrees. Is subject expertise something that one can master on the job solely through use of information resources, interactions with patrons, and self-guided research training, including non-MBA business-related workshops and seminars? For many business librarians, the answer is certainly in the affirmative. However, though there is no empirical evidence to show that the quality of information services by academic business librarians is enhanced specifically by the possession of the MBA degree, common sense relates that the possession of a graduate degree in a specialized field will increase depth of knowledge. Certainly in the case of business, in which many of the disciplines require the application of quantitative operations based upon formulas and standards, such as in accounting, finance, and operations management, it is unlikely that a librarian will fully grasp what a patron is seeking if that librarian has not actually engaged in some of those calculations himself or herself. Based on personal experience, I found that taking classes within the MBA program enhanced my own specialized knowledge. Also, the experience that I gained as an MBA student provided additional benefits in terms of personal growth and enhanced communication skills.

CONCLUSION

This article offers an overview of, and commentary on, graduate education for academic business librarians. The author submits that the MBA degree provides a valuable credential for academic business librarians by enhancing their knowledge of business topics. In addition to delivering formal academic instruction, the nature of the MBA curriculum contributes in a positive way to the academic business librarian's interpersonal skills. The intention of this article is to argue that the pursuit and attainment of the MBA will increase subject knowledge and very likely will enhance the skill sets and competencies of academic business librarians who possess it.

REFERENCES

AACSB International Accreditation Website. (2007). Retrieved June 1, 2007, from www.aacsb.edu.

Bergevin, P. M., & Winston, M. D. (1998). Meeting the mission: The role of business librarians in addressing the challenges of regional business education. *Journal of Business & Finance Librarianship, 3*(3), 19–32.

Dvorak, P. (2007, February 12). Theory & practice: MBA programs hone "soft skills." *Wall Street Journal*, p. B3.

Education Committee of the Business Reference and Services Section. (October, 2006). Core competencies for business reference. *Reference & User Services Quarterly, 46*(1), 40–43.

Edwards, D. H., & Fiscella, J. B. (1996). Collection development. In C. A. Sheehy (Ed.), *Managing business collections in libraries* (pp. 76). Westport, CT: Greenwood.

Fidel, R. (1991). Searchers' selection of search keys. *Journal of the American Society for Information Science, 42*, 490–527.

Forman, J. (1999). Management communication and MBA education: An argument for management literacy. *Selections, 15*(3), 9–16.

Hay, A. (2006). Seeing differently: Putting MBA learning into practice. *International Journal of Training & Development, 10*(4), 291–297.

Hsieh-Yee, I. (1993). Effects of search experience and subject knowledge on the search tactics of novice and experienced searchers. *Journal of the American Society for Information Science, 44*, 161–174.

Hunton, J. E., Stone, D. N., & Wier, B. (2005). Does graduate education contribute to professional accounting success? *Accounting Horizons, 19*(5), 85–100.

James, S. (1989). Understanding management principles and practices: Management training for business information professionals. *Education for Information, 7*, 355–363.

Kendrick, A. (1990). The educational background and work experience of academic business librarians: Results of a survey. *RQ, 29*, 394–399.

Knight, M. (1999). Management communication in US MBA programs: The state of the art. *Business Communications Quarterly, 62*(4), 9–32.

Lawrence, J. J., & Dangerfield, B. (2001). Integrating professional re-accreditation and quality award processes. *Quality Assurance in Education, 9*(2), 80.

Liu, L., & Allen, B. (2001). Business librarians: Their education and training. *College & Research Libraries, 62*(6), 555–563.

Mintzberg, H. (2003). Unconventional wisdom: A conversation with Henry Mintzberg. *Leadership in Action, 23*(4), 8–10.

O'Connor, L., & Marien, S. (2002). Recruiting quality business librarians in a shrinking labor market. *The Bottom Line: Managing Library Finances, 15*(2), 70–74.

Pagell, R. A., & Lusk, E. J. (2000). A professional photo of academic business librarians worldwide: The present picture and a future view. *Journal of Business & Finance Librarianship, 6*(1), 3–21.

Pfeffer, J., & Fong, C. T. (2002). The end of business schools? Less success than meets the eye. *Academy of Management Learning and Education, 1*(1), 79–95.

Spender, J. C. (2007). Management as a regulated profession: An essay. *Journal of Management Inquiry, 16*(32), 32–42.

White, G. (1999). Academic subject specialist positions in the United States: A content analysis of announcements from 1990 through 1998. *Journal of Academic Librarianship, 25*(5), 372–382.

White, G. (2004). Business information courses in LIS programs: A content analysis. *Journal of Business & Finance Librarianship, 10*(2), 3–15.

Winston, M. (1997). *Recruitment, education and careers of academic business librarians.* Unpublished doctoral dissertation, University of Pittsburgh.

The Value of International Experience

David A. Flynn

INTRODUCTION

My main career goal in 1992 was to become a business librarian at a major university. My geographic preference was Hawaii by the year 2000. Presently, I am happy to be sharing this with you from the beautiful island of Oahu, where East meets West, and international business is key.

No doubt, I also enjoyed a very interesting path of work and adventure before landing in Hawaii. A truly fulfilling part of my career path—the leap beyond my comfort zone to the other side of the globe—may have been a considerable factor in securing my current post. Although I suppose I also brought a worthy inventory of the more routine professional qualifications to the interview, I still believe that my international experience gave me an advantage that is highly regarded at my culturally diverse campus and not easily attained by reading the latest guidebook to "doing business internationally."

Much like the bulk of literature on this topic, my observations here are merely anecdotal. This should not be terribly surprising, however, because most writings on this subject are limited to entertaining accounts of overseas assignments and reflections on how the author feels he or she may have benefited from the experience. Obviously, without a controlled study of inputs and outcomes, these claims of benefit are more in the vein of perception, or subjective value. Still, I feel completely convinced that my experiences abroad were very valuable to me.

Following a quick sweep of some of the more recent literature on librarians (and other professionals) working abroad, I share some sentiment from my four years in Japan. I also will offer some advice on how you might prepare for and benefit from a little expatriation of your own.

LITERATURE REVIEW

Standard indexes for library science and general business return very little on the topic of value to the individual from temporary work assignments abroad. Still, there are a handful of relevant articles on how international experience might affect a career. Other articles touch more on the areas of repatriation, unique international experiences with perceived benefits, one's suitability for work abroad, and how to prepare for and locate a position in another country. For additional articles on global work adventures (not specific to librarianship), consider browsing the free Web-based resource centers of support organizations such as Transition Dynamics or Families in Global Transition.

Obviously, not everyone is in a hurry to bid adieu to family and friends in exchange for an extended appointment overseas. Borstorff, Harris, Feild, and Giles (1997) summarized research on factors associated with employee willingness for taking expatriate assignments. After reviewing studies on personal characteristics (such as age, sex, marital status, and prior international experience) and attitudes toward relocation (such as international interests, career focus, and ethnocentrism), the authors suggested several guidelines for employees and employers when considering expatriate assignments. Related studies confirmed reluctance by many employees to make such a move due to concerns of financial burden, spouses' careers, disruption to children, and even negative impacts on the individual's career.

A move of this type is a no small decision. For those in the consideration stage, Beagrie (2006) served up a snapshot of advice and emphasized the importance of careful research of the potential host culture and a thorough self-analysis to make sure such a drastic move will be personally and professionally rewarding. Similarly, Lomax (2002) outlined some of the essential questions you might ask yourself and your family to evaluate your suitability for an expatriate posting.

If you are ready to commit, Lacy (2006) helps you prepare for the international job search and provided several options for locating short- and long-term posts with private sector and government-sponsored operations. Although the article provides general guidelines for the international job search process, it focuses more on intern opportunities and other short-term options.

Sound advice for all potential expatriates is to talk directly with others who have already worked abroad, or to read firsthand accounts of their work experiences and daily life in another country. Ferguson, Nesta, and Story (2007) shared their experiences of working as library directors in Hong Kong. The authors recalled their original motivations for seeking overseas assignments and then explored differences and similarities in management styles and library operations, as well as their challenges with the new culture and language. Similarly, while exploring transferability of management knowledge across borders, McKnight (2007) recounted her experiences as an expatriate library director in the United Kingdom and provided practical advice for others contemplating an international relocation. Although not specific to librarians, *The Adventure of Working Abroad* (Osland, 1995) uses numerous anecdotal episodes to describe the peculiar challenges of living and working in an unfamiliar culture and how these experiences can transform a person emotionally and professionally. Using Joseph Campbell's *Hero with a Thousand Faces* as a framework, Osland provided an entertaining illustration of the physical and mental journey abroad and back.

Some seek adventure, and others are hoping to advance a career. Richardson and McKenna (2003) interviewed 30 British academics with overseas experience to explore their decision making for originally taking the assignment, as well as their perceptions of any favorable impact on their careers. These participants clearly believed they were more marketable afterward and should be rewarded for what they gained from their international experience. MacDonald (2005) explored the careers of more than 200 Canadians who had worked abroad and found that the value of international work experience for career development was generally positive. Unlike earlier research on the same topic, many repatriates in this study were promoted upon return or decided to continue education in areas

similar to their international work. A recent study on "leadership with political awareness" conducted by the Chartered Management Institute (United
Kingdom) found that managers who had worked outside the United Kingdom scored higher on all dimensions of the survey instrument (Hartley,
Fletcher, Wilton, Woodman, & Ungemach, 2007). The authors are convinced that these scores indicate a definite leadership advantage for those
having gained exposure to different cultures.

Although there is not an abundance of empirical research on the benefits of international work experience, there is no shortage of advisory
publications. For selected writings on general expatriate experiences and
transitioning your work to another culture, browse the listings at the *International Job Exchange: Bibliography* maintained by American Library
Association's (ALA) International Relations Round Table. Also visit Tran-
sitionsAbroad.com, Transition-Dynamics.com, or other similar Websites.

POTENTIAL BENEFITS

I can profess that there is indeed value in international experience because I do not find it difficult to realize benefit from good and bad experiences, particularly when I am learning and growing along the way.
However, professional and personal growth from an experience abroad
is not at all universal or automatic. There are far too many variables involved to guarantee heaps of reward for everyone. Some expats will enjoy
a favorable experience abroad, others will not. Some will discover greater
career opportunities upon return, others will feel overlooked and a step behind. Luckily, my experiences abroad and since then match closely much
of what I have read in other expatriate accounts espousing the benefits
of overseas assignments. There are known risks, as outlined below, but
potential rewards seem worth it to me.

Let us start with how it might affect your résumé and cover letter because
those are often your first introduction to a new organization. Your résumé
should illustrate your applicable skills for a new assignment by describing
prior achievements and ongoing responsibilities. Potential employers may
see you as having a stronger awareness and more tolerance for cultural
differences, a genuine global perspective, greater flexibility, adaptability
and endurance, creative problem-solving skills, comfort with risk, and a
drive for new experiences. If you sell them on paper, you may get the
invitation for an interview to discuss further how the skills you learned
overseas are transferable to the position you now seek. Do not be surprised
if an employer spends a considerable portion of your interview asking
about your adventures abroad.

Global awareness and related diversity issues are increasingly important for many businesses and academic institutions. Your international experience could make you more marketable to these organizations. Remember, your international experience is more than a claim on your résumé that you are broad minded; it is an actual demonstration of your versatility and flexibility for adapting to new surroundings and new ideas. In a study by Richardson and McKenna (2003) academics who had worked abroad believed that "as higher education becomes increasingly international, international experience would become more valuable" (p. 789). They clearly perceived themselves to be "more marketable" than those without international experience. The same can be applied to the global business setting and to the world of business information services.

Although some of the operational and managerial approaches may differ abroad, many of the professional skills gained or improved during your international experience will be transferable to the work environment in your home country, and vice versa. Ferguson et al. (2007) went as far as to say that, "with the exception of Medicine, Librarianship may well be the most transferable skill in the world" (p. 223). Studies also have shown that those with previous international experience are more likely to succeed in subsequent foreign assignments, even when the previous experience was in a different country (Borstoff et al., 1997). This certainly can make you more marketable when pursuing additional posts abroad.

A fringe benefit of working abroad will be your new opportunity for travel to neighboring countries. I would not have had the same opportunities for multiple trips to Thailand, South Korea, Hong Kong, and mainland China had I been working in the geographical center of the United States. However, from Japan these trips were easy and relatively inexpensive. Compensation packages for expatriates are often quite generous, making regional travel very affordable. You also may be able to negotiate airfare for travel home once per year.

During your time abroad, you will develop lasting friendships and extend your professional network. If you maintain these relationships, they will be very special to you and will endure subsequent moves. Additionally, it is very likely that you will discover new hobbies, music, literature, and foods that will enrich your life forever.

EXPLORING EXPATRIATION

Are you genuinely wondering if a stint abroad will invigorate your life or career? The stranger in a strange land can be exhilarating, but be careful.

This decision demands due diligence. Before you pack your bags, do the research necessary to make sure your experience will be a positive one. I watched several expats come and go rather quickly during my time in Japan because they were not prepared, nor willing to learn about the culture at a deeper level.

First, evaluate your suitability. Is this really the right time, the right job, and the right location? You should ensure that an adopted country suits your lifestyle and be mindful not to romanticize at the expense of your long-term career. Determine how long you want to work abroad and how you will resume your career at home. Then, begin your cultural training as early as possible. Try to get a realistic understanding of what it will be like to work and live in your country of choice. If you hope to enjoy your new situation after the novelty wears off, you will want to have a sincere interest in the people and language(s) of your new land.

Often, this kind of move can be costly beyond the initial moving expenses. Financial arrangements at home need to be evaluated, including ongoing taxation and real estate implications. Preparing early allows you to address practical matters and be better prepared to cut through miles of red tape. If you are planning an extended stay, seek advice on legal matters, educational options for your children or spouse, immigration requirements, options for health care, housing and transportation, and basic business etiquette. It will not take long in your new work setting before you are reminded that you are not in Kansas anymore.

CULTURE SHOCK

For many, the culture shock is not at all negative. In fact, it can be rather amusing. Early in your experience, many things that might otherwise be annoying back home are instead cute or quirky abroad. These odd moments might slow you down, but they should not bring you down. If your stay is a short one, you may even return home before growing out of that euphoric stage where everything is captivating. An extended stay, on the other hand, will allow you to develop much deeper understanding of the new society. Eventually, you will be able to spot a fresh expat from 20 paces just by the twinkle in his eye. Your integration into society is not automatic, however. I knew long-term expatriates in Japan who took no interest in learning the language or customs of their host culture. Naturally, this was a constant source of frustration for the individuals and those with whom they interacted. The simplest of things remained troublesome.

Premove training might help lessen the culture shock to just a few minor jolts here and there. Of course, reading about a culture and actually living it 24/7 are very different things. My general advice is to remember who you are and where you are. Be sincere and interested in your host culture, but do not pretend to be someone you are not. For example, if you are an American in Japan, it might be better to behave like an upstanding American loving your new life in a fascinating new country, rather than an American trying to be Japanese. The locals will see right through you and wonder why you want to be someone you are not nor ever will be.

It is also quite possible that your shocks (and the lessons thereof) will begin early in your search for a new life abroad. I discovered during job interviews in two different Asian countries that the inquiry might drift well outside of what we might consider "normal." For example, during one interview I was asked out of the blue, "How do you feel about homosexuals?" Excuse me? That is not a typical job interview question in the United States. Indeed, practice is changing throughout Asia, but very personal questions about lifestyle are common in some situations. While being recruited for a position in another country of Southeast Asia, I was asked how I planned to "deal with" the part of the book trade controlled by organized crime (worded differently). I was completely unprepared for that line of questioning, but I stayed calm and focused, and it seemed to go well. The key in those and similar situations is to not pretend nor become rattled. You also should prepare yourself for the possibility of rejection and discrimination. If you have never felt discrimination based on appearance, you just might while living abroad. It did not happen often, and it was never a major incident for me, but there were times when I was judged on looks alone and then treated in a less-than-desirable way during my travels. It felt very strange the first time it happened, but it was another eye opener that helped me to see and contemplate issues from a new perspective.

Many people cannot begin to even try to see something from a perspective other than the one constructed by their upbringing. As a young adult, I always thought I was progressive and open minded, but I realized abroad that I typically limited my understanding of an issue to a rather narrow American perspective. Far too often, Americans have little respect for perspectives that do not already match their own, almost as if they are not worthy, or even a real point of view that someone is experiencing.

I recall a time when I was struggling with a stalled work issue and a more seasoned expat colleague of mine (a real student of the local society) helped me to understand where we were getting bogged down. I kept insisting that a particular practice was wrong "in principle." My colleague explained that

I was failing by examining the issue only from a Western perspective, as if there was only one way (the American way) to do something. I was not appreciating that my Japanese counterpart's perspective on the same issue was very real and very sensible to him. His understanding of the issue was of a reality viewed through a mental map created from an upbringing in a society quite different from my own. Who was I to assume that my way was automatically the right way, particularly in his country? That lesson helped us get to resolution then and remains with me today. This is where the value of international experience lies. The key is the actual experience of organizational behavior and interpersonal relations. It is one thing to proclaim hypothetically that you will respond in a certain way, and quite another to actually experience your response and learn from it.

REPATRIATION

Culture shock grabs the headlines, but it is the reverse shock during repatriation that is often more noticeable and negative. After spending three or more years in another country, you will have developed new attitudes and behaviors that helped you to integrate into your foreign society. You will have changed during your time abroad, but your friends and family back home will not fully recognize it and will not be able to understand what you are feeling. Most of them will have no way to relate to your emotions of feeling like an alien in your own country.

Some aspects of your birth culture that were "normal" prior to your departure may now irritate or disappoint you upon return. Native citizens of your home country might seem more like foreigners to you. They may appear to be self-absorbed and have little interest in affairs beyond their own neighborhood. When I returned to the mainland United States, many things suddenly felt excessive, such as always needing to be bigger or better than the guy next door. I was also disappointed by the frequent lack of customer service in retail establishments and was surprised when friends or family would not notice anything "wrong." I kept feeling poorly treated by cashiers having nothing more to say to me except, "next." After spending time in Japan, I had become used to an enthusiastic greeting, a smile, and a thank you. Perhaps some of the greetings and expressions of gratitude were not heartfelt, but they were almost always there. You get used to it.

These negative aspects of repatriation sound like a downer, but I now see that they fuel the value of your international experience. Your newfound sensitivity allows you to recognize (not overlook or take for granted) the strengths and weaknesses of very different societies. You get to apply the best of both worlds in your approach to work and life. This will not happen overnight, however. In an outstanding literature review on reentry transition, MacDonald (2005) showed that the reverse culture "shock" lasts three to ten months. After this extended period of doubt, frustration, and feelings of not fitting in, the stage of "readjustment" occurs beginning somewhere between 11 and 20 months after returning home. This is a time of "finding balance between the old life and the new one, incorporating the international experience into one's persona, and finding one's place in society" (p. 35).

Ten years after returning to the United States, I still exhibit distinctive behaviors learned in Japan. Luckily for me, most are also accepted norms in Hawaii's culture, as it is heavily influenced by generations of Asian immigrants.

POTENTIAL RISKS

Tourist travels outside of your borders often pose health and safety concerns that must be addressed. Expatriating, however, presents a number of additional risks to negotiate. For example, working and living abroad may affect your pension and retirement plans. You will want to consult a financial advisor to learn about taxation and savings implications. You also will need to prepare for your local medical and dental coverage. I did not plan on getting hurt while abroad, but accidents happen. I can tell you with certainty that bizarre and terrible things can happen during and after treatment, particularly in remote areas.

The biggest risk may be the flip side of this article's basic premise that international experience has value for your professional life. Some may say that the expatriate assignment is overrated and could easily interrupt your career path. I do not believe it is necessarily or frequently the case. Please note, however, that if you plan to return to your home country, there definitely is a cost-benefit analysis that needs to be probed. The United States is among the leaders in librarianship. Our efforts toward an informed citizenry, free inquiry, and support for research within a widespread technological infrastructure are fundamental. Your experience abroad, on the other hand, even in the more developed countries, may be one of much less privilege regarding the library's infrastructure and the overall support for resources and access. Likewise, in many areas, the professional trends will not keep pace. If you do not make efforts to stay current with advancements back home, you will fall well behind the cutting edge. This can be compounded each year you are away to the point that your international experience becomes a liability and could lead to you being overlooked for promotions or new positions that might otherwise have been within your reach had you remained in your current professional track. Similarly, if you do not stay in touch with your colleagues back home, your professional network will deteriorate. Maintain your old network and build a new one. I found it very helpful to become involved in a regional professional association in my host country.

Other challenges can be as basic as not being able to utilize many of your known resources back home, such as interlibrary loan services or expensive subscription databases. Or, they can be as complex as employee relations. For example, as an outsider, you might become frustrated by not being able to command the same level of trust from the local workforce as you did from colleagues in your previous homeland organization. You also may find that your options for promotion at your overseas institution are very limited or nonexistent. And, along with all of the feel-good stories from abroad, there are also expatriates who experience depression, loneliness, health problems, financial stress, and an assortment of restricted freedoms.

There is also risk with your reentry to the homeland workforce (unless you are returning to the same position). For example, it can be very challenging to conduct a job search from overseas. Libraries will be interested in you but might find it cost-prohibitive to fund your international airfare for an on-site interview. Returning to your home country prior to securing gainful employment can eat quickly into your savings, but it may become necessary.

RESOURCES FOR FINDING INTERNATIONAL POSITIONS

Richardson and McKenna (2003) found that "taking an overseas assignment was often down to chance, luck and serendipity" (p. 789). If you do not want to wait for serendipity, you might begin by exploring some of the resources outlined below. Library positions and internships are available in private international schools, military installations, universities (including your "sister" colleges), multinational corporations, investment houses, government agencies, and more. Of course, you do not have to limit yourself to work in a library. Related endeavors can shine on your resume as well.

IFLA's LIBJOBS
http://www.ifla.org/II/lists/libjobs.htm

Mailing list and Web archive (updated automatically) for librarian and information professionals. International in scope, but includes many U.S. postings.

International Schools Services
http://www.iss.edu/
Postings and recruitment information available for ISS and non-ISS schools.

Department of Defense Dependents Schools
http://jobsearch.usajobs.opm.gov/a9dd16.asp
Vacancies for Department of Defense Education Activities (DoDEA) positions are searchable via USAJOBS.

Transitions Abroad
http://www.transitionsabroad.com
From the 30-year-old magazine of the same name, this is one of the main portals for international jobs, internships, study opportunities and volunteer positions.

Fulbright Teacher Exchange Program
http://www.fulbrightexchanges.org/
The program includes opportunities for librarians and matches U.S. and overseas candidates during the spring of each year.

For developments and opportunities in international librarianship, read *International Leads*, the official publication of the International Relations Round Table, American Library Association (ALA) (http://www.ala.org/ala/irrt/intlleads/international. cfm). Also visit the standard job listing sites of ALA, Special Libraries Association (SLA), and the *Chronicle of Higher Education* (www.chronicle.com).

For those currently studying, most universities will have programs that can help guide you to organizations that match students with international internships. See also the Institute for International Education's online headquarters for studying abroad (http://www.IIEPassport.org). The Peace Corps is another option for spending two years in a developing country, typically working in the areas of health care, education, or business. Also, many of the English language newspapers in foreign countries provide position advertisements online. For information about international opportunities to teach English as a second language, visit http://www.tesol.org.

CONCLUSION

There is a widely held perception today that international experience, particularly in business-related fields, is extremely important.

Globalization, multinational corporations, and cross-cultural management are no longer electives at my university, they are core requirements. However, while the classroom provides a great start, there simply is no substitute for actual experience abroad.

My experience in Japan is irreplaceable. I believe it is a highlight of my life and career, and there is no question that I would do it all over again. If you find a suitable opportunity abroad and feel that the timing is right, I would encourage you to give it serious consideration. Pursue it with passion and you will be rewarded.

REFERENCES

Beagrie, S. (2006, September 5). How to . . . gain international experience. *Personnel Today, 41*. Retrieved November 28, 2007, from Business Source Premier database.

Borstorff, P., Harris, S., Feild, H., & Giles, W. (1997). Who'll go? A review of factors associated with employee willingness to work overseas. *Human Resource Planning, 20*(3), 29–40. Retrieved November 28, 2007, from ABI/INFORM Global database.

Ferguson, A., Nesta, F., & Storey, C. (2007). Managing across cultures: The experiences of three Hong Kong academic library directors. *Library Management, 28*, 213–223. Retrieved November 28, 2007, from Emerald Fulltext database.

Hartley, J., Fletcher, C., Wilton, P., Woodman, P., & Ungemach, C. (2007). *Leading with political awareness: Developing leaders' skills to manage the political dimension across all sectors* (Executive Summary). London: Chartered Management Institute.

Lacey, J. (2006, Fall). Working abroad. *Occupational Outlook Quarterly, 50*(3), 2–18. Retrieved November 28, 2007, from Business Source Premier database.

Lomax, S. (2002, April). So you want to work abroad? *Business & Economic Review, 48*(3), 12–18. Retrieved November 28, 2007, from ABI/INFORM Global database.

MacDonald, S. M. (2005). *Building international work experience into career development* (Doctoral dissertation, University of Calgary, 2005). ProQuest Dissertations & Theses, AAT NR05644.

McKnight, S. (2007). The expatriate library director. *Library Management, 28*, 231–241. Retrieved November 28, 2007 from Emerald Fulltext database.

Osland, J. S. (1995). *The adventure of working abroad: Hero tales from the global frontier.* San Francisco: Jossey-Bass.

Richardson, J., & McKenna, S. (2003). International experience and academic careers: What do academics have to say? *Personnel Review, 32*, 774–795.

INDEX

Page numbers in **Bold** represent Figures. Page numbers in *Italics* represent Tables

academic business library 106
academic clientele 113
academic culture 112
academic librarians 42-3, 106
academic libraries 105; difference to public libraries 107-8; transitioning to **109**
academic positions 110-11
accountant 120
accounting firm library 106
accreditation 216
adaptation 140
administration 57, 66, 200-1
administrative team 87-8
administrators 72, 94
Advanced Leadership Institute for Senior Academic Librarians 78-9
advancement 132
advancement strategies 140
adventure 224
The Adventure of Working Abroad (Osland) 224
advertisements: job 4, **5**, 41, 64, 101, 211
advice 123; from practitioners 42-3; working abroad 224-5
advising 153
advisors 146
age 67; starting career 203-4, *204*
alert services 172
Alice in Wonderland (Carroll) 51
allbusiness.com 54

alliances 138
alumni directories 180
American Association of Law Librarians (AALL) 158, 163
American Association of School Librarians (AASL) 159
American Library Association (ALA): annual meeting 46; contacts 178-9; Emerging Leaders Program 157; mentoring activities 159-63; New Members Round Table (NMRT) 162-3
applicants: unsatisfactory 3-4, **8**, 65, 210
appreciation 113
argumentation 213
Ask.com 171
assignments 15-16, 20-1
Association of College and Research Libraries (ACRL) 160; Harvard Leadership Institute for Academic Librarians 73-80
association leadership 156
Association for Library Collections and Technical Services (ALCTS) 160
Association for Library Service to Children (ALSC) 161
Association of Public Data Users (APDU) 179
Association of Specialized and Cooperative Library Agencies (ASCLA) 161
Association to Advance Collegiate

Schools of Business (AACSB) 215-16
attitudes 34, 125; positive 145-6, 163
audience 136
audio conferencing 78

background: educational 28-9, 40-1, 63-4,
  205-7, 210; relevant 16
bad days 193
balance 99, 103
balcony approach 75-6
bench strength 68
bibliographic instruction sessions 44
billing 135
birth culture 229
Bizlink 173
Blackboard 115
Bloglines 170
Blue Cross and Blue Shield Association
  (BCBSA) 152
books: love of 202
boomers 61-3
breaks 191
budgets 89; changing 135
burnout 182; defining 184
business: appreciating 126; interest in
  205
business classes 123
business community: partnering 124
business course quality 117
business degree content *217*
Business Ethics Links Library (BELL) 44
Business and Finance Bulletin 48
Business and Finance Division 46-7, 158
Business and Industry Data Center
  Program (BIDC) 181
Business Information Alert 172
business information courses 41, 211
business information literacy 218
Business Intelligence Center 174
business intern 16-17
Business Librarians Ning site 173
business needs 30-1
business owners 180
business plan tutorial 19-20

Business Reference and Services Section
  (BRASS) 45-6; annual preconference
  46, 100, 174; meetings 177
Business Research Guide 14
business schools: evaluating 215-16
business-related careers 201
BUSLIB 172, 181, 196

California State University Long Beach 147
Canadian libraries 62
candidates: assessing 68
career: advancing 224; interrupted 230;
  past 54-5
career change 92; decisions 202-3, *203*
career development 56-7; mentoring 153;
  strategic 87
career goals 222
career mentoring 163
career path 127
career resources 48
career satisfaction 205-6, *206*, 207
career transitions 98-9
careers: previous *198*
case studies 76
centrality 84
certificates of advanced study (CAS) 132
challenges 169-71, 188
change 72-3, 95; adapting to 140;
  addressing 83-4
classroom technology 78
Click University 132
clientele: types of 112-13
clustering search engine 171
cohort groups 89-90
collaboration 18-19, 26
colleagues 95, 172-4; alliances with 139;
  knowing 182; lack of 123; relating to
  102; supportive 186
collection development 31, 39
collections 107
College Library Directors Mentor
  Program 157
College and University Business Libraries
  Section 47

Colorado State University 148
comfort zone 73
command and control 95
Commerce Library 121
commitment 75
Committee on Interinstitutional
  Cooperation (CIC) Academic
  Leadership Program 73
communication 103, 126, 150, 216-17;
  gap 63; skills 213-14
community: building 90; supportive 186
community involvement 192
compensation 6
competencies 67; core 41-2, 212; training
  68-9
competitive advantage 43
competitive arena 75
competitive edge 177
competitive information 122
competitive intelligence 135
competitive intelligence courses 117-18
Conference of Newer Law Librarians
  (CONELL) 164
conference presentations 22
conferences 25, 45-7, 174-5
confidence 25; building 91
conflict resolution 65
Connecticut Library Association (CLA)
  164
consultation 91; peer 21
contacts 143, 178
content manager 134
content plateauing 53
continuing education 56, 132
contract jobs 133
cooperation 215-17
coping strategies 191-2
core competencies 212; guides 41-2
corporate culture 153
corporate environment 137
corporate librarians 29-30, 42-3, 106;
  client relationships 112; research studies
  207
corporate libraries 197

Corporate Library Excellence
  (Matarazzo) 129
corporate social responsibility 44-5
corporations 60
counselor 22
course development 44
courses: specialized 29
cover letter 225
cross-sectoral mobility 52
cultural training 227
culture: corporate 153; different 225;
  organizational 33, 75, 88; of patrons 33;
  unfamiliar 224-5
culture shock 227-9
curiosity 34, 125
currency 168; demand for 31
current career 55
current events 125
curriculum development 44
customer service 230
customers: types of 112-13
cynicism 184-5

data organizations 179
data sources 31
databases: advice about 21; creating 35;
  unfamiliar 31
*A Day in the Life: Career Options for
  Library and Information Science*
  (Schontz and Murray) 129
decision-making influence 185
degrees 3, 6, 14, 29, 63-4, 110, 210;
  business 120
dehumanization 184
delegating 91
demand 176
democracy 136
demographic data 31
demographics 40; analyzing 67
departmental alliances 138
departmental relationships 100
depersonalization 184, 187
depression 185
desk time 107

detachment 184-5
development opportunities 56
directors: recruiting 64; training 81-95
discrimination 228
discussion group 46
distance learning 52, 98
diversity issues 226
diversity problem 65-6
DocuTicker 174
dynamic content 35

e-communication 151
e-mail requests 134
e-mails 100
e-mentoring 151, 165
economic development 124
education: continuing 56, 132;
   customizing 130
educational background 28-9, 29, 40-1,
   63-4, 205, 210; academic business
   librarians *110*
educational opportunities 49
emotional exhaustion 187
employee relations 231
employees: burnout 190-1; potential 67
employers: nontraditional 11; satisfaction
   3-4, 9-10, 65, 210
employment survey 196-7
encouragement 93-4
enthusiasm 21-3
entrepreneur's workshop 19
entry-level librarians 29-30
ethics: corporate 44-5
events: attending 182
exhaustion 184
ExLibris website 171
expansion 14
expatriate assignments 223
expectations 87
*Expectations of Librarians in the 21st
   Century* (Bridges) 130
experience 9, 143, 197, *198*; practical
   121; prelibrarian 201-2, *202*
experiential learning 73

experimentation 140
expertise 218-19; shortage of 29
explaining 126

face-to-face mentoring 151
face-to-face work 114
facilitator 93
faculty: collaboration with 18-19, 44;
   communication with 214; directory 39;
   networking with 180; relationships with
   113; research interests 39; stability of
   77; understanding 115
faculty status 99-101
fairness 186
family involvement 192
FAQ server 173
feral professionals 156-7
Financial Institutions Section 47
financial literacy 123, 124
five year itch 63
flexibility 114, 226
flexible scheduling 191-2
forecasts 31
frames 75
friendships 226; sustaining 90
functional specialists 101
funding 135
future career 55

general programs 130
getting away 86
global awareness 226
globalization 233
goals: assessing 54; corporate librarian
   136; meeting 56-8; setting 103
good days 193
Google: beyond 171
Google Reader 170
graduate degree 219
graduates 62-3; business education 119-
   20; MBA 212-15; professional positions
   102
grass is greener perception 66
gratitude 230

group work 214-15, 216-17
growth: professional 54-5, 225
growth experience 73
growth opportunities 63
guidance 143
guide 22

Halifax plc 151-2
hard skills 215
Hawaii 222
headlines 125
horizontal growth 55
hot job 128
human resource 75
hurry 122-3

immersion 82
in-house training 32
independent study 131
individualized training 35
inefficacy 185
influence 115, 185
information: interest in 136; structuring
    24
information crises 135-6
information delivery 30
information literacy 218
information needs 34-5, 112-13
Information School interns 15-16
information style 33
Information Today 170, 175
Informed Librarian 172
InfoTip 170
inquisitiveness 125
instruction 137
instruction sessions 44
instructors: respect for 77-8
integration 227
intensive program 82
intensive training 74-5
interests: personal 54
internal candidates 101
internal postings 64
International Association for Social

Science Information Service and
    Technology (IASSIST) 179
international librarians 108
Internet Public Library 174
internships 15-17, 131; international 232
interpersonal communication 215
interventions: burnout 190
interview 134
interview question 228
investment 124
Investment Services Section 47
inward growth 55
irrelevance 139

Jacobsen, T. 52-3
jargon 122
job demands 190-1
job duties 114
job engagement 186
job functions 202-3
job market 4-11, 63-6
job search: international 224; overseas
    231
job security 138
job settings *197*
job stereotyping 111
job titles 6, 7
job-person fit 185
jobs: finding 132-4, *see also* positions
*Journal of Business and Finance
    Librarianship (JBFL)* 48, 172
journals: professional 172; publishing in
    47-8
just-in-time training 35

keeping up 169, 175
Keller, H. 80
Kirkwood, H. 43
knowledge: requisite 39; sharing 116;
    specific 35; thirst for 125; transferable
    115-16
knowledge management 130
Knowledge and Special Libraries
    (Matarazzo and Connolly) 130

Kresge Business Administration Library 173

labor shortage 1-4, 61-6, 65
labor supply 6-10
language: business 138; command of 176-7; learning 33
leader partnerships 90
leadership 56-7; association 156; defining 72; literature review 83-4
leadership development 72-3, 166; program 81-95
leadership institutes 57, 68
leadership mentoring 155-6
leadership program 86
Leadership for Research Libraries (Woodsworth and von Wahlde) 83
leadership skills 64-5, 68
leadership styles 76-7
leadership supply 61-3
leadership workshops 94
learning 137; collaborative 76; interest in 21-3
learning environment 77, 93
learning forum 46
learning tool 19
liberal arts 121
librarians: best 125-6; challenges 122-3; future 147; international comparison 108; newsletter 171; pairing 22; relationship with patrons 106; respected 72; shortage of 1-5, 61-6; survey *109*
The Librarian's Career Guidebook (Shontz) 130
librarianship: growth of 5; love of 202
Library Administration and Management Association (LAMA) 161
Library Advisory Program 146
library committee 44
Library of Congress Business Reference Service 173
library and information science (LIS) degree 97-8

library and information studies (LIS) programs 41; teaching 115-18, *116*
Library and Information Technology Association (LITA) 161
Library Instruction Round Table (LIRT) 162
library instruction sessions 39
library school 40, 130-2; alumni 181
Library Student Internship Program 17
life plateauing 53
lifestyle questions 228
Lists of Lists (LOL) 174
literature: professional 172
local government 124
local practices 33
Louisiana State University Library 148
Lynch, B. 93-4

McDonald's Corp 60
management 57; strategic 94-5; teaching 23
management problem 74
management skills 65, 68, 211
managerial literacy 213-14
managers: demographics of 108; exposure to different cultures 225; MBA programs 212; shortage of 63-6
market forces 218
marketing 45, 135
marketing data 31
marketing plan 14-15; tutorial 17-18, 24-5
marketing research 120
Maslack Burnout Inventory (MBI) 187
Massachusetts Institute of Technology 173
master's degree: second 132, 210
MBA 132, 210
medical coverage 230
Medical Library Association (MLA) 164
meetings 135; mentoring 145-6
members: developing 160
membership: selling 156
mentee perspective 24-5
mentor 100; responsibilities 149-50

mentoring 57; American university programs 143-8; defining 142-3; Senior Fellows Program 92-4

Mentoring in Action (Clutterbuck: Garvey; Stokes and Garret-Harris) 150-1

Mentoring Program Coordinator 145

mentoring programs: successful 151-3

mentoring workshops 146

mentors 39, 43; lack of 123; recruiting 163

mentorship programs 17-18

microphones 78

midcareer development model 53

middle management 62

mismatch conditions 186

MLS graduates 62-3

mobility 139

mutual mentoring 165

narrow perspectives 228

National Academies 148-50

negativity 185

networking 85-6, 94, 131, 139; international 179; professional associations 177-9

new broom theory 66

New Ideas Forum 147

New Jersey Library Association (NILA) 164-5

New Librarian FAQ 147

New Members Round Table (NMRT) 162-3

newsletters 134-5, 171

nominations 67

nonlibrary jobs 199-200

numerical data sources 31

off-desk time 108

one-to-one training 32

open planning 66

open-ended research question 113

organizational culture 33, 75, 88

organizational issues 55-6

organizing 169

orientation mentoring 144

outreach 124-5, 134

page 120

pairing 22, 148

paraprofessional jobs 199

patrons: business 122-3; culture of 33; distance from 184; diverse 126; negativity of 188-9; networking with 180; relationship with 106; time-sensitive 30

peer groups 172-4

peer mentoring 148

peer tutoring 20-1

peer-review 48

Pennsylvania State Harrisburg School of Business 215

Pennsylvania State University 99; mentoring 145-6

pension 230

people skills 215

People's University 124

performance evaluations 212

personal accomplishment 185

personal development 23, 86

personal efficacy 187

personal growth 54, 225

personal questions 228

personal resources 191

personal satisfaction 103

persuasion 213

philosophy 137-8

phone requests 134

physical resources 191

placements 97

planning 51; in-depth 24; strategic 83-4

plateauing 53

Popovich, C. 43

position advertisements 4, **5**, 41, 64, 101, 211

position change 92

positions: international 231-2; vacant 10, *see also* jobs

positive attitude 145-6, 163

postlibrary school 130-2
practical experience 121
practitioner advice 42-3
prelibrarian occupation types 199-200,
  200
premove training 228
presentations 25
prestige factor 117
prioritising 169
Private Equity Section 47
proactivity 138
problem-solving 34
products: knowledge of 138-9
professional associations 139; business
  education 45; mentoring 155-66;
  networking 177-9
professional development 22-3, 34, 56,
  81-95, 102-3, 132; enhanced 90-1;
  mentoring 153; opportunities 174;
  supported 94
professional growth 54-5, 225
professional jobs 199
professional librarian 101
professional mentoring 144
professional satisfaction 103
professional trends 230-1
projects 24-5; new 135
promotion mentorship 144, 145-6
promotions 64-5, 87, 139
public libraries 105; clients 112-13;
  difference to academic libraries 107;
  outreach 124-5; preference for 121
Public Library Association (PLA) 161
public policy issues 88-9
public service 39
publications 30
publishing 47-8, 100

qualifications 2-4, 6, 39, 40-1, 63-4, 67,
  110, 210
questionnaire: mentoring 151-2
questions: difficult 33; enjoying 121

readjustment 230

readvertising 10
Real Estate Round Table 47
recruitment 2-4, 18, 23, 210; internal 65;
  management position 64; mentoring
  158; statistics 61-3
reentry 230
reference: improving 45-6
reference courses 117-18
reference questions 121, 217-18
reference training 32
Reference and User Services Association
  (RUSA) 156, 162
referrals 31
reflection 103
*Reframing Organizations: Artistry Choice
  and Leadership* (Bolman and Dean) 74
reframing theory 75
Reid, B. 52
relationships: professional 85-6;
  strengthening 214
relocation 98
renovation 190
reorganization 190
repatriation 229-30
repetitive tasks 188
requests 134
research 106
research agenda 48
research guide 20
research instruction 19, 23
research libraries 83-4, 86-9
Research Mentor Program 20
research needs 26, 113
research questions 218
research skills 24
research support 14-15
resources 41-2; awareness of 15;
  international jobs 231-2; Internet 42; job
  190-1; knowledge of 30-1; training 33-4
résumé 225
retention 63
retirement plans 230
retirements 1-2, 61-3, 155
reverse mentoring 165

rewards 186
risk-free rate of return 33
risk-taking 92-3, 140
Rutgers University 32-3

sabbatical 86
salaries 3, 6, *8*, 132-4, 210, 218-19
satisfaction 218
scheduling: flexible 191-2
school librarian 98
science and technology librarians 2-3
search engines 171
search process 34-5
searching skills 170-1
second-career individuals 198
self-assessment 52, 53-5; time
  management 169
self-awareness 87
self-discovery 76
self-training 56
sensitivity 229-30
service 48
service quality 218-19
shadowing 133-4
shelver 120
situations: misreading 75-6
size 106, 107
skill gaps 68
skills 9, 41; enhancing 212; potential 68;
  quantifying 72; transferable 206, 226
SLABF 196
social activities 178
social networks 102
social resources 191
socialization 153, 156-7
soft skills 213-15
sources: information on 117-18; job
  hunting 133; scrutinizing 113
speakers 78
special librarianship 130-1, 207
Special Librarianship As A Career
  (Special Libraries Association) 129
special libraries 197
Special Libraries Association (SLA) 164,

174-5; Business and Finance Division
  46-7, 158; membership 178
specialists: functional 101
specialized mentoring 145
specializing: age of *204*; reason for *205*
specific knowledge 35
specificity 31
Staff Development Program 149
staff librarian 100
staff numbers 65
*Staff Planning in a Time of Demographic
  Change* (Whitmell) 69
staffing issues 101-2
state data centers 181
statistics 126; understanding 219
stereotyping 111
stimulation 188
strategic management 94-5
strategies 169-71
stress 135, 188; chronic 183
stressors 188; response to 184
structural plateauing 53
structure 75
student perspective 16, 18
students: collaboration with 18-19; needs
  of 25; respect for 77-8; supporting 15;
  working with 113
study groups 76
subject associations 179-80
subject guides 173
subject knowledge 42, 109-10, 212, 218-
  19
subject specialists 119; labor shortages
  2-3; positions 211
succession planning 60, 156, 165-6;
  design 66-9
Sullivan, A. 80
Sullivan, M. 74, 79
Supersearchers 170
supervision 57, 115
support system 89-90
supportive attitude 145-6
surveys 11
symbolic frame 75

symbolic value 84

teaching 79, 106, 200-1; enjoyment of *117*; interest in 116; Library and Information Science (LIS) programs 115-18; masterful 77-8
teaching tool 19
team-building 87-8
team-work 214
technology background 45
temporary jobs 133
tenure 49, 189
tenure mentorship 145-6
terminology 33, 122, 206
theories: business 212-13
time management 169-70
time-sensitive patrons 30
training 29, 32-4; competencies 68-9; intensive 74-5
training manual 32-4
training stages 31
transfer 192
transferable skills 206, 226
transformation 79; preparing for 74
transition 230
transition difficulties 111-12
transitioning: challenges for 137-9; reasons for 109-10, *111*
travel 136, 226
trust 90
Tucker, J. C. 32
tutorials: automated 32; web-based 17-21
tutoring: peer 20-1
two cultures 112

undergraduates 113
unions 114

university: library mentoring programs 143-8; mission 84; role of library 88
University of Nevada Las Vegas (UNLV) 32
University of Utah 146-7
University of Washington 146
University of Washington Bothell (UWB) 13
user base networking 180-1

vacant positions 10
validation 91
value: symbolic 84
value chain theory 43
vendors 31
vertical growth 55
virtual networking 181-2
volunteer mentors 144-5

web resources 42
web search strategies 170
web-based classes 98
Web-based Information Science Education (WISE) consortium 131
web-based tutorials 17-21
website: company 134
Western perspective 228-9
Womack, R. 32
work abroad 223-32
work community 186
work experience 99
workload 185
workplace planning 60

Yale University Library 147
Young Adult Library Services Association (YALSA) 162